HOPE THROUGH

THE Tie Between

Compiled by Suellen J Strite

Illustrated by Lois Ann Eby

What Is Grief? page 11 From ministering to the grieving. Used by permission of Still Waters Ministries.

Whose Loss Is Worse? Jerry L Sittser page 62 Taken from A Grace Disguised: Expanded Edition by Jerry L Sittser. Copyright © 1995, 2004 by Gerald L. Sittser. Used by permission of Zondervan. www.zondervan.com.

From Horizontal to Vertical, Sharon Yoder page 70 From To Have and To Hold—Hope Restored for Single Women. Faith Builders Resource Group, Guys Mills, PA 877.222.4769. Used by permission.

The Cold Cottage, Suellen J Strite page 112 Appeared first in Family Life Magazine. Used by permission.

What Can I Say? Titus Hofer page 189 From Ministering to the Grieving. Used by permission of Still Waters Ministry.

The Widow's Answer, Eva Metz page 305 Adapted, reprinted from Gospel Herald, August 15, 1940. Mennonite Publishing House, Scottdale, PA. Used with permission of MennoMedia.

ISBN: 978-1-933753-81-2

Text design by Larisa Yoder
Illustrations by Lois Ann Eby

Carlisle Press
WALNUT CREEK

2673 Township Road 421
Sugarcreek, Ohio 44681
800.852.4482

The Tie Between

Hers was a world of sunshine,
Of beams that no cloud could dim,
A radiant life of contentment,
Complete and secure with him.

And then in a moment he left her,
To live where there is no night;
And a cloud settled down like a curtain,
Snuffing away the light.

It seemed that the cloud would crush her,
Would smother her breath away,
Till it blackened the brightest blushing
Of the vigorous dawn of day.

But while daily the cloud engulfed her,
And towered to heaven from earth,
A faintness of glory spread through it,
And beckoned new hope to birth.

In that cloud hung a hint of heaven,
Through the scent of the fresh-turned sod;
For the cloud was a link between them,
A tie between her and her God.

From the cloud that had been so heavy,
A rainbow set foot on earth's lap—
A bridge between earth and heaven,
A promise that spanned the gap.

Lucy A Martin

Dedication

To all brave souls who are reaching out for the hope that lies beyond the clouds…and to those who are buoying up the outstretched arms.

Foreword

My dream of one day writing a book began when I was a teenager. The projected topics of my future book varied with my age, but never in my wildest dreams did I consider writing a book like the one you hold in your hands. I did not even like to *read* books about widows, let alone compile one, because they made me feel sad. But then…neither did my sister, Lydia Hostetter, dream that her happy marriage would end in sad widowhood after thirteen short years. The accident that ended her husband's life sent her on a search for a book that she could not find. She found books on grief everywhere, widow's life stories she found here and there, devotional books for widows were readily available; these were all helpful in some way. But the book she was searching for, the book she wanted and really needed, was not for sale. She discovered it was to be found only in the thoughts and hearts of people.

Out of empathy for her, I proposed with trepidation, "Should I compile that book for you?"

"Would you?!" She swallowed my offer in one happy gulp. And me? I've been up to my neck in words ever since, as generous folks bared their hearts and shared their thoughts to make the book my sister was looking for.

With gratitude to...

…our Heavenly Father, for providing a rainbow for every cloud.

…my husband, Dennis, whose kindness and encouragement cannot be overrated.

…our six children who almost believed me when I told them that by washing dishes, they were helping with this book.

…my sister, Lydia Hostetter. Bless her heart; she was not willing to fill out a survey, or tell her life story on these pages, but she did step way out of her comfort zone to contribute a few pieces. You will find them with the initials LMH; it is to be understood that no other words in this book are hers.

…Grace Shirk for sharing her story. I hope she receives as many friends as she anticipates through this contact.

…each contributor, anonymous or otherwise. One of you wrote: "I am not sending much, but hopefully if we each send a morsel, there will be enough for a meal for us all." Well said. My sister wanted a book for widows; I wanted it to be more than that. I have faith that this manuscript holds words which will satisfy more than one searching widow, fatherless child, or supporting friend.

…my writer's critique group for chasing the flies and gnats off this meal, Sharita Horst for adding salt and pepper to the bland portions, Jennifer Perfect for measuring out proper servings, and Seth Williams and Larry Weber for checking for nutritional value.

…Lois Ann Eby, for enhancing this rather somber manuscript with her unique flair.

…Marvin Wengerd and Larisa Yoder of Carlisle Press for turning my compilations into a book!

Contents

You cannot direct the wind, but you can adjust the sails.

Adjusting the Sails

Woe is me for my hurt! My wound is grievous: but I said, truly this is a grief, and I must bear it. Jeremiah 10:19

Adjusting the Sails

SUELLEN J STRITE

As well-wishing witnesses looked on, the groom took his bride's hand and helped her into their ship. After pausing to ask God to be their Captain, they hoisted the mainsail and started across the ocean of life. They knew they might face storms, but they were young, strong, and full of hope. They were in love, and love covers many sailing stresses. They enjoyed helping each other change the sail from starboard to portside depending on the direction of the wind.

Their little craft was big enough for children, and several times they moored up and thanked God for the new blessing He placed in their arms. Now their days were fuller and their nights shorter, but the stars still shone across the ocean at night. They were content. They sailed joyfully for a few years.

But then, a terrible storm came up. The boat listed dangerously in the wild waves. The children's mother sent them frantically to the hold below, then she ran up to the stem, where her husband's strong tanned arms were desperately manning the helm. Then another wave whipped across their craft and the stern shot into the air. She saw the mad wave fling her husband overboard. The fact barely registered, as she clung to the side rail for dear life. The boat tossed and rolled in a dangerous position. Suddenly the waters calmed and it righted itself.

A splash here. A ripple. A wave lapped the deck. But her husband's capable hands were no longer on the helm! Gone! Just like that! Adding her own salty tears to the ocean, she ran down to the hold. Safe! All the children were shaken, but alive.

She was shaken too. How could she steer without her husband? How could she ever hope to get her children safely across the great ocean? No one on the boat understood sailing as well as he: which way the wind was shifting; where to watch for quicksands and icebergs; when to cast the anchors and wait for calm waters. None of the children were old enough to help her decipher the map and compass. What could they do? Drift aimlessly in circles?

At first, she merely reefed the sails and floated along. She gathered her children around her and they wept together great buckets of tears. Each child took a turn dumping the buckets into the wide ocean which had swallowed their father. In the evenings they sat on the deck and talked of him, and of his goals for their journey. The nights were black, and the days were gray, but they watched for the stars to shine and the sun to rise.

Time and again they went to their Captain Father for help and strength and courage. She felt His divine hand sustaining her, and her children grew older and stronger and wiser. Finally, one day they all felt they were as ready as they ever would be to adjust the sails around to the leeward and press ahead.

Sailing was not what it had been. Now she stood at the helm, and her arms were not as strong and capable as her husband's. She had to make decisions and give orders, and she was not as wise as he had been. But she was at peace with their decision to sail on. It would be worse to drift in hopeless circles, eventually drowning in despair.

Underneath the newfound laughter and joy that spilled from the deck was an ongoing healing grief. It was not the happy voyage she had dreamed of sharing with him for a lifetime. She realized now, as never before, that humans cannot direct all the winds that blow their way; but that they can choose to adjust their sails to accommodate the shifts in such a way as to sail on.

Above that, she clung to the promise that as long as sailors keep their eyes on the Captain, He will guide them safely to the *harbor* where there will never be another storm.

Question 1

What were some of the physical, emotional, and spiritual challenges you faced during your hardest grief?

Widows answer:

• I had a loss of appetite. Food went around and around in my mouth and I could not swallow it.

• I ate, but I could not taste the food.

• My main physical problem was a tiredness that lasted for months; I had no motivation or energy for anything. After a few months, I dealt with anxiety; I was uptight and could not sleep soundly. Then, for some time, I felt detached from life. I went to social events merely because that was what was expected of me, and I left feeling relieved that one more gathering was behind me. Spiritually I felt like I couldn't (didn't) trust God. I still believed in Him, but felt somewhat like I couldn't trust Him anymore with the rest of my life if this is how He is going to plan things! I felt carried by prayer initially, then later felt shaky faith. I felt a distrust toward God for a long time and I still struggle to really trust Him like I should.

• I felt it would be easier for the whole world to just stop. But I knew life must go on and I must try to be brave for my family's sake.

• I struggled with the deceptive thought that if only I was married again everything would be all right.

• I was weak and shaky. Emotionally, I was in shock at first. My brain felt numb; therefore, nothing felt real. But I feel strongly it was God's mercy and grace at that time. He never gives us too much at a time. It was harder for me as time went on and reality set in.

• I felt detached from the rest of the world; like I was in my own little shell. I felt like I was looking through sunglasses those first weeks. I

4

wanted no pity; I just wanted understanding, sympathy, and love. I could not cry in front of others. But alone in my bed, I would cry my heart out to the God Who understands. It really upset me to see a couple with marriage problems.

• Of course, I could not function normally. An hour or two of sleep was the norm. And I had never expected fear. I am not a fearful person by nature, but fear would hit me, especially at night. Fear of what? Fear that I simply could not make it through the terrible anguish of grief and loss. I clung to God, but in my worst pain I could not feel Him. I knew He was always there, and I hoped someday it would get better. But hopelessness was flung at me. How could it get better when there was no chance of this changing? My husband is gone! One night peace settled over me as the picture of God's hands tenderly holding a nest of blue eggs in the midst of a storm came to my mind. This picture was from a card someone had sent me. It seemed Satan knew to hit me just as I came out

> Grief is shock…There stood my husband's boss. Right away I knew something was wrong. "Tell me. Is he hurt bad?" "No, he is gone," was the response. The finality of those words! My brain froze. Anonymous

of sleep when I was weakest. I always flew to God and envisioned Him holding me in His arms, under His wings, where Satan could not get at me. Then peace came.

• Everyone around me seemed to know all the answers or glibly said, "You will be taken care of. God makes no mistakes." Those things can be easily said from a feather pillow. I had a hard time seeing that God can

> You must find someone to talk to.

bring something good out of something so bad. I learned that God gives us more than we can handle (when I am weak then He is strong), but He will help us carry it. He puts us to the end of ourselves so we can appreciate His strength.

• I had a hollow feeling in my stomach often associated with meeting people. This went on for a long while. I think it was related to knowing people would be watching to see how I was coping. I did feel like God was far away part of that first year. I read somewhere that those are the times we need to depend on others' prayers for us. I feel the state of shock we are in may be in relation to the way our husband was taken.

• I was physically spent, drained, tired. I was in denial for a long time. Your good days will eventually outdo the bad ones. Widowhood puts faith to the test. I learned to trust like never before, remembering God does love and care for me. Those He loves, He chastises, and we shall come forth as gold!

• I wondered how I could still function normally—it hurt so inside—when it seemed as though I should be physically maimed.

• God seemed far away. While others may assume that we feel God's presence when we need it most, I found the "Footprints in the Sand" poem to be more realistic. Often it is only as we look back on life's hardest experiences that we can see how He carried us through.

• Eating and cooking were necessary evils. Sleeping was an ongoing struggle. Many times I would doze off, only to jerk awake with subconscious anxieties coming to the surface. Tight muscles made it hard to relax and rest, and lack of sleep made that tension worse. While I did not use a chiropractor regularly before my husband's death, I found it to be a necessity that first year or two, and was encouraged by others to just figure that into my budget as a necessary expense.

• The toll of grief compounded by not having our husband's listening ear is a heavy burden to carry alone. I found myself feeling that if I don't have my husband to talk to, I'll just have to cope with this myself, because who wants to tell anyone else the emotional struggles you were accustomed to sharing with your husband? But I found out the hard way that it was more than I could cope with alone. I remember one appointment when my neck and back muscles were so tight, I told my chiropractor that I wasn't sure how much she could help, because it felt like a tightness coming from the inside out. That day, before I left, she told me, "You must find someone to talk to." She offered to listen if I wanted to talk, but assured me that she knew I have a network of support in my church and encouraged me to find someone who could listen. That was the nudge I needed to reach out for more support. And I came to recognize that when the muscle tension got out of control, it was a symptom of emotional overload. Time to lighten up the schedule for a bit, find some quiet time, or call someone to unload.

• I had an emotional breakdown in the third year after my husband's death. Our dear children approached me with the question, "Will you go for help?" They knew I was struggling so… My heart had gone along with my husband, because finally he was no longer suffering. I went to Green Pastures, PA for 4½ weeks, then I upgraded to Spring Haven, Ohio. Now I am at Share and Care in Ohio. I am so glad for all the help and encouragement I received. God is so good, and He answers prayer.

Remember: it is OKAY to take medication if your mental health is suffering too severely. Talk to your family doctor if you are not getting any sleep, are losing touch with reality, or are otherwise unable to function. Stress of any kind affects our mental health, and the death of one's husband is certainly not the least of stresses. *Anonymous*

Dear New Widow,

As you walk this lonely path of widowhood, you will discover that grief has changing seasons. Perhaps by sharing a few snatches from my journal, you will see that God helps me, and will help you as well, as you turn your calendar, page after page.

Here where I live it is spring. I hung out the laundry and wished I could bring the beauty into the house. It seems nature is awakening with the clear blue skies, warm sunshine, and songs of the mourning doves, cardinals, and robins. Is that why I feel a quiet joy? I am so thankful that God has my life in His Hands. I have no answers for the questions my heart sometimes asks. But somehow, I know and feel God will lead me the way He sees best. I kneel at His feet; only there can I find peace, and bow my head in thankfulness for His constant care, love, and forgiveness. I need His help in the day-to-day tests. It is a miracle to see the frail snowdrops peeping from behind the snow after our long, cold winter.

Last evening I read Mark 6. This chapter tells how Jesus healed the multitudes and fed them. Then how He departed into a mountain to pray, alone. It is touching to me to read how Jesus also needed time alone. Then Jesus saw His disciples toiling in rowing; He walked on the sea and would have passed them by, but they saw Him and cried out. Jesus called to them, *"Be of good cheer: it is I; be not afraid!"* As He sees us toiling on this pilgrim way, He would pass us by if we would not call on Him for help. "Saviour, Saviour, do not pass me by..." He is longing to help us. His heart is moved with compassion. He can cheer and comfort us in many ways, through His Spirit.

And now it is brilliant summertime. The green trees look magnificent against the blue sky. "My Father, You created all these beauties of nature. Look down on me, Your child! Do You understand the tears that fall on this page? I feel as if I'm at the end of the rope, at the end of my patience and childlike trusting faith. It seems bitter thoughts want to crowd in. Every day I struggle to submit all to Your Hands. With Your help I want to take in stride the things that deeply pain my heart, and cope with the deep, deep longings, which only You know and understand. Lord, it's these desperate moments, these moments just You and I know, that I need You desperately. Otherwise I would go under completely and give up." It is so heartrending to hear my three-year-old daughter pleading to go to heaven to see her father. She said, with tears in her eyes, "Jesus is calling me. May I go now?" No words can express a mother's heart as she sees her child look up to heaven with tears, longing to see the father she never saw. How can I comfort her, when my own heart is also filled with the same longings? I can keep looking to my one, true Friend who never forgets, or leaves, or forsakes. He has promised to be a Father to the fatherless and a Husband to the widow...

The sun has set in a cloudless sky. My daughter and I went for a walk tonight. I got tears as I thought how special it would be if her father, my husband, would be along. I looked back to the farm and saw the tall, lone pine tree sharply silhouetted against the sunset. I thought it fit so well to my life. That loneliness! But I am richly blessed, for God is faithful.

This morning as I was working in the garden, I glanced up and saw a lone Canada goose winging its way silently, swiftly, across the gray sky, just above me. It touched my heart, and gave me courage and a longing to follow its example, going on silently. "May Thy will be done."

Today is a frosty fall morning. I felt encouraged to tread into this day, with my hand in God's hand. I feel unworthy of His constant care and protection. But now it is evening. My daughter is tucked into bed after a day of playing and asking questions. The moon is shining down on me; it feels comforting after my day of stirred longings and memories.

I cleaned the upstairs. There is a lot behind those words. It means I aired all the tiny baby garments (that I used only once), then tucked them all away again. It means I aired my dear husband's suits, hats, and shoes then I put them all in the closet and shut the door.

Cleaning the upstairs means I faced stark reality again. I felt the pain, the memories, the longings, again. Then I tried to put them all away and with effort I got up and am trying to go on. What will my future hold?

Will I ever again need the items I aired? God knows. God cares. God guides in His time and way. I trust Him.

I awoke early this morning to winter's snow swirling outside and words circling in my mind, "All the way my Saviour leads me, what have I to ask beside? Can I doubt His tender mercy, Who through life has been my Guide?" How comforting to know I can rest in His arms.

Today in the services we heard about eternity, how our minds cannot grasp what that is. How very short life is, compared to eternity...If a little bird would come to a large stone once in a thousand years to sharpen its beak, until the stone is worn down to nothing, it would still be only a drop in eternity. How indescribable! It makes our toiling and pain seem very small and short, and it brought a surge of hope to my heart. "This too shall pass; it did not come to stay..." I want to keep that vision deeply ingrained in my heart. We are here to prepare for eternity.

Now another calendar year is drawing to a close. Another year without my husband. A step closer Home. One less year to live through, before I too can go. "Here, Lord, I give myself away, 'tis all that I can do." As I looked out across the graveyard through the pouring rain I had to think, "Oh, how fleeting this life is! My own dear husband...Years have passed now since I last saw you and felt you...since I heard your voice... Grass has grown over your grave, and faded... rains have beat against your gravestone, storms have swept across your grave, the sun has shone, rising and setting many times over your grave...All that is left is a gravestone and memories. Yet your soul is living on...and someday I hope to meet you again. But till then, I want to keep on, ever trusting in my Guide and Comforter."

Spring has returned. It is such a mellow evening. This morning I cried when I awoke, for I had such a real dream about my husband once again. I saw him and went to him and told him I have such a longing for him. I asked him if he still loves me. He put his arm about me, looked into my eyes, and said, "Oh, yes." Then he took my hand and said he'll explain why we cannot be together. We went on a long walk. It is beyond words how I felt, walking there beside him. I just looked down, for I felt like a child beside him. But oh, the thrill of feeling his touch! That deep feeling of BELONGING to someone! Yet all the time I felt a deep sadness in my heart for I knew we would part again.

"Lord, help me to really feel I belong to You...bring me close to You again, that the echoing deep void in my heart need not feel so aching. Help me leave life's vast unanswered 'why' in Your Hands."

Through every changing season, we must look up, and remember the source of all good things. We need to cultivate the attitude of a thankful heart. Always. Our reason for thankfulness is God Himself; not things. The only way to be thankful in any situation is to think about God. This we must do through snow and rain and sleet and hail. "Lord, here I give myself away, 'tis all that I can do..." I need the prayers of others through all the changing seasons. And of course, I will continue to pray for you, as well.

Sincerely,

"Begonia"

What Is Grief?

TITUS HOFER

Grief is the intense emotional suffering caused by loss, according to a dictionary definition.

Grief is shock and denial, especially when death is sudden. Usually the first thing we say when we hear of a sudden and tragic accident is, "No, it can't be true!" God made us this way so that our mind does not receive the full impact all at once.

Grief is tearing. There is never a clean cut. Which is easier or harder: to experience a sudden death in the family, or to experience a death after an extended illness? The one says, "You didn't have to see your loved one suffer." The other says, "You had the opportunity to say good-bye." Both conclude it is a tearing experience.

Grief is a wave. It is actually many waves, one right after the other, that leaves the bereaved gasping for air. The grieving person may be having a fairly good day, then something like a song, a picture, or a certain place triggers that rush of emotion and aching emptiness all over again.

Grief is love. The reason grief hurts so much is because we love so deeply.

Grief is guilt. What have I done to deserve this? If only I had tried something different. Was I careless? If only we had sought a different treatment. If only, if only.

Grief is overwhelming loneliness. Nightfall comes, but there is no one with whom to share the events of the day. We listen for the footsteps of our loved one, only to be struck with the overwhelming realization that we will hear them no more. Satan savagely attacks the lonely person and scatters a haze of question marks over the goodness of God.

Grief is deep weariness. It brings physical lethargy and a lack of motivation that makes little choices look like mountains and a new morning impossible to begin. It is the feeling that the world must stop and let one off because the demands of life are too overwhelming.

Grief is resentment. Thanks to the grace of God among our Christian brotherhoods, we seldom see displays of anger or resentment at a time of death. But Satan often tempts the grieving with these very feelings.

Grief is bewildered questions. It has been said that we can ask why, but we cannot demand answers.

Grief is depression. Job said, *"My soul is weary of my life…He hath destroyed me on every side, and I am gone: and mine hope hath he removed like a tree."* These words express the deep depression of a father who had lost his health, his entire living, and every one of his children.

Grief is a heart reaching out for comfort and understanding. Reproach *hath broken my heart; and I am full of heaviness: and I looked for some to take pity, but there was none; and for comforters, but I found none* (Psalm 69:20). God forbid that anyone in our brotherhood would ever be able to honestly say that no one cared.

Grief is a journey. It is not a quick pain that you experience once and then it's over like a vaccination or a bee sting. Grief is a painful healing process that takes days and weeks and months.

In the end, *Grief is acceptance.* This is the result when grief is properly processed and has done its healing work. Acceptance is the wholehearted embrace of God's will as the all-wise, ever-loving sovereignty of my heavenly Father. This is not just the grudging admission that God is bigger than I am and therefore I must reluctantly knuckle under, but the firm belief that God is too wise to be mistaken and too good to be unkind. We acknowledge the truth that even when we cannot trace His Hand, we can always trust His heart. We may wrestle long and hard to come to that acceptance, and we may struggle to always maintain it. But to move on in life, the grieving one must come to embrace the fact that *As for God, his way is perfect* (Psalm 18:30). That is true even though we will always hurt, and our loved ones will always be missed.

Grief's Exhaustion

ARLEN & KETURAH MARTIN

Grief is emotionally exhausting. We cry buckets and buckets of tears, only to see something that reminds us of our loved one— and we cry some more. We go to church and we choke back the tears that threaten to surface. We attempt to talk around the lump in our throats. We try to smile while inside we feel like a hot, dry, barren desert. We stand at the yawning abyss of anger and bitterness and we struggle for a toehold as we feel ourselves slipping. We look around and marvel that the rest of the world is going on as before, and we long to go back to the time when family life as we knew it was normal.

Grief is physically exhausting. Grief is hard work! We literally ache all over from it. We get up in the morning exhausted and go to bed exhausted. We feel as if we have been stabbed with a dull, serrated knife and the knife is slowly rotating—slicing, tearing, and ripping. The wound that we carry festers, scabs over, reopens, and festers some more, draining us of vitality and requiring years to heal. We gaze at the wound and we can't help but think back to that time when life was normal.

Grief is mentally exhausting. We cannot think. We cannot focus. We cannot concentrate. Grief overwhelms us and we often function on autopilot. Our thoughts are a boiling, churning cauldron of *what ifs* and *if onlys*. The turmoil leaves us feeling scorched and suffocated. Through the haze of questions, we look back to that time when we were a complete family and life was normal.

Grief is spiritually exhausting. We kneel to pray, and our needs, thoughts, and petitions are too deep for words. They are truly *groanings which cannot be uttered.* We struggle to trust a God who has allowed this devastation in our lives. We wonder where He is and if He really cares. The darkness overwhelms us and we can't see the Light that beckons us onward and upward. We feel adrift on the sea of life. We flounder and grasp for our Anchor. The waves crash over us and threaten to sink us. Through the storm, we look back to when life as a family was normal.

Time moves on. Days turn to months and months to years. God works His healing touch and the wound is not quite as sore, the desert not quite as dry, and the darkness not quite as black. We thank God that once more we can glimpse the Light. We thank Him that He doesn't forsake us, that He is the Anchor for all of life's experiences. We thank Him for loving us when we doubted Him. We thank Him for strength to face each day with His help. We thank Him for the friends who show they care. We thank Him that He sent His Son so that someday we can be reunited with our loved one in heaven. God gives us the courage to trust the future to Him while we as a family create a new normal. 🌹

Don't be surprised if you can't eat or if you want to eat continually, if your hair falls out for several months, or if your heart flutters and flips and your blood pressure surges. Expect headaches, fatigue, and churning stomach. These are just a few of the possible physical problems and are listed simply to alert you to the physical side of grief. *Light Through the Dark Valley*

Lessons on Grief

SHEILA J PETRE

Grief feels like hunger does, that weight of emptiness carried below my heart. It's physical, and the pain grows, and then I realize it is hunger—I've forgotten to eat. I eat, and the pain leaves. That pain.

Grief is like sitting under a blanket tent, and the light is dim, and I can't decide whether to hunch my shoulders under it or hold the blanket up with my head, and it's not sharp, or hard, or physically describable. It is just there and my body aches with the burden of keeping that blanket far enough away that I can breathe and do something else at the same time. Maybe I should concentrate on breathing only and let the other things go for now. But do I have a choice?

Grief is selfish, intruding into thoughts, letters, conversations, everyday decisions, when I want to do something else—have a normal conversation with my mother about child-training, wear a light dress to church, write to a friend about picking green beans.

Grief is lonely; not just because you have lost someone who loved you, but also because everyone else draws back into their busyness, and leaves a bubble of space around you: since they have never been where you are, and might say the wrong thing, they think they'll stay away from you and, lest they seem callous, not have a normal conversation about child-training, dress patterns, or picking green beans.

I wrote the words above in a letter to a friend, a month after I watched my six younger brothers carry our youngest brother's discarded body across the parking lot of a church in Washington State, and lower it into a gash of earth. It was the first grave in the cemetery, and the first death in our immediate family.

Edward drowned in July 2015. He was fourteen. Any of you who have lost a loved one at or near the age of fourteen will agree: this is one of the hardest ages to lose someone you love. I never knew that—until that summer. There was a lot I didn't know about grief; some days I wish I had never had to learn.

One of the most important things I learned is that the best context in which to lose someone you love is a caring church community. The phone rang the morning after Edward died, as I packed numbly. It was my mother-in-law; she was dropping everything she had planned to do that day, to help. The phone rang again; it was a friend whose brother had drowned; she was praying. It rang again. It was our deacon, calling to say he was thinking of us and praying for us. It rang again. It was another friend, saying she was coming over. Cards poured in; food came. Friends sent money to help pay for our unexpected trip.

At my parents' church, the community exhausted themselves providing food, tea, Kleenexes, and comfort for the extended family. One friend came to the house and picked up all the Sunday shirts and shoes we had for her—she took them home and must have spent hours pressing shirts and polishing shoes. I thought of her for months afterward when I put on my shoes, which had received at her hands the best polish job of their lifetime.

This friend had suffered many losses in her family; she was a great comfort. Ironically, while some fellowmourners can be the greatest comfort, others are the cruelest. I was speaking tongue-in-cheek when I wrote that fourteen is the hardest age. It is—because Edward was fourteen. But believe me, the age and the way you lost your loved one will be the hardest age, the hardest way. A sympathetic mourner will keep silent about her convictions on this subject when she goes to comfort someone who has lost a loved one in another manner or at another age. Because…

No matter how hard you try to keep from doing it, you will compare. I had observed this in grieving people before I was one of them. But after I was one of them, I realized my mind did it on its own; there was no stopping the thought.

I learned that, because of this comparison game, and for other less explicable reasons, grief disrupts friendship lines. The people who come with empty arms to hug you and full arms to bless you are not always the people you would expect to see. You wonder whether some friends ever heard of your loss, for they never mention it—or they do so with strange, hurtful words. Others send comfort, again and again—you hadn't realized they felt so close to you, but now you feel closer to them.

I learned that "why?" is often a better response than "because." We heard a lot of becauses in late 2015 and since. Though the Bible does exhort us to comfort with the comfort wherewith we were comforted, the standard "because when you suffer, you can relate better to others who suffer" creates a chicken-and-egg dilemma in my mind: If that's why I suffer, then why did they suffer? And if no one suffered, would anyone have to?

In the book of Esther, Mordecai said to his cousin, "This is why you came into the kingdom, Esther." Wait a minute. He didn't say that. He said, *"Who knoweth whether thou art come to the kingdom for such a time as this?"* Because Christ Himself, Who knew the past and the future (and Who not only knew, but is God), asked, "Why?" on the cross, I believe mortals can ask the same. When loss strikes a community, too few of us are willing to let the circumstance stand at "who knoweth?" Yet in tragedy, no one knows, and perhaps ever will know, except God.

Also—God doesn't always answer, but the answers He has already given come alive in new ways. In the raw weeks following Edward's death, passages of Scripture which had always rested calmly on the page kept leaping up and singing.

One of the hardest things I learned is that grief goes on and on. We wake in the morning and the one who was gone yesterday is still gone today. All that personality, all that potential—gone. At some point, the realization trickles down from head to heart knowledge: He will be gone for the rest of my life. There's no getting over this. If I live until then, will I weep for him in 2065? The answer is a difficult one: I probably will—unless I lose someone closer.

I learned that few people are as annoying as the person always telling you everything she has learned about grief. For this reason, you'll be glad to know I have here shared only a fraction of what I have learned. 🌸

Fifteen Things I Wish I'd Known About Grief

ANONYMOUS

After a year of grief, I've learned a lot. I've also made some mistakes along the way. Today, I jotted down 15 things I wish I would have known about grief when I started my own process. I pass this on to anyone on the journey.

1. You will feel the world has ended. I promise, it hasn't. Life *will go on*. Slowly. A new normal will come. Slowly.

2. No matter how bad a day feels, it's *only* a day. When you go to sleep crying, you will wake up to a new day.

3. Grief comes in waves. You might be okay one hour, not okay the next. Okay one day, not okay the next day. Okay one month, not okay the next. Learn to go with the flow of what your heart and mind are feeling.

4. It's okay to cry. Do it often. But it's okay to laugh, too. Don't feel guilty for feeling positive emotions even when dealing with loss.

5. Take care of yourself, even if you don't feel like it. Eat healthy. Work out. Do the things you love. Remember that you are still living.

6. Don't shut people out. Don't cut yourself off from relationships. You will hurt yourself and others.

7. No one will respond perfectly to your grief. People—even people you love—will let you down. Friends you thought would be there won't be there, and people you hardly know will reach out. Be prepared to give

18

others grace. Be prepared to work through hurt and forgiveness at others' reactions.

8. God will be there for you perfectly. He will never, ever let you down. He will let you scream, cry, and question. Release your emotions to Him. He is near to the broken-hearted.

9. Take time to truly remember the person you lost. Write about him or her, go back to all your memories with them, truly soak in all the good times you had with that person. It will help.

10. Facing the grief is better than running. Don't hide from the pain. If you do, it will fester and grow and consume you.

11. You will ask, "Why?" more times than you thought possible, but you may never get an answer. What helps is asking, "How?" How can I live life more fully to honor my loved one? How can I love better, how can I embrace others, how can I change and grow because of this?

12. You will try to escape grief by getting busy, busy, busy. You will think that if you don't think about it, it'll just go away. This isn't really true. Take time to process and heal.

13. Hobbies, work, relationships, etc. will not take the pain away. If you are using anything to try and numb the pain, it will make things worse in the long run. Seek help if you're dealing with the sorrow in unhealthy ways.

14. It's okay to ask for help. It's okay to need people. It's okay, it's okay, it's okay.

15. Grief can be beautiful and deep and profound. Don't be afraid of it. Walk alongside it. You may be surprised at what grief can teach you.

> Grief is real... Grief is complex... Grief is neither right nor wrong...(although there are some unhealthy ways of dealing with grief)... Grief is deep...Grief has many facets...Grief also has stages and each stage has NO determined length or intensity... But Grief is a personal journey... which no one can determine about another person. Each of us deal with grief differently... and yes, age, hormones, circumstances, can play a part (a havoc!) to one's journey. MP

Consolation

PHEBE J MARTIN

Sorrows too crushing to speak of
Griefs that my tongue cannot frame
Troubles too many to number
Burdens too heavy to name
But the Spirit hears all of the groanings
And in infinite wisdom and love
He bundles them up, and in mercy
Bears them to the Father above.

God has placed us within a brotherhood of believers for many good reasons. When we face a deep need in our lives we discover more of those reasons. We should open up to caring friends and tell them how we feel. They are probably wishing to talk with us but do not know how to open the subject. In most cases the brotherhood does very well in showing love and care to those in grief. However, sometimes a well-intentioned comment may be imprudently given. If the comment did not sit well with us, we should forget it. We must not add it to our list of struggles. *CLE Jr*

Doubt struggles with the tangles on the underside of life's tapestry. Faith believes God is designing the top into a beautiful masterpiece.

Tangled Black Threads

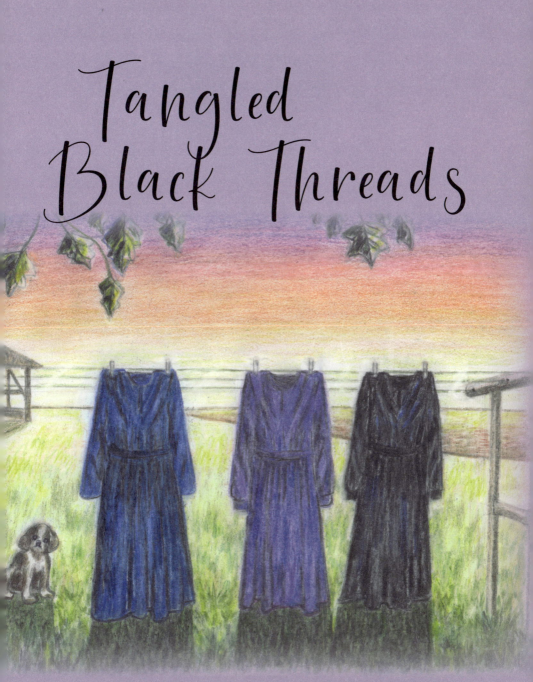

Oh my Lord, if the Lord be with us, why then is all this befallen us? And where be all his miracles which our fathers told us of? Judges 6:13

Denial Rectified

S U E L L E N   J   S T R I T E

Oh No! NO! No! This…Can't…Be…True!
This great knot of pain where my heart used to be. No.
It is not True. I will not believe it. Of course not.
Our kind loving Father would not *do* it. He would not even
Allow it.
His Father-Heart is too kind to snatch (steal!) this young man…
This tender-hearted husband…
This compassionate daddy
from his wife (my sister!) and six young children (they call me aunt!).
It is not true.
My mind is flying. Around. The Maypole.
My stomach is following suit.
There are not many tears on this ride…
Just groans, and silent screams of protest.
It is not true. So I shut it off. I go into shock mode…
I hang on the phone—making plans—No! I'm NOT making plans
because of the horrendous accident.
Because it didn't happen.
I am just making plans for…for the day—just portioning out my
children to babysitters

Because…

Because…

well; so I can go be with my sister, but NOT because she doesn't have her husband.

My sister's husband did NOT die.

I am NOT buying this piece of
BLACK FABRIC
For her. NO.

Of course not.

I'm not. Am I? No.

Of course, I am not buying it. The clerk *gives* it to me.

"Because of the situation," she says.

The situation?

But this horrible situation that everyone is talking about
IS NOT TRUE!

This is not my sister in her new
BLACK DRESS,
Pulling—   dragging—   her—   feet—
  Into church…to attend…her…own…husband's….visitation…NO!

I scream a silent denial!

I could pull my hair out!

This is NOT true!

If this did actually happen…

If this is actually true…

Then WHY…WHY…WHY can't she view his earthly body
    One
                Last
                        Time?

My body shakes with sobs. At last.

Friends grip my hand in sympathy.

"Tell me it's not true!" I holler at one of them, in a whisper, in a torrent of tears.

She pats my shoulder and walks on.

I look over at my sister hunched with grief in her new
BLACK DRESS.
And I know why my friend walked on, silently.
I know.
But I still think—at least I hope—it is
Not. True.

My husband sees that my mind is still spinning on the Maypole. So, he tries to comfort me
in his gentle way. I want to cling to him.
Yet I want to push him—away.
My sister needs her husband, too! It's not Fair!
It's not right for my husband to comfort me!
My mind is spinning so fast I cannot get my thoughts to function even into a prayer…
Except this: Why, God?
Why?

At last, I allow my husband to grasp the Maypole in his firm grip and he
slows it down.
"We need to accept comfort," he says, "so that we can comfort your sister wherewith we have been comforted." Together, we pray…more than just a little *Why?* Prayer.
Together, we read Words from God's Book:
Come unto Me…heavy laden…I will give you rest. Matthew 11:28
I will not leave you comfortless: I will come to you. John 14:18
The Lord is good, a strong hold in the day of trouble. Nahum 1:7
But though he cause grief, yet will he have compassion according to the multitude of his mercies, for he doth not afflict willingly nor grieve the children of men. Lamentations 3:32-33
Yea, though I walk through the valley of the shadow of death, I will fear no evil: for thou art with me; thy rod and thy staff they comfort me. Psalm 23:4
Put thou my tears into thy bottle: are they not in thy book? Psalm 56:8
And God shall wipe away all tears from their eyes; and there shall be no

more death, neither sorrow, nor crying, neither shall there be any more pain: for the former things are passed away Revelation 21:4

It hurts to do this together. My sister is going to bed
alone.

Yet if I hope to be any comfort at all to her in the morning, then I must accept comfort tonight, together, from the Source of all comfort.

He alone can completely stop the Maypole and give me rest in the midst of grief and turmoil and questions.

The questions linger on—and on.

Today, I asked God hesitantly,

"Did You…Really…Know…What…You…Were…Doing?"

I never asked God that before.

And I don't know if it was even right for me to ask Him today.

But why?— Why?— Why? Why did it need to be this father?— This young?— Why did he die in this way?— Why when he was so needed?— Why when his children are so little?— And some will not remember him. — Why, when he was a husband, a father, a brother, a friend?— Why? Why this man?— At this time?— In this way?

It is bringing so much grief and stress and sadness into our lives.

"Was this really Your will, God? Really?"

And His answer came in an unexpected way. But it came:

"You do not need to know the answer to all your *whys*, Daughter. Just trust the Father.

Some of your questions will only be answered in Eternity.

Some questions you will think you discover answers to…sometimes your supposed answers will be right, and sometimes wrong.

Please understand that your Father did not willfully cause this gruesome death.

He only allowed it.

God was there, at the scene, on that terrible Saturday. His angels were there.

And as soon as the victim's soul left his mangled body, the angels carried it straight into the

Father's Keeping. Weep not as those who have no hope!

God is loving and kind.

He is waiting…longing…for you to let Him work.   His work.

He wants to bring something good out of something bad.

He wants to take all the ugliness of this accident, and turn it into something beautiful.

Then slowly…I begin to understand.

God was trying to tell us this when He placed a

DOUBLE RAINBOW

In the sky, the night of my sister's husband's death.

And when He painted that

GORGEOUS SUNSET

the night of the funeral precisely for all of us who were grieving.

He was trying to tell us that if we become clay in the Potter's Hand, then He can work even an ugly

BLACK

DRESS

into something much more BEAUTIFUL

Than a DOUBLE RAINBOW or a GORGEOUS SUNSET! 🌹

Time heals grief. As time goes on, changes take place. No, we never forget our loved ones. Dates and certain happenings bring the past back to us with a crash. The most important thing is to find ourselves in the will of God, and say as well as live out "Thy will be done." So often in life our plan is plan A. We tend to look at the here and now. However, there are times that we need to go to plan B. Plan A is not plan B, but if we adjust our mindset and our will to the will of God, then plan B can prove to be a tremendous blessing because it is God's will. C Lester Eby

Question 2

Many widows struggle with *why*? How did you cope with your own *whys*?

Widows answer:

• I wondered why my five-year-old son had to still be in the hospital and could not be at the viewing and funeral of his daddy. Why was my husband taken when he was a dad and minister who was needed at home and at church? Why did my husband die after our debt was finally paid off and we had dreams for the future? The *whys* can go on and on. This is a broken world. Our *whys* need to be put at the feet of Jesus. There are a lot of *whys* which we will never understand. But God's ways and His will are perfect for us. Embrace it; accept it; and you will have peace.

• For some reason I feel I never really struggled with *why*. I felt like I just accepted his death from the start.

• The biggest *why* I grappled with was wondering why, if God has such a tender, caring heart for the widows and fatherless, then WHY does He make them?? Then once, in my devotions, I was reading about the children of Israel. Mention is made of how God delivered the Israelites from bondage and led them to Canaan with His mighty hand so that other nations could see His power and bring glory to His name. And then I wondered, *Does He do that for the widows, too? Care for them in such a way, and supply strength to go on, so that others can see His power and might, and bring glory to His name?* I need to remind myself over and over that this is for a purpose; God's way is best; all things will work together for good.

• I felt I could hardly say, "Lord, Thy will be done," when my family and I needed husband and father and brother so much. Then God sent me a few visions that were a great comfort where I saw my departed husband and sons; they seemed so at peace. How can I wish them back to such a world? It was hard, not being able to view our loved ones'

27

bodies. At first that did not bother me so much; I was just thankful their bodies were found in time to have their funeral the same day. Needless to say, as time went on, the *whys* came. Why were my husband and two sons taken at once? Why could there be no viewing? I knew I had many failures, but I blamed myself, wondering which failure this accident was a result of. But with much prayer, I came to rest in the thought that if this is what it took for me and my family to reach heaven, then I will accept it. Jesus suffered much for my sake. Heaven will surely be worth it all. God promised to be our ever-present help, and a husband to the widows.

• We dare not linger at the question *why*. We need to accept again and again. Since God has my best interest in mind, why do I think it would be so much better if my husband was here to help with teenage challenges? God must not have thought so!

• I couldn't understand why my husband was ordained as a minister only to be snatched away two short weeks later. What was the purpose? Then I thought of all the praying he did, and how we felt God's presence in our lives, and how much closer we were to each other over that time. I think that was God's way of preparing him for death, and me too. I grew in those few short weeks, becoming closer to God. I also struggled, wondering why our baby had special needs, and we only found out after my husband died. I wondered what he would have to say about it. But I knew God knows best, and my husband's soul is cared for.

• Why? When God Himself said that it is not good for man to live alone, why did He separate us? Or can a woman be alone better than a man? Yet, man is to be the leader. What is a woman to do without a leader? I always stop myself with the thought of the many single girls who never had a man to complement their weak points, or to lead them; yet the thought enters, "Yes, but neither do they have children to raise alone." I must always come back and rest in the fact that God knows best. He works things out for the best of our souls even though we cannot understand.

• Time after time I asked my heavenly Father, "Why? Why me? Why my children? Why this on top of everything else? If God is almighty, then why did He not prevent this from happening?" My best coping suggestion: Go to God, talk to Him, tell Him how confused, angry, frustrated, and hopeless you feel. Tell Him how little you understand, how you don't understand your own reactions, let alone everyone else's. Tell Him, vent to Him; He already knows what you are feeling. Be honest. Then ask Him to open your eyes to see the positive in a negative situation. Ask Him to show you how to go from here, and just do the next thing. Thank Him for something even when you don't feel thankful. Then take the next step and then the next and then the next...

• Why did my husband have to die now, when my children were still so young (ages 2-10) and could hardly help manage the farm work? Why did this happen when our farm was still in debt? Why did this happen to me, who am so young and not very smart? It was comforting to know that God chooses the weak things of the world to confound the mighty. By choosing our family, perhaps He could perform His work better than if we would have been capable to continue without so much help from others. Because of my husband's death, a non-Christian native found a church and started to attend. Another couple repented of sin in their lives. All to God's glory.

• How did I cope with my own *whys*? Let me tell you, those *whys* do come, and they are real. People told me, "God makes no mistakes." True, He doesn't. But the *whys* still come. Why did God take my husband away when we thought we were not nearly done with him? I had to decide myself that I will probably never know in this life; my *whys* will not be answered here. This actually gave me a sense of peace and overwhelming trust in my heavenly Father. He knew already before my husband was born that He would take him again that day in July of 2013. My *whys* are still not answered, but they don't have to be. God just wants me to put my hand in His and follow Him. That is enough for now.

• "WHY?" Is there any answer that satisfies? Personally, I find I have to keep eternity in focus all the time. Only eternity will explain the many unanswered questions of life on this earth. Sometimes we hear or read that Christians should never ask why. But hurting people find comfort in reading the groanings of Job, of the Psalmist, and of the prophets like Jeremiah. Even Jesus asked, *"Why hast Thou forsaken Me?"* I was blessed by a sermon about Job that pointed out that while Job did question God, he did not deny Him, and though he raised questions, he did not demand answers. At the same time, though God never answered most of Job's questions, neither did He condemn him for them (Job 42:7,8). That clarified some things in my mind, and I found them so much closer to where the rubber hits the road than some things I had read or heard.

• I did not really struggle with whys when my husband died because I had already worked through those feelings years ago when I went through a broken courtship with an altogether different person. After dating one and one-half years, he just simply quit with no explanation. It was not nice. But I had a dear dad that helped me talk things over time and again, and also a dear aunt who helped me realize this was God's plan for my life. If we pray, *"Lord, not my will but Thine be done,"* and humbly try to keep on keeping on, God makes it possible.

• Our hearts ask the *why* questions. Some people tell us we should not ask, "Why?" but rather ask, "What?" (What will You have me learn from this?) Is that what Jesus asked? Did He not also ask His Father, *"Why? Why hast Thou forsaken Me?"*
Jesus knew God's plan from the beginning. He knew God's purposes for His sufferings. And yet in the garden He wrestled with God's plan. Not once, not twice…but three times, He asked that God's plan would be changed. Were His wrestlings over after His third time of "nevertheless…?" Was He finished with His *whys?* Was God displeased with His Son for struggling with His plan for Him? Isaiah says He saw the travail of His soul and was satisfied.
David also had many questions for God. *"My God, my God! Why hast Thou forsaken me? Why art thou so far from helping me? Awake! Why sleepest*

Thou, O Lord? Oh God, why dost Thou cast us off forever? Why dost thine anger smoke against the sheep of Thy pasture? Why withdrawest Thou Thy face from me?" Yet we do not read that God condemned David for his questions. Rather, David was said to be a *man after God's own heart.*

Admittedly though, we cannot spend our entire life asking *why*. Finally, we need to realize that we simply do not know why. Even if we think we figure out why, we might still be wrong. Mordecai did not say wisely to Esther, "Thou art come to the kingdom for such a time as this." Rather, he humbly acknowledged, *"Who knoweth whether thou art come to the kingdom for such a time as this?"* (Esther 4:14).

The fact remains that only God knows the answers to all our *whys* and we find peace only as we leave our questions with Him. 🌺

> Grief is like a winding valley where any bend may reveal a totally new landscape. CS Lewis

31

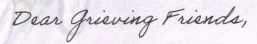

Dear Grieving Friends,

And God shall wipe away all tears from their eyes; and there shall be no more death, neither sorrow, nor crying, neither shall there be any more pain (Rev. 21:4).

Our thoughts and prayers have been with you much over the past few months. Oh, how well we remember those mind-numbing first hours as we reel from those harsh words... "Life has fled." We know the bitter anguish of standing around our loved one's casket, trying desperately to grasp something stable, hoping somehow we will wake up and this is all a horrible nightmare. We re-member the echo of that click as the casket lid is lowered and his face is forever closed from earthly sight. We sit at the gravesite and watch, watch, watch as gradually the casket slides from our view.

And oh, the utter finality of those shovelfuls of dirt slowly, slowly, slowly cover-ing up the last possibility that we will wake and find it was all a bad dream. The thud of those shovelfuls will be forever etched into our minds. We remember the frantic feeling of wanting to tell everyone to STOP, please stop. You cannot cover up my loved one! But... the casket is buried, buried along with countless hopes and aspirations we had for them.

And then ...we turn to the grueling task of living. An atomic bomb has blasted our landscape apart, leaving utter devastation in our path. The fallout leaves us gasping for fresh air. We gaze at the fragments scattered at our feet, the shards from that masterpiece we called "family." The task of piecing it back together appears unfeasible. And we come face to face with the stark realization that even though we may find most of the pieces, the jagged edges and gaping holes will always remind us of what we once had.

We remember the suffocating numbness that envelops our whole being as we walk through each day on autopilot. We remember the intense yearning to see him again, to hear his voice, to fix his favorite meal, to hear him enjoying life along with the rest of the family.

We know the turmoil of the "why" and "if only" that plagues our minds and leaves us feeling wilted and unable to cope with our life that has been reduced to rubble. We know the agony of grieving, the constant surrendering of our will until we are physically, emotionally, mentally, and spiritually exhausted.

We know the physical pain of grieving, the seemingly constant surrendering of our will over and over again until we are physically, emotionally, mentally, and spiritually exhausted. We sift through his belongings as tears stream down our faces. We set the table for meals...and one plate is missing. We do the laundry and fold the wash...and someone's clothes are missing. The family comes home... and there is one missing. His schoolmates talk together after church...and there is one missing. We sing together...and there is one missing! The chasm they left behind is bigger than the Grand Canyon and the mountain ahead of us looks as unachievable as scaling the Himalayas. The wound in our heart festers and we wonder if we will ever heal. Time marches on. Days turn into weeks, weeks turn into months, and months turn into years. We move farther and farther from that life back there where we were all together.

BUT! Thank God, we also know firsthand the One who stands by our side weeping with us. We know the One who whispers, *"Peace, be still,"* and soothes the storm that rages in our hearts. We know the One who promises to never *leave us nor forsake us.* We know the One who assures us that He will take the grief of today, mend it, and make it into something beautiful. We trust the One who provides us with the courage to get up in the morning and face the day one hour at a time because He has pledged to walk it with us. We know the One who will carry us when the valley of grief looming ahead looks too treacherous, the night too black, the path too rock-strewn, and we are simply too bone weary to take another step. And...*praise God* we know the One who sent His Son so that some sweet day we can be reunited in heaven, together as a complete family once again.

So, dear friends, *keep on*. Time does heal. Now when grief is fresh, we are not sure we want it to because we are afraid if we heal, we will forget. We will never forget!! You will never forget! We promise the footpath will not always be this impassable, the dark will not always be this opaque, and each day finds us one day nearer Home.

May God continue to be with you each day, comforting your hearts and bless-ing you with His presence. May He remain your Anchor and Compass on your voyage of life and the Light that illuminates your shadowy valley of grief.

Sincerely,

"Mr and Mrs Carnation"

What Should I Do With "Why"?

MARY E MARTIN

Moses wondered WHY…
Why must I lead these people?
Why must they grumble so?
Why must I fetch them water?
He let his burden grow,
Frustration overtook him.
Alas! He raised his rod,
And struck the rock in anger;
He disobeyed his God!

Balaam wondered WHY…
Why can't I go to Balak?
Why can't I give him aid?
Why can't God give permission?
So once again he prayed.
Alas! His prayer was selfish,
He twisted God's reply,
His stubborn will rose early;
His soul began to die!

Elijah wondered WHY…
Why can the heathen prosper?
Why must I stand alone?

34

Why must they seek to kill me?
Just let me die unknown.
He waited in his cave door;
He heard God's still small voice.
He left his cave behind him;
He made God's will his choice.

My Savior wondered WHY...
Why do My friends lie sleeping?
Why must I drink this cup?
Why did My God forsake Me?
Then He gave His Spirit up.
His will was crucified,
Temptation's war was won,
And by His resignation
Salvation's plan was done.

Today I wonder WHY...
Why did God let this happen?
Why did He take this man?
Why must I stand here weeping?
How can this be His plan?
Frustration overwhelms me,
I want to raise my rod,
My stubborn will is begging,
To strike against my God.

But when I wonder WHY...
I'll pray for resignation.
I'll listen for God's voice.
I'll leave my cave of burdens;
And make His cross my choice.
To win frustration's battle,
My stubborn self must die,
Then someday up in heaven
I'll know the reason WHY.

The Reason

Thoughts gleaned from a sermon by DARREL MARTIN

Jesus was the Son of God, the Son of Man, the Son of David, the Son of Mary, and often called the Son of Joseph. What an unusual situation! If Jesus would have limited His thoughts to what seemed normal, He would have had ample reason to feel very strange. But Jesus was blessed with the conviction that God was His Father, and all other situations were subject to that "verity."

Our lives also include some situations that seem so unique. Satan wants each of us to feel so alone in our situation, that we will use that as a reason to take our own course in life. The temptation to hide our lives in our situation is dangerous.

Why are there unique situations? The most honest answer to that question is, "That is how life is." That is not a very satisfying answer, but it needs to be understood. Life is a collection of unusual situations. I really cannot tell you the reason your life is how it is now. But be assured, God has a reason.

In Genesis 12:1, why did Abram need to leave Haran when he was comfortable there? Why do people need to be called away from what is comfortable? Life is going to include challenges. Why must there be such a drastic change when I thought I was satisfied? Most of us have familiar territories in our lives where we have experience and feel comfortable.

We think we "about know" how things are going to go, and then…! Genesis 12:1-3: It was not because of how Abram thought or reasoned, but because of God. So God could do what He intended.

In Genesis 50:19-20, why did Joseph need to forgive and show mercy to his brethren? Why give opportunity to others? Why relate mercifully to those who don't deserve it? God is reserving His place, and I must respect the place of God. God is overshadowing all of life's events with His control. When I become consumed with where I am, I need to consider where God is. Then He is recognized as the source of mercy. It is not radical to forgive…it is reasonable. GOD thinks first, but means it unto good. Reason doesn't begin with the human mind, but the eternal mind of God. Even when it hurts. V.20…to save much people alive. V.21… nourish…these are kindly words. Why should we use kindly words? God did for us. Read: Ephesians 4:32. This is what God has first and most perfectly done for us.

In Deut. 1:37-38, why did Moses need to concede and let others do what he could not do? God, in mercy, provides significant measures of blessing. He took Moses to see Canaan. God has His portion for us. Maybe we cannot go into the land, but…. God is correct. Not outwitting. He is just. We are most blessed when we say, "All right." The fact is that some can, and I cannot. God is most wise and most just by what He determines.

In Matt. 26:53,54, why did Jesus need to personally suffer when the angels could have delivered Him? Jesus knew all about the cross, the death, the resurrection, the future, but He still desired to be delivered from the cup of suffering, if possible. Jesus knew a lot about angels, and their power in heaven and on earth, so it would have seemed reasonable and special if some angelic power would take over at this time. Jesus knew angels could do all He needed. But…the Word of God stood. God spoke first. The Word of God says the pain-filled, suffering, dying Christian must suffer. Persecution is a reality. Challenges remain. Suffering is personal. There is a portion of the cup for me. Each has his own circumstances that no one else knows. But One did know. Before we get caught up in the sensation that no one else knows, we must remember that God in heaven knows. We are believing His Word. When challenges come, we can say,

"Nevertheless, not my will." God's reason must always exceed our own will.

In 1 Cor. 9:5-12, why did Paul need to live without a wife? Jesus' life inspired Paul to live in submission. God respects married, single, widows… a variety of social disciplines. God is working in disciplines in social life. God's work is worthy of our best and our all.

There is where life starts, and must be built. When God says *no*, He is really saying *yes* to another, better way. A person in such situations finds meaning in a different way; and different sources of "fullness" when life seems to deny, or not give what others have. Maybe we cannot determine the reason. But we can help each other to find meaning where we are in life.

In the wake of a tragic accident, the almost inevitable question is…why did God allow it? Although we might wish for more and better answers to that question, it is a relief to be relieved of the necessity of viewing God as having made it happen. And it is comforting to know that God is great enough to use for benefit every pain-inflicting experience that comes our way, even that which He Himself does not send. Such experiences may actually give God the opportunity to do what He otherwise could not do in the lives of the sorrowing survivors. For we are given the blessed assurance that *all things work together for good to them that love God*. Having a promise like this eliminates the need for having all our questions answered.   Merle Ruth

Confidence in the Providence of God

Thoughts gleaned from a sermon by LARRY WEBER

*U*nder whose wings thou art come to trust (Ruth 2:12).

Boaz realized that Ruth had come to trust God. Psalm 91:1-4: There is no safer place than under God's wings.

1. We must choose to trust, to have confidence in His providence. "Providence" means loving guidance and protection. Our sovereign God is *able to do exceeding abundantly above all that we ask or think...* Physical safety is secondary to spiritual safety. God wants every man to be saved. He doesn't find pleasure in sickness or in accidents...but He finds pleasure in His children trusting Him.

2. We must claim God as "my God" (Psalm 91:2). This conviction carried Ruth through life. It doesn't matter if we have a heart attack, if we are exposed to danger, or if we are threatened, God is all-wise and all-powerful. Trust God for everything. We are under God's care. What is the secret place? Near to the heart of God. The world does not know the secret place. Sometimes the world looks on and marvels at the composure of one who is in a stressful situation; this is the result of learning to trust.

The secret place is under God's authority. Keep it clear: sickness, disease, and bad things are not the direct will of God. In spite of that, we can say, "God is my God." The secret place is a fixed place. We don't ask for leave of absence and expect God to take care of us. Sorrow and despair come into our life, but God is our refuge. We are under God's wings. The devil is cunning, but he does not tell us that his end purpose is to destroy us. God's power is greater than the devil. God *will* deliver us. His truth is our shield. Let's choose God.

We can learn of birds' wings to learn of God's care. This provision is for all of life.

A. God has swift wings, like the swallow. The swallow can go around the world 89 times in 10 years. God is swift to help His children. Are we looking for physical health? No. We have something better. When our physical life is threatened, God's grace is there, swiftly. God's care, God's grace…is swift. Sometimes we wonder how someone can cope with their trials; God's grace is there when the time comes.

B. God has broad, strong wings, like the eagle. The eagle's wings span seven feet from tip to tip. God's wings are overshadowing each of us all the time. No situation is so large that God's wings won't cover. Eagles are so strong, they have picked up a child and rescued him from danger. God's strong wings can save us….and those wings can destroy and defeat the enemy.

C. God's wings are gentle. He will cover thee with soft feathers. A bird swoons gently over the nest. God relates gently. Trouble is harsh, but God comforts and assures. *Thy gentleness hath made me great… Thou shalt not be afraid of the terror by night or of the arrow by day.* We need to choose God. We choose to say, "I will not be afraid." Develop this conviction ahead of time: "Even though I am threatened, I will trust in God." Information causes fear to rock our faith. Godly men get hurt; they get sick; they die. But don't be afraid. How does God see things? He knew everything from eternity past. God is not responsible for all the bad things that happen. Maybe the car tire blows and we are hurled over a precipice; God is still good. He saw it happen. At times God does protect. We should pray for protection, if it is His will. Sometimes it is His *permissive will* for us to be hurt. It is always God's *foreordained will* to give us grace. God could have told Satan, "You aren't going to disturb the hedge I have around Job."

God is not the planner of tragedies. He allows them, but does not plan them. God did create the law of gravity. If a man sets up a ladder and reaches beyond his limit, he will fall. Why did God tell the Israelites to put a fence around the perimeter of their flat roofs? God wants us to use safety laws to protect ourselves. Sometimes we are careless or foolish. This sin-cursed world will bring death. If things were preordained then what would be the use to follow safety laws? God does permit us to make choices. But God doesn't leave us to bear those happenings alone. We must exercise our faith, and trust that God will bring something good.

What are some conditions we must meet? We need to dwell in the secret place. God's Word, His church, and fellowship with Jesus Christ: this is the secret place. We need to set our love upon God, not upon earth. We need to call upon Him. Are you praying? Asking God for help? Ask…then receive. If our prayers in general are in the spirit of helplessness, God will be there at all times. Ask for Him to show His will. Ask for His protection.

The more we learn to know God, the more we trust. The more we love, the more readily we serve. The more we serve, the greater our joy and peace.

Make the best of life by as full a knowledge of God as our present life will allow. God's wings offer full protection. To trust and obey will take the worry out of life. Turn your body, mind, and soul over to Him. God wants us to be industrious, but never worry that He won't care for us when we are limited.

Under His wings is fresh air and pure water. We can be restful and satisfied.

Give God your troubles. He will keep them forever, or until you want them back. Raymond P Brunk

Prospect
LYDIA HESS

Someday these clouds will all be rolled away;
All shadows gone, a golden, vast array
Of brand-new vista shall unfold before our eyes.
Rejoice! And hope beyond these starless skies.

Between You and God

Mother Teresa

People are often unreasonable, illogical, and self-centered; Forgive them anyway.

If you are kind, people may accuse you of selfish, ulterior motives; Be kind anyway.

If you are successful, you will win some false friends and true enemies; Succeed anyway.

If you are honest and frank, they may cheat you; Be forthright anyway.

What you spend years building, they may destroy overnight; Build anyway.

If you find serenity and happiness, they may be jealous and scornful; Be joyous anyway.

The good you do today, they often will forget tomorrow; Do good anyway.

Give the world the best you have and it will never be enough; Give the world your best anyway.

You see, in the final analysis, it is between you and God; It never was between you and them....Anyway!

Of all sad words of tongue or pen, the saddest are these, It might have been! John Greenleaf Whittier

When the Camera Clicks

Oh that I were as in months past, as in the days when God preserved me; When his candle shined upon my head, and when by his light I walked through darkness; As I was in the days of my youth, when the secret of God was upon my tabernacle. When the Almighty was yet with me, when my children were about me. Job 29:2

43

When the Camera Clicks

SUELLEN J STRITE

A photographer goes to great lengths to get a perfect picture. He arranges the scene much as one would arrange a vase of flowers. Everything is symmetrically pleasing to the eye, from the bright poppy backdrop, to the sprigs of dainty baby's breath sprinkled throughout the kaleidoscope of lilies and ferns and daffodils. Once all is to his satisfaction, he clicks the camera…and beholds a beautiful work of art which he shares with friends and copies onto calendar pages and hangs on the wall.

Although this makes a good picture, there are other, more majestic photos which capture the eye. Imagine the photographer who wants to take a photo of the old family barn, along with the stately windmill. He takes his paraphernalia out to the edge of the pasture, sets up his tripod, and squints through the camera lens.

He smiles in satisfaction. The brilliant blue sky and lush alfalfa make a perfect setting for the scene. He is about to capture the moment on his camera when…

Suddenly two deer bound out of the woods from the right! Beautiful, graceful. Leaping across the alfalfa, the white of their stubby tails flashing and their ears perked. And then they…stop! They stand perfectly still for one moment, their beady eyes darting, considering their next move….

Snap! The photographer is ready and he catches the moment. And none too soon! With quick twitches of their pointed ears, the long, thin legs vault the barbed wire, leap across the soybean field, and are gone from sight over the hill.

But the camera has clicked. The picture is permanently recorded. There is no way to ever capture the exact same photo again. Unlike the vase of flowers which can be arranged and rearranged, it is virtually impossible to pose those two particular deer under an identical blue sky in the same lush alfalfa.

What's more, there is no way to go back and change the scene. Maybe it would look better if the deer were standing closer to the barn. Maybe one has its head a bit too high, or too low. Maybe…

But the camera has clicked. The picture is recorded just as things were at that moment. A few moments before, a few moments after, and the scene would have been drastically different. Can we compare this to a sudden death?

Perhaps a long illness preceding death could be likened to the vase of flowers…there is time to rearrange the scene…time for last words… last directives….last apologies….last good-byes. Whereas, with a sudden death, the camera clicks, and the scene is captured "as is."

Think of visiting three countries: 1. WHY do I have all these trials? If we remain here, our spiritual progress is likely to remain at a standstill. 2. WHEN can I get out of all these troubles? Here, too, all we do is spin our wheels. 3. WHAT can I get out of these troubles? Then rise to the challenge! *God hath caused me to be fruitful in the land of my affliction* (Genesis 41:52). God knows how much we can bear. He shields us from being overloaded. Merle Ruth

Question 3

What regrets do you have, and how do you cope with them?

Widows answer:

• I regret that my husband cannot see the children growing up. The youngest ones do not know him at all. And they get this deep longing to see him. He was full of life and love, and it seems he is missing it all. But we know God makes no mistakes. He is at a place much better than here, so we continue on, hoping all to meet some sweet day.

• I regret that I did not build up my husband and trust him like I should have. Bygones are bygones. I cannot redo the past. But I can (and have) repented to the Lord, and I can learn from past mistakes to trust and submit to those over me, and whose advice I ask.

• I regret that too often I took my husband for granted. Too often I looked to him for happiness and fulfillment, when in reality that was unfair. Only God is able to provide that entirely. I wish I would have done better at fervently praying for my husband, and allowing God to speak to him instead of nagging so often. I wish I would have learned better housekeeping skills sooner, so my husband could have benefited from them as well. I wish I would have been less negative, and visited with him cheerfully instead of using him as a dumping station for my petty woes and trials.

• I wish I would not have cared so much what other people might think if they knew what long hours my husband was gone, or how late our suppers often were because of his job. Or what they might think of us when we didn't make it to an evening gathering, or if I came by myself because of his work schedule. I would have enjoyed having my husband home more, and apparently, I was ashamed that he wasn't. Did I assume people would then think we don't have a good marriage?! Now when I go to a meeting where most people come in couples, I admire the ladies who are brave enough to come without their husband. I actually find it easier to go to such events alone now, than I would have when my husband was still here, because now I know it's out of the question that he'd go with me. Back then, I would hope that maybe it would still suit him in the end. Sometimes it felt like he might not have really cared or tried hard enough to make it work. How do I cope with these regrets? I don't dwell on them. Besides, I know that my husband would not want me to feel bad about any of it, and that he would tell me I was a good wife for the most part.

• My biggest, most painful struggle in dealing with my husband's death is that there were things in his life that should not have been. I questioned if he was ready to meet his Maker. That was very hard for me at first, but praise God, I feel at peace about it now for the most part. I felt God gave me some special tokens of assurance during those first weeks and months that spoke peace to me. But there were some painful issues in our marriage, and I feel we did not have the solid Christian marriage that I longed for, and still long for. My husband was an excellent provider for us physically and financially, but emotionally not so much, and spiritually even less. I was at fault as well, by not being the unselfish, loving, trusting wife that I should have been. I still struggle with wondering if I have dealt with/worked through those past hurts in a healthy way.

• Yes, I have regrets. Often, since my husband is not here, I think of the many times I failed him. He was patient and easygoing, while I was strong-headed, and wanted to get things done fast. But we did have a lot of memories that are so good. I struggled with wishing I could tell him again that I am sorry for all the times I failed him. I told it to God whenever I could not go on, and that helped. Also, I needed to accept God's forgiveness, and trust He does forgive. I also talked to family about it, and they told me they know my husband wouldn't hold anything against me. Just hearing them say that helped me cope and feel forgiven. If we have regrets of the one who is no longer here, it can help us be kinder and more loving to the ones who are still with us.

• My husband seemed to have something on his mind awhile before he died. It seemed he was trying to sort it out. I regretted that I didn't probe more to get him to voice his thoughts. I coped by assuring myself that if he would have really known what those feelings were, he would have shared. I believe God was preparing him for this parting, and at the time I would not have been able to handle it anyway if I had known.

• I was sorry we never could discuss our son's special needs and what is to be done about it. My husband never knew our son had Cohen's syndrome. I was sad he could not help me cope with it, yet I think it would have been hard for him to accept. I wish he could have watched him grow up to be such a sunshine in my life. I felt our son was my gift from him.

• We did talk about his upcoming death, but I wish we would have discussed it more. Maybe we could have made more plans for when he is gone and I am alone. But I remember he did not want to bind me to anything, not knowing what the future would hold. He gave me to God, knowing He would always be with me. And I know one reason I did not talk about his death was because he was sick and weak, and finding it hard to leave me and the children. I had to be the strong one then, and I still must be the strong one.

• My only regret was, "WHY did I push my husband to go fishing that night?" Maybe it would not have happened! Maybe he would still be here! I had to let go and let God be God. I had to accept the fact that God had a plan and a purpose even before my husband was born. He had our path in mind and we are created to glorify Him so who am I to say, "O, Lord, not this!"

• I wish we had talked more on the future here for my children and me, should he leave. Things like finances, how much to give at what age? But situations are so different even within families and children's jobs.

• I wished I would have known how soon it all would end…our marriage, his business, and so much more. There are so many things we could have done differently if we had known…relocating, a different occupation, and so on. But I have to realize that apparently God wanted us where we were. And all those little details that are too miraculous to be just a coincidence can be reassuring that if God worked those little things out, He has the bigger picture in His plan too.

• I wished I could have known all the things I learned about my husband after his death. In the comments and memories people share, we see a different side to the person we lived with. Impressions that school friends, co-workers, and business acquaintances share are special, and I wished I could have asked him more questions and expressed appreciation for some of the things I learned only now. I wish I would have been able to understand him better, like I can now with the new things I learned about him. It was good for me to realize in relating to older widows, that no matter how many years a couple had with each other, when death comes, it never feels long enough. There would always be more to learn about each other, conversations we wish to continue, dreams that didn't come true.

All Things for Good

LYDIA HESS

At times our route is altered by a providential hand;
Our muscles loathe the climbing over rugged mountain land.
Though. We marvel at the summit views, the wonder we would miss
If we had not been ushered up a scenic road as this.

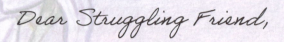

Dear Struggling Friend,

I once read of a widow who struggled with regrets. She was asked, "But if your husband had lived, would the scene have changed into something prettier?" She answered vibrantly, "Of course! We always settled our arguments and made peace." She was advised, "Then you will need to ask the Lord to help you do away with the ugly photo and focus on the beautiful pictures left in your memory file."

A widow of many years says, "Never ask a widow if her husband was saved." Everyone wants to meet their loved ones in heaven. Who knows her husband's weak points as well as his wife? When the camera snaps suddenly, with no time for apologies or good-byes, the widow may be overcome with feelings of fear for her husband's salvation. But the wife also knows her husband's desires and sincerity. Don't forget, *A bruised reed shall he not break, and smoking flax shall he not quench, till he send forth judgment unto victory* (Matt. 12:20).

On the other hand, sometimes the one left has regrets about things for which she never had time to apologize to her husband. One young girl struggled with regrets after her father was snatched from this life. The advice was given to her, "If Daddy were here and you apologized to him, would he forgive you?" She replied that yes, of course she knew he would. "Then you need to rest in that knowledge. The past cannot be changed, but what we do from here matters." The same holds true for the sorrowing widow who wishes she could recall that last sharp word. Finally, we need to move on; we do serve a merciful God who *understands our frame and remembers that we are dust* (Psalm 103:14).

Sincerely,

"Dahlia"

♡ *We can never change the past. When the camera clicks, it is all over. We may wish with all our heart that things could have been different, but that will not change the past. It can change the future. We need to live and plan and relate to others today so that if it is the last day, there are no regrets.* C Lester Eby

That Secret Struggle

SHEILA J PETRE

In many ways, my fourteen-year-old brother's funeral was full of triumph and hope. He had committed his life to God the previous year, and been baptized less than three months before he drowned while swimming with his brothers. He had chosen to live a godly life, and now—he was in glory! The joy of that, the hope, lined our grief with something light enough to see and strong enough to cling to. Together we talked about it, and were grateful.

Alone, in the dark hours, doubt slithered in. How could we be sure? We knew our own secret thoughts; all the ways in which we did not measure up to the perfection of the One Who offered our salvation. What about my brother? What unconfessed sin might he have harbored? He was so human! What if…?

At these times, I remembered my friend Miriam. Miriam lost a younger sister to an autoimmune disease. Her sister was a quiet, vibrant person, calmly carrying out her roles as daughter, sister, aunt, and friend. None who had known her would have questioned her Christianity. But Miriam told me, when she called to offer sympathy and the promise of prayer the morning after my brother died, that sometimes she worried about her sister's salvation. She knew of no thing which was amiss in her sister's life, but she still sometimes…feared.

Until she realized that this fear carried with it no redemptive quality. It could only come from Satan, wearing her down as it did, filling her mind with venomous confusion. After she recognized the source of her doubt, she was able to overcome it, to say *"Get thee behind me, Satan"* by the power of God.

I shared Miriam's thoughts with a widow friend from the West Coast, and she responded with these words in a letter: "this is a common struggle. But I think it is one we tend to struggle with alone, because we are afraid of bringing it up… lest we reflect on our husband's character or raise questions in other people's minds."

The lonely struggles can be the hardest ones. Widows knew their husbands as few others did. They saw the weaknesses, the failures. As a wife, you may have struggled to overlook some imperfection—or many imperfections—in your husband. Perhaps you discussed these things with him, and no lasting change occurred. As a widow, these memories are worrisome—but who do you tell?

Find another trusted widow friend, or perhaps your mother-in-law, and share your heart; you will discover you are not alone. Sharing your worries with someone else does not mean you didn't love your husband. Despite how the rest of the world may appear, we are all, each of us, flawed individuals needing grace.

If you can think of no other person with whom to share, take your fear to God. He alone knows your husband better than you did. These doubts do not come from Him. The cup He gives you to drink is strong with grief and heartache, but taste and see that He is good; He offers triumph and hope.

> Ere thou sleepest, gently lay
> Every troubled thought away;
> Put off worry and distress
> As thou puttest off thy dress.
> Drop thy burden and thy care
> In the quiet arms of prayer...
>
> Henry Van Dyke

52

A victim feels desperate and pouts a lot; a survivor feels dependent and prays a lot.

Under the Juniper Tree

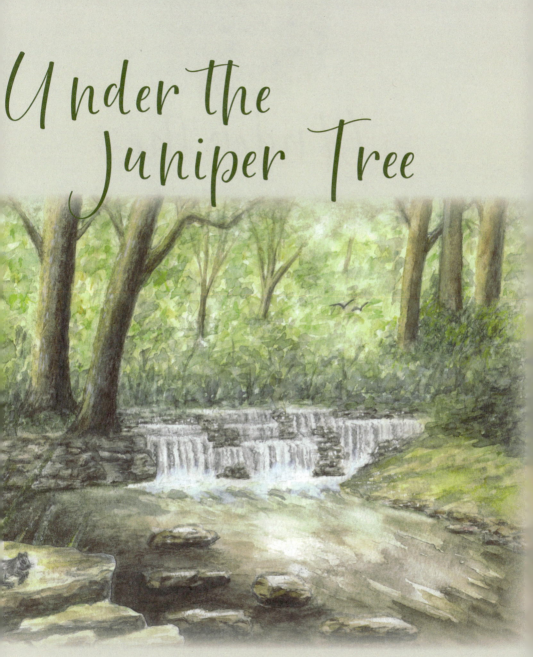

...[Elijah] went a day's journey into the wilderness, and came and sat down under a juniper tree: and he requested for himself that he might die; and said, It is enough; now, O Lord, take away my life. 1 Kings 19:4

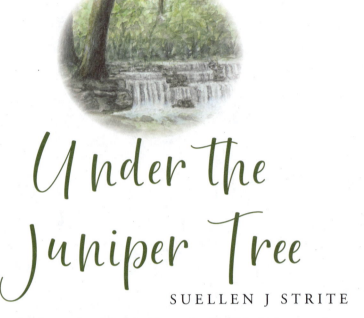

Under the Juniper Tree

SUELLEN J STRITE

Anne Steele was the oldest daughter of an English timber merchant. She was only three years old when her mother died. Anne's father, in spite of his grief, was a good man and he raised Anne for the Lord. He also pastored a church in Broughton, England, for forty years without a salary. Anne joined the church of her father when she was fourteen years old.

At the age of nineteen, Anne's hip was severely injured, leaving her an invalid in the prime of her life. But then, brighter days came her way, when she met a young man, Robert Elscurot, whom she learned to love. In spite of her handicap, he eventually proposed to her.

But, alas! Her beloved drowned the day before their wedding. Anne suffered much as an invalid, and an *almost widow*. I think there must have been many times she could have sat down under a juniper tree and wished for death.

Instead, Anne began writing devotional material. When she was in her mid-forties, she submitted some of her writings for publication. Her father prayed as she sent off her manuscripts, "I entreat a gracious God, who enabled and stirred her up to such a work, to direct in it and bless it for the good of many…I pray God to make it useful and keep her humble."

God answered that prayer, and many of Anne's poems were converted to hymns which we still sing today. We can hear Anne's heartfelt pleas to God in the following two hymns which she penned when she was forty-four years old:

My God, my Father, —blissful name,—
O may I call Thee mine!
May I with sweet assurance claim
A portion so divine!
Whate'er Thy providence denies,
I calmly would resign;
For Thou art good and just and wise;
O bend my will to Thine.
Whate'er Thy sacred will ordains,
O give me strength to bear,
And let me know my Father reigns,
And trust His tender care.

Father, whate'er of earthly bliss
Thy sovereign will denies,
Accepted at Thy throne of grace,
Let this petition rise:
Give me a calm and thankful heart,
From every murmur free;
The blessing of Thy grace impart,
And make me live to Thee.
Let the sweet hope that Thou art mine
My life and death attend,
Thy presence through my journey shine,
And crown my journey's end.

Anne Steele's earthly journey ended on November 11, 1778. As she closed her eyes for the last, her weeping friends heard her whisper, "I know that my Redeemer liveth."

Day after day, widows observe married couples; they watch other people's children holding their daddies' hand; they notice complete families with a father and a mother; they witness new homes being formed and the process starting all over.

These sights can leave the widows feeling alone, deserted, overworked, and misunderstood. These miserable feelings can pile up high enough that one day they call from beneath their mountain, "I am a worthless victim of unfortunate circumstances! Nothing good will ever come of all this. Just let me sit under a juniper tree and die!"

Human nature will take the widow to the juniper tree often. The devil would like to keep her there, too. God noticed Elijah sitting there under the tree and He did not want him to stay there. But He did not harshly condemn Elijah; instead He brought Elijah nourishment and encouragement. He helped Elijah focus on facts rather than his feelings of the situation. Elijah responded rightly. He arose and went in the strength of that meat for forty days.

If Anne Steele spent time under a juniper tree, she did not stay there either. She "arose," looked to God, and focused on being an encouragement to others.

Sometimes the widow drops down under the juniper tree and…just wants to stay there. Not always does her tree even look like a juniper; it might look like a birch tree, with a scenic waterfall in the background. But if she is staying there feeling sorry for herself, and believing that no one has life as tough as she does, well, then it is a juniper, no doubt. And however difficult it may be, she eventually needs to accept her heavenly Father's nourishment and encouragement to get up and continue on as Anne Steele and the prophet Elijah did, for another "forty days."

God could have kept Daniel out of the lions' den. He could have kept Paul and Silas out of jail. He could have kept the three Hebrew children out of the fiery furnace. But God has never promised to keep us out of hard places. What He has promised is to go with us through every hard place, and to bring us through victoriously. Rosell

Question 4
How do you cope with feelings of self-pity?

Widows answer:

• Self-pity must be cast aside as soon as it enters your mind! Otherwise, you will go down. Acceptance is part of healing. Others do not have it better, even though it might appear that way. Overcome self-pity by reaching out and thinking of those who do not have a blessed married life, or have health struggles. Do an act of kindness. Call or visit a friend. I am prone to pity myself on Sundays, driving the horse, alone, after I raised nine children alone. Seeing couples together on Sundays is hard. But the Lord has promised us to be overcomers. He is our comfort.

• I feel most sorry for myself when I think of the possibility that even though I am young I might never experience the special closeness of marriage again. It feels like I am being deprived of one of the biggest joys of life by not being married anymore. If I am not careful, I can feel (believe) that being married would really be the answer to happiness, when in reality I know it is not true. Life can be joyful and fulfilling in Christ no matter what our marital status is. It is good for me to focus on ways God can meet spouse-needs in my life, and then thank Him for it. "Thank you, God, that You can be my Husband, my Worth, My Encourager, my Motivator, my Best Friend, my Advisor, my Director, my Listening Ear." The list could go on and on. The key is to make sure I am allowing Him to meet my needs by being open to Him. Sometimes I feel sorry for myself that no human knows me as personally as my husband did. No one who sees my bad and good sides, and yet encourages and affirms me anyway. I am guessing all widows, widowers, and singles could use extra encouragement and affirmation. But no flattery, please!

• If pity wants to surface, the best I found was to think of our many single sisters, or those with marriage problems; then pray for them, and count my blessings that we had a blessed and lovely marriage even if quite short. I am left with children, so I feel we still have part of my husband with us. And now they are all grown and have families of their own, yet they still care so deeply for their mother in many loving ways. What a blessing.

• Usually when I find I am pitying myself, there is only one thing that helps me overcome; that is being *thankful*. Being thankful for what I had; being thankful for what I still have. It is only by the love, grace, and mercy of God that we have these gifts. Weddings are not easy for widows. It helps me to remember that we were also at one time in the new couple's shoes. We were happy together. And it is right and good for them to be happy as well.

• I feel sorry for myself when I ask someone to do something and then wait weeks and weeks until it gets done. Or when it seems my life is harder than other ladies' because I no longer have my husband to pull the heavier load. I can really feel that way when I have to make umpteen trips carrying heavy buckets of water to fill up the trough because the hoses stay frozen day after day. I cope by praising God in song, going over my list of blessings, or simply throwing myself at the Lord's feet and telling Him the battle is too hard for me; will He please take over? Of course, doing something for someone else, even one of my children, helps me forget myself.

• It is a deal to work through to see happy couples. But far worse is to see unhappy, or "pretend happy" couples and seeing women who do not support their husband. Woe to their children in the future when they get to teenage years. Pray for them.

• I feel sorry for myself when I see other couples going places together and enjoying their retired life after raising their families; I don't get included because a single person is such an odd number. To go alone can be too awkward. To cope, keep busy at home and remember widowhood is just for this life. Once we enter heaven's gate, we no longer will care how hard our situation felt at times; we will be Home!

• I had a hard time accepting that we were so young, and our life seemed to have barely started. I would look at couples who had been married thirty or forty years and wonder why we had to part so soon. But it was easier to accept when I compared our marriage to my sibling's unhappy one. I felt blessed that ours was happy and we were true to each other. A long, unhappy marriage is far worse than a short, happy one. So, I try to be content.

• The time I am hit hardest with feeling sorry for myself is when I see a husband take care of his wife and when I travel with couples and watch a husband bring his wife to church. But maybe the hardest of all is dinner invitations. The woman is left out at the end of the walk, then the husband takes care of the rig. Thinking about God and heaven does not really help, for it seems that will be a long time in coming. The best way I cope is to get involved with other people's joys and trials. Especially those with ongoing trials. Who can better empathize than one who has to work through the process of acceptance again and again?

• When I see women and children living life the way God intended, I have an ache inside. If only I would not know what I do. If only I and my children could have remained innocent of so much hurt, heartache, disappointment, and acceptance. If only life would look so blissfully full of promises of hopes and dreams without the knowledge of reality. I did not know what tired was until I became a widow. I did not know what depression or hopelessness felt like. I did not know what forgiveness or acceptance took until I had to do it. I did not know Who God was until I became a widow and He was all I had left. I also learned what true joy is, and yes, God has been good and I can finally thank Him for giving me, *treasures of darkness and hidden riches in secret places* (Isaiah 45:3).

• In the recent months before my husband's death, for some reason I was especially dreaming of growing old together. Things like going on business trips together once our children were grown. (His work took him out of the area at times, and with several young children, he was needing to curtail some of those jobs since we couldn't all come with him anymore.) While I still feel cheated sometimes, it is good for me to remind myself that even those couples who do enjoy 50 or 60 years together don't always have opportunity to fulfill those dreams. Sometimes there are special-needs children who still need care when others their age are empty nesters. Or one, or both, of them may struggle with health difficulties that limit those possibilities.

Sometimes it is so hard to see other couples our age whose lives continue on where ours was so abruptly cut off. Most couples have years of sharing daily life and raising children, while they learn to know more about each other. For those of us whose life together is cut off after only a few years, we feel cheated out of those years of deepening relationship, of merging backgrounds and ideals, of raising our family together with the combined strengths from each home. One thought that crystallized in my mind that first week was, *We still had so far to go together!*

And yet, we don't want there to be more widows; we do want to see happy couples like God planned for most people! If we cut ourselves off from them because of the pain, we are also cutting ourselves off from the ways God uses normal families to fill in some of the void in our home. I find that in rejoicing with others whose home and business life continues like we dreamed of ourselves, we are blessed along with them in so many ways. And it is good for us to enter into the setbacks and disappointments that they too experience along the way, even though they may feel so minor in comparison with what we have lost. To quote Nikki Haley who grew up in an immigrant family who had a different background and dressed differently than most of their contemporaries… "My mom would say, 'Your job is not to show people how you're different. It's to show them how you're similar.'" I take that as a personal challenge. Often those differences feel much bigger to us than to those we relate to, and there is a lot to be gained in continuing to relate to friends and family like before.

• I struggle with pitying myself because I feel so lonely. A dear sister sent me a card that said, "Loneliness is our friend…when it causes us to enjoy the companionship of God as much as that of a friend." That helped me realize that I have enough when I have God.

60

Dear Young Widow,

It is so easy for us widows to pity ourselves! But as an older widow, I would like to encourage you to steer clear of that pit. It is easy and human to feel cheated, especially if people around you are living the dream you have now lost. You wanted to raise a family and grow old with your husband. And here you are left struggling to raise the family alone, make a living, and give your children a healthy view of a loving God...

When at times God feels so far away, remember, He did not do this to punish you. He has a plan and a purpose. We live in a fallen world; bad things will happen. But if we allow it to, God can use this to His glory and your life can be made richer than you can imagine.

After many, many dark days, when healing comes, you will be able to appreciate the better days so much more. Yes, acceptance is a work in progress, and can be frustratingly elusive! But fight for it, grab for it, and hang on to it. Then once again, joy will come into your heart and life will seem manageable again. You will be able to say, "God is good, even if life isn't."

Sincerely,

"Dianthus"

If you want to be miserable, look inside. If you want to be distracted, look around. If you want to be peaceful, look up.

Author Unknown

Whose Loss Is Worse?

GERALD SITTSER

Gerald Sittser lost his wife, daughter, and mother all in the same vehicle crash.

We tend to quantify and compare suffering and loss. We talk about the numbers killed, the length of time spent in the hospital, the severity of abuse, the degree of family dysfunction, the difficulty and inconvenience of illness, the complexity of details during a divorce, or the strings of bad luck. I have done so myself. After the accident, I found myself for the first time on the receiving end of this process. The newspapers covered the story for several days running. I received hundreds of telephone calls and thousands of cards and letters. I became an instant celebrity—someone whose loss could not be imagined or surpassed. Consequently, I often heard comments like, "Three generations killed in one accident!" Or, "All the important women in your life gone, except for poor Catherine!" And most frequently, "I know people who have suffered, but nothing compared to you. Yours is the worst loss I have ever heard about."

But I question whether experiences of such severe loss can be quantified and compared. Loss is loss, whatever the circumstances. All losses are bad, only bad in different ways. No two losses are ever the same. Each loss stands on its own and inflicts a unique kind of pain. What makes each loss so catastrophic is its devastating, cumulative, and irreversible nature.

What value is there to quantifying and comparing losses? My own loss was sudden and traumatic, as if an atomic blast went off, leaving the landscape of my life a wasteland. Likewise, my suffering was immediate and intense, and I plunged into it as if I had fallen over a cliff. Still, the consequences of the tragedy were clear. It was obvious what had happened, and what I was up against....

On the other hand, I have a cousin, Leanna, with multiple myeloma, an incurable form of cancer. Her loss has been gradual and subtle, as it probably will continue to be. The landscape of her life is being destroyed slowly, one square inch at a time. Her suffering lingers on and on, and pain wears her down like friction wears down metal. Little inconveniences, like walking with a cane, remind her at every turn that she is sick. She has no idea what is going to happen to her in the next three years or even in the next three months. She worries about her two teenage children and about her husband, who has Parkinson's disease. That cancer looms over her, casting an ominous shadow over her entire world.

So, whose loss is worse, hers or mine? It is impossible to give an answer. Both are bad, but bad in different ways.

Is it really useful to decide whose losses are worse?

Catastrophic loss of whatever kind is always bad, only bad in different ways. It is impossible to quantify and to compare. The very attempt we often make in quantifying losses only exacerbates the loss by driving us to two unhealthy extremes. On the one hand, those coming out on the losing end of the comparison are deprived of the validation they need to identify and experience the loss for the bad thing it is. They sometimes feel like the little boy who just scratched his finger, but cried too hard to receive much sympathy. Their loss is dismissed as unworthy of attention and recognition. On the other hand, those coming out on the winning end convince themselves that no one has suffered as much as they have, that no one will ever understand them, and that no one can offer lasting help. They are the ultimate victims. So, they indulge themselves with their pain and gain a strange kind of pleasure in their misery.

Whose loss is worse? The question begs the point. Each experience of loss is unique, each painful in its own way, each as bad as everyone else's, but also different. No one will ever know the pain I have experienced because it is my own, just as I will never know the pain you may have experienced. What good is quantifying loss? What good is comparing? The right question to ask is not, "Whose is worse?" It is to ask, "What meaning can be gained from this loss?"

Victims have no power to change the past. No one can bring back the dead. There is no going back. But there can be going ahead. Victims can choose life instead of death. They can choose to stop the cycle of destruction in the wake of the wrong done, and do what is right. Forgiveness is simply choosing to do the right thing. It heals instead of hurts, restores broken relationships, and substitutes love where there was hate. Life is mean enough as it is; they choose not to make it meaner.

It was the brokenness of my children that reminded me every day that they had had their fill of suffering. I did not want to see them suffer anymore. I realized that my unforgiveness would only prolong their pain. I knew they were watching me, whether deliberately or unknowingly, to see how I responded to the wrong done to us. If I was unforgiving, they would most likely be unforgiving. If I was obsessed with the wrong done to me, they would too. If I lived like a victim for the rest of my life, they would probably do likewise. If I drove all mercy from my heart, they would probably follow my example. They, too, would insist on fairness, and when that failed them, as it surely would, they would want revenge. I did not want such a plague in my home. I did not want to raise bitter children. So, I chose to forgive, for their sake as well as my own. 🌹

A thought: I know not why,
There comes to me today,
The thought of someone,
Miles and miles away,
Unless there be a need,
That I should pray.

Author Unknown

64

Widowed but Whole

DELMAR AND DARLETTA MARTIN

In the human life cycle, a person matures from a completely dependent infant to a whole, independent adult. This wholeness is not a self-sufficiency that is without need of close relationships. Rather, it is a stable maturity that benefits from giving and receiving in close relationships. While marriage is not necessary for a person to become a whole adult, marriage can contribute to a healthy maturation.

In an ideal marriage, two individuals merge their wholeness to create a union of greater capacity than either could have alone. This union can provide the ideal relational environment for a new generation of dependent children to be cared for.

When death comes to a marriage, the intertwining of two whole persons who have become one whole, must separate. This is hard work. In addition to the loss of the gender qualities of the deceased spouse and the increased responsibilities of caring for the children, you have the work of becoming an independent, whole person again. This involves taking back the part of yourself that you have put into your spouse, and letting go of the part of your spouse that he has put into you.

In a sense, this defines the work that is required for the successful recovery of a survivor. It cannot be done quickly, but it must be done if you are to have the capacity to face life as a healthy, happy single or remarried person. This does not mean that you completely separate yourself from your identity with your deceased spouse. Your spouse has helped to shape who you are. This is yours to keep. In that sense, the life of your deceased spouse will live on in you, and everyone you relate to will be touched by that part of your spouse. It is a true honor to a spouse to successfully grieve the death, and to retain the capacity to give and receive in healthy relationships.

Misunderstood

MARY E MARTIN

Today my sister shared with me
A basketful of bread.
She saw my lonely, starving heart,
And thought I should be fed;
But when I tried to eat, I found
Some lemons there instead!

"What shall I do, O God," I groaned,
"With such a raw mistake?
My soul cannot absorb this food,
I think my heart will break.
Just let me crush these lemons, Lord;
I simply can't partake!"

My Father's answer came to me,
Descending like a dove,
"Just crush your lemons with My grace,
Add sweetener with My love;
The water of forgiveness pour
With power from above."

As I repent of bitterness,
My grief begins to fade;
For by the death of God's dear Son,
This recipe was made.
With healing heart, I reach my hand;
My soul sips lemonade.

Through Faith, I Can

ANONYMOUS WIDOW

When the dark cloud of widowhood shrouded me, I felt like giving up. What was the use to try to meet the needs of my family without my husband's help? But someone told me there is no room in a widow's life to say, "I can't."

Since then, Hebrews 11:11 has blessed my soul and given me strength many times. God had promised Sara the impossible. She could never have had a child in her old age, of her own strength, and she knew it. But, through faith, Sara herself received the strength she needed from God to achieve the impossible.

Through faith we too can receive strength from God to:

1. Rise each morning and face the day, knowing it will be another day of aching loneliness and grief.

2. Meet the needs of our families to the best of our abilities. We need to claim the promise that God will give wisdom liberally to those who ask without wavering. And as He gives answers, He will also give strength to carry them out.

3. Attend weddings and funerals without our companion by our side. Weddings, in particular, focus on couples; not to mention the painful reminders of our own joy and youthful innocence on our wedding day.

4. Assemble three meals a day even when the one whom we used to

cook for is not here to enjoy our efforts. Our children deserve their mother's attention, too.

5. Make mealtimes cheerful and full of friendly conversation when the empty chair at the head of the table is cutting holes into our already hurting hearts.

6. Lead the family in daily worship, even though it should be Daddy's role. More than ever, our families need to be taught to find comfort in God and the promises of His Word.

7. Sing as a family, even though the bass voice is missing. Though it may cause tears in our eyes and pain in our hearts, our children should never get the message from us that singing is no longer approved of because of the grief in our hearts.

8. Forgive the misunderstandings, the ignorance, the criticism, the callous indifference, and the gossip. We must remember that there may be those who hurt with us who simply do not know how to express comfort as they would like to.

9. Drive the children to school on snowy mornings and meet fathers bringing their children.

10. Remain calm during a severe summer thunderstorm. Our children may be extra fearful since Daddy is no longer here. Our example of trust can be their security.

11. Let go, when necessary. It can be a challenge to not become overprotective. At times it is best to let our children be with other families to learn the give and take of normal family life with a strong father figure.

12. Ask for needed help, whether financial, emotional, social, or spiritual. Admitting that we are unable to meet some of the needs of our family is humbling. But God has not designed us to bear our burdens alone. That is why He *has placed the solitary in families.*

13. Make the evenings a time of pleasant family togetherness, even though we don't feel like a family anymore. Sometimes putting a puzzle together may be the last thing you feel like doing, but we need to focus on the family members we still have with us.

14. Review memories of happier days.

15. Crawl into a cold and lonely bed, knowing our heavenly Maker-Husband is with us and will watch over our family all night. He will be

awake when we waken at midnight. He will be listening for our daily plea for strength to "keep on keeping on" in the dark valley of the shadow of death.

Sara could have sat down and protested that she simply could not have a child. Instead she was given strength because she had faith in God. I am strengthened by Sara's example of faith and strength. God will strengthen you too, if you will ask Him in faith. *For He is faithful that promised.*

Eye of the Whirlwind

S W

Peace to you, Job
Peace in the ashes
Peace in the oozing boils
Peace in the empty pastures
Peace in the silent barns.
Peace at the ten grave mounds
ALL
Is in My hands
ALL
Is in My heart.
Much you do not know
My hedge is threatened,
But
It shall not be broken through.
Peace be unto you,
Job.

From Horizontal to Vertical

SHARON YODER

Sharon Yoder offers the following helps from her book, *To Have and To Hold*. Although written from the perspective of a single woman, widows can benefit from her insights as well.

"[E]very woman has] intense desire for emotional intimacy with a male. Emotional connection validates her need for belonging and security. For women, emotional connection is fostered through conversation and kindness. When a man patiently listens to her expressed feelings and responds with kind words, she is quickly charmed and drawn to him" (p. 107).

"How then can a woman's need for emotional intimacy be met outside of marriage? Her connection with men in general cannot provide a substitute for the intimacy of marriage. Neither can she capture a surrogate satisfaction from other relational sources, and live with every desire met. Intimate connection with a man is reserved for a committed relationship. But remember, marriage does not fill every hunger either. Only God is enough. There are many times when we as women must offer our unfulfilled longings to Him, allowing His love and comfort to satisfy us in a way no human relationship can" (p.108).

"Meaningful, appropriate male and female relationships do exist outside the marriage covenant. When we learn to draw our belonging and security from relationship with God, we are freed to share in a wider spectrum of male and female completion. In God's economy, femininity and masculinity offer to each other unique and precious gifts that cannot be received from any other source" (p.108).

"One of a woman's most basic needs is for emotional bonding and intimacy. A woman's hunger for connection is like a funneled chalice which needs continual assurance of a committed love. If her funneled chalice runs empty, she will deeply desire to give expression to her need for emotional bonding and intimacy. In her emptiness, she is tempted to fill her need in the context of herself. She may succumb to [temptations] that make her feel fully alive and beautiful as a woman. Strangely, she ends up feeling empty and shameful afterward" (p.122).

"Women have been frustrated with their strong desires for marriage and intimacy, feeling the tension of godly boundaries. How does one remain pure in the throes of desire? Certainly, being a Christian does not eradicate desire! God designed and created the physical bodies of men and women. They are distinctly male and female. In His infinite wisdom, He placed in these bodies hormone levels that would induce desire, creating in each a need for the other. These desires are not wrong; nor are they unscriptural. Quite the opposite!

"We must recognize that the physical and emotional realms make us most acutely aware of desire. Our bodies and souls have needs and cravings. They stir up desires when they become aware of a perceived lack. They crave the comfort of fulfillment. When our bodies are exhausted, we long for sleep. When they are hungry, we desire food. When our hearts are lonely, we yearn for companionship. Desire seeks fullness" (p. 111-112).

"God calls single women to live in the submission of deferred hope. He wants us to know He sees what we cannot see. In submission to Him we find rest and freedom. When our hearts are at rest, we are freed from the need to engage in compulsory, impure habits" (p.124) .

"The sacred joining of a man and wife is, in part, a picture of what God intends for the consummation of all things in Jesus and His bride, the church. What is now withheld [for the widow] will not be withheld in the new heaven and new earth. Single and married people alike will then experience in their redeemed bodies what the union of oneness was only foreshadowing, as they bring their gifts of fidelity to the marriage supper of the Lamb" (p.130)!

"Psalm 68:5,6… God provides solutions for those in need. When He reaches out to the fatherless, He becomes a Father to them. He tells the widows that He will become their Advocate. Now, both the widows and fatherless may already have learned dependency through existing supportive relationships. The fatherless often have mothers. Widows most often have families. In their distress, God now calls them to turn from horizontal relationships to a vertical relationship that places their trust and faith in Him" (p.223).

"Who is there…to love us unreservedly, exclusively, and unendingly? Who is there to hold us in an eternal embrace—to protect us, shelter us, and fight for us? You do have a Prince. I have a Prince. The Prince of Peace has come to us, and will come for us. When He comes, all that is wrong with the world will be made right. It is this hope that gives us the ability to live in a fallen world, a world that is in opposition to everything that points toward God" (p.255).

"Life is not found in having the perfect Christian husband. Life is not found in beauty or popularity. Life is not found in comfort, connection, or competence. No, fullness of life is found in turning ourselves toward the scrutiny and gaze of a Redeemer whose eyes are full of love and mercy. Life is in opening our hearts to the Lover of our souls who walks with us in all of our relationships. And finally, life is turning our spirits toward the Tree of Life, who fills all our desires with His wholeness. Thus, our shameful fig leaves will be exchanged for a robe of God's righteousness, and we will bask in the glory of His freedom and truth forever" (p.100-101)!

We take the care and kindness of our brotherhood for granted…but where are we for those hurting silently? The "bile ducts," the "arthritic joints," the "thyroid issues," the "ulcers," the "skin rashes," of our church body. Even the little "paper cuts"…they hurt too! *Mary Petre*

If any lift of mine may ease the burden of another,
God give me love and care and strength to help my ailing brother. Anonymous

Catching Fish

Pure religion and undefiled before God and the Father is this, to visit the fatherless and widows in their affliction. James 1:27

Catching Fish

SUELLEN J STRITE

In 2016, our 13-year-old had surgery to put a pin in his hip due to the growth plate slipping out of kilter. Our 11-year-old had his inflamed appendix removed. Our 17-year-old had 25 stitches in his hands to shut up what a garage door spring tore open. And my husband faced major surgery to repair achalasia, which is a malfunction of the sphincter muscle between the esophagus and stomach. Bills were making a mountain on our desk, and questions were making piles in our minds.

One night as our son was under anesthesia, my husband reached for the Bible and read the account in Luke chapter five where the disciples fished all night and caught no fish. Dejectedly, he informed me, "I feel like those disciples."

Quite soon after this, he had his surgery. It turned out to be even more major than we expected, recovery took longer than we imagined, and our faith felt weaker than we had anticipated. My brother stopped in to see how we were faring. We threw the question to him, "How is it that we keep casting our nets and casting our nets, yet our boat never fills up?"

He studied a bit, but gave up. "I will have to think about that one," he confessed. He turned to leave, and then suddenly whirled around. "Did you have anything for lunch today?"

"Oh, yes," we told him. "A kind sister from church brought us a steaming bowl of potato soup."

"There is your first fish," he said simply. He grinned like he had caught that guppy himself.

We stood flabbergasted and watched him leave. In the following weeks, many "fish" came in our front door. It was almost exciting to see the different species…bass, trout, mackerel, tuna…several oysters and clams. Even a few whales! Now we had food to eat and help to pay our bills, but more importantly, our faith was boosted. It was comforting to know our church family cared that much.

Not as soothing was the realization that apparently God did not intend for us to catch all our own fish right now. That takes a lot of sputtering and gulping, but what are the options? Drown? Starve? Give up our faith?

There are many reasons God placed the church here. One of those purposes is so there is someone available to help us catch fish when our efforts are not enough. There is no way a widow can catch enough physical, emotional, and spiritual fish for herself and her children, all by herself. It is depressing for her to realize that if her husband were here, fishing would be much simpler. In fact, sometimes when she and her children are out in the black night casting their nets, she feels like wailing, "This is impossible." But what are her options? Drown? Starve? Give up the faith? NO! When the widow's feeble net comes up empty, let the church family give from their nets to supply her need. 🌸

To love at all is to be vulnerable. Love anything and your heart will certainly be wrung and possibly be broken. If you want to make sure of keeping it intact, you must give your heart to no one, not even to an animal. Wrap it carefully around with hobbies and little luxuries; avoid all entanglements; lock it up safe in the coffin of your selfishness. But in that casket—safe, dark, motionless, airless—it will change. Your heart will not be broken; it will become unbreakable, impenetrable, irredeemable… The only place outside of heaven where you can be perfectly safe from all the dangers of love…is hell. CS Lewis

Question 5

In what way does your ministry support you that you most appreciate?

Widows answer:

My ministry:

... cares about us.

...promises to pray for us... and then they do.

... prays aloud for us.

...helps to teach our children spiritually.

...provides someone for me to go to for advice with decisions.

...sends us mail and scrapbooks.

...helps us financially, especially when we have major medical bills.

...brings in Sunday meals, or invites us to their place for Sunday dinner.

...is available.

...shares tidbits with us from the ministers' meetings. (Things the deacon has shared with me from ministers' meeting discussions about us have always inspired me. It helps me know they really care about us and want to help us have a home as normal as possible and develop children that can be an asset to the church, rather than a drain.)

I have become aware of an area needing attention: Those who are standing by need support too! Those standing by are the ones who are picking up the pieces behind the scenes...the ones filling in where needed...the ones who hurt, cry, and mourn just as deeply, but they may lack support because this is not their personal loss. We have stood by several times and hurt and cried and gave and gave and then came home and crashed alone. I know it is more blessed to give than receive and I do not want any of my dear ones to suffer, but it was a loss to me too...my nephew, my close friend's child, my aunt... Let's remember to support and pray for our ministers and their wives as they shepherd the widows and fatherless among us. Mary Petre

Dear Widow's Supporters,

If you have been called to step in and work with the new widow and your husband has been asked to be a father figure for the widow's children, then I am writing to you. Many years ago, my husband and I stepped into such a situation which was fragile with new grief. We felt keenly alone in the daunting task we were called to. We longed for someone with experience to give us encouragement and advice. Thus, I feel led to share with you who are today where we were years ago.

If you are newly married, then your job looks extra daunting. You wonder how you will ever guide and train someone else's children, when you don't have children yourselves. We were told, "Think of the schoolteachers. Many of them do not have children of their own, yet we trust them to teach and train other people's children about seven hours every day." That tidbit gave us courage.

Your job will be hard. So hard. You are newly married and you will want to hold your husband's hand when you walk out to check the back forty. But first you need to check if the widow is looking out her window; you don't want to cause her extra pain. You will want to take a snack out to your husband where he is shoeing the horse, but what if the widow is hanging out her laundry? You dart behind buildings and bushes, hoping she won't notice. Not that you think she is spying on you, but her husband used to shoe that horse, and *she* took *him* snacks. You manage to make it inside the shop door without her seeing you, and you think you will have a few special moments together...only to find three little children sitting on the bench watching your husband work. If you can cheerfully share your snack between the four of you and walk calmly back to your house, that is love and gentleness and meekness all mixed together and you will have peace in your heart. You remind yourself that your husband will come in the house tonight and you can have him all to yourself; those little children on the bench will never see their daddy again on earth.

But remember, you are human. You had peace that day, but two days later when you dodge the buildings and shrubs to give your husband a fresh-baked brownie, only to find those same children sitting on the buggy seat waiting to go along to town, you feel angry. You hide the brownies; no need to give them any of your treat. You give your husband a dark look and raise your eyebrows. He catches the hint and asks them to run an errand. As soon as they disappear, you hiss, "I thought surely this time I would find you alone!"

You won't really enjoy the date, in this frame of mind, so you plod back to your house, and your steps are not peaceful this time. Each step says, *this is not fair. Why did God take her husband and make me share mine? No one knows or understands what we face. No one else has to train children before they have any of their own. No one else spends hours discussing child-training with the widow. And stomp, stomp! Of all things, just last evening you were going to ride along to town with your husband, but the widow's oldest son was planning to go with him. You didn't mind then, because you knew the boy missed going to town with his dad, and he deserved this quality time with a man.* But now it makes you mad. Why can't you just be alone?

You'll reach your house, swish the dishes through the water, dark thoughts broiling through your brain. And then the doorbell rings. It is the widow's three-year-old daughter bringing you a little container of potato soup. The note says the soup is a thank-you to you for sharing your husband with her children. You are glad the little girlie is too young to notice the color you feel creeping up your neck. You thank her, and when she leaves, you cry. You are glad the widow could not read your tumultuous thoughts. But you know God can, and you tell Him all about it. And that evening when your husband gets home, you will serve him hot potato soup and tell him with a smile, "Thanks for taking Junior along to town. We got soup in repay!"

There are several things to remember as you begin your new role:

1. This was not the widow's choice to be a widow and she does not like to be a burden.

2. This is God's will for you to be in this situation at this time and He will give you the grace you need.

3. You and your husband have recently been married. God plans for your marriage to be joyful and rich. But you cannot have a good strong marriage if you do not take time for each other. Yes, you want to be careful you do not cause the widow extra pain by seeing you together, but remember, you are not the only couple she is seeing. Are the other husbands and wives going separately to church? Do they not sit beside each other at a meal?

There are things that are very unkind and thoughtless to do in a widow's presence. Refrain from those things, but you do not need to treat your husband like he is a stranger.

You *must* tell your husband your struggles. You cannot let yourself think that because the widow does not have someone to share with, then you shouldn't share either. Understand and believe there is no way you can be a support to the widow and her family, if your marriage is running on low. So, take time for yourself and each other.

You are not the only people in the world; the widow has more family and church family. You might say, "No one else is offering to help." But did you think about the possibility that other people might be scared to offer? Maybe they are worried you will feel you aren't doing your job right if they step in. Ask for help. Maybe someone else could put the widow's buggy wheel back on, so your husband has time to fix your wringer washer.

4. There will be misunderstandings, but don't take them personally. You are all new in this. A new widow, new fatherless children, new workplace for you, maybe even a new state, new church, new friends. You are all facing lots of adjustments. You all have God to help you. But you have your husband for a sounding board and the widow doesn't. Many times, you will need to be her sounding board. You will need loads of wisdom to always know how to answer the many questions. But don't think you need to always have a ready answer. The widow no longer has her husband, so instead she is talking to you; sometimes all you need to do is cluck your tongue and reassure her of your prayers and support. Then she can go to bed feeling relieved that someone listened who will keep it confidential; you didn't need a good answer, just a good ear.

5. When you feel you have it tough, remember the widow has it tougher. She did not ask God to take away her husband...the man who knew her and her children up and down and in and out. She did not ask that their dreams would all be shattered...dreams of raising their family together, taking their family to church and teaching them the way to heaven, working together with their children in the produce patch and harness shop. Instead, she has this inexperienced young couple to help her teach and train her children. How can she know you won't make a financial disaster? How can she be sure her children won't be wrongly influenced by something you do?

How would you feel if suddenly your husband's shop and horses and equipment were all given to another man, and you had no idea if he would take care of them or not? The new man doesn't know how many horses your husband looked at until he found this one that he liked and trusted; nor how hard he had worked and saved to be able to buy it. The new caretaker cannot have the same appreciation for those things as your husband did. So sometimes it helps to try to see things through her eyes.

6. When you feel discouraged and alone, think of others who carry a heavy load. There are ministers and their wives who carry the weight of their whole congregation. There are the mentors, committee members, and support groups who are giving up things, too. There are families who care for special-needs children, and families who work through health crashes.

7. Once in a while, give yourself liberty to fast-forward your thoughts several years into the future. When we were handed the responsibility of being the widow's primary support couple, someone else with experience told us, "The first year is the hardest. Easier days will come." I would say the same to you. You will never be able to say it is fun to help the widow, but a new normal will come and you will all get to know each other better. Her young children will grow up only knowing your husband as the father they look up to. You will learn what to expect of each other and how each one responds to different things. You have proved yourself worthy by this time and she trusts your husband with all the financial decisions. That makes you want to do your best. You will feel so responsible for her children's souls and you'll wonder how you would ever cope if one of them wouldn't accept Christ. As her teenage sons enter courtship age, you will worry over them as if they were your own children. By this time, you have children of your own, and their joy and innocence helps ease the pain and turmoil and challenges of training teenagers. There will be times you think you cannot wait until the widow's children are all grown and you can live your own life. But yet, you almost don't really know how it will be to just be your family. And when you think how interwoven your two families have become, you will wonder how you could ever separate when there are so many good memories.

If you are like we were, you would never have chosen this calling to be the widow's main standby. But as you submit to this load, you will experience blessings you never dreamed of. God go with you.

Sincerely

"Geranium"

Relating to the Fatherless and Widows Among Us

Thoughts gleaned from a sermon by DANIEL WEAVER

Relating to the widows among us is a subject dear to the heart of God. If God tarries, there will be more widows. Psalm 146:9: *The Lord… relieveth the fatherless and widow.* Exodus 22:22-24: God hears their cry. Psalm 68:5: *A father of the fatherless and a judge of the widows.* Many Scriptures speak of the stranger or the fatherless and widows.

Deut. 24:17-22: God reminded Israel that they were not to take a widow's raiment to pledge. They were to show kindness and generosity to the stranger, the fatherless, and the widow.

While God made provision for the widows, they still needed to labor. The widow at Zarephath was asked for her cake. The widow was to use the oil she had. Ruth needed to glean in Boaz's fields. I Tim 5:10,14: Widows' families should be busy meeting their own needs, yet with extended family helping, so they are not overburdened.

Acts 6:1: Here the widows were neglected; leaders were assigned; joy resulted.

Viewings and funerals sometimes get late. Is it worth it? It is part of our church life, and we should go. It does something to us. As we express our sympathies, may our prayers go with them.

Family life for the bereaved will never be the same. Another family member cannot take the place of a departed parent. Adjustments and

81

decisions will need to be made.

Many times, the family's business comes into focus, and most times it is good if the business can keep going for a while. Someone will need to be appointed to be in charge of the decision making. If possible, this should be a father or a brother or a son. This helps to leave the right image and helps preserve his marital fidelity. The appointed one must be sympathetic and respectful of the way things were run before.

Others need to support the person who is in charge. Everyone would like to help, but if we are not careful there will be too much help. Sometimes when there is too much help, the children learn where they can go to get what they want. These families are not exempt from the enemy of our souls. Children still need to learn lessons of obedience and submission and support the one in charge. Children, especially boys, can develop an independent spirit, but they must learn accountability to their mother. The business is still their mother's. The children may need help and encouragement for this to happen.

Friends of these children have a powerful influence on their life. We need to beware: what kind of friends are our children being to the widow's children?

As time moves on, the children grow up. They need direction in choosing a life companion. They will likely choose their companion from the type of friends they have. We need to help our children be the right kind of friends. The power and influence of example of other young people reaches far.

Fathers, we have a responsibility when God brings a fatherless family into our midst to be the example that we should be. An illustration would be the automobile I buy for my son. Would I want the widow's son to have one like it? Can the widow afford it? There are many areas in business life where this comes into focus. Widows' children, especially boys who have no father, are looking at other fathers as an example. They may at times feel a little inferior and they want acceptance. They do not want to be considered different, so they may do something to prove that they're not.

God has given a special calling and responsibility to the congregational life in these situations. The congregation should relieve the widow (James

1:27). They can do this by prayer and visiting. It does not have to be big or outstanding things, just small things along the way. Involve the widowed family in church activities; help them enjoy the joy of service. Sometimes when a person is on the receiving end too much, they expect to always be there. The children need help to be satisfied with what they have, but at the same time be ready to help if they need it.

Sometimes in the stress and hard work of the daily routine of life, we may feel too exhausted to attend church services. But that is when we probably need it the most. It may take some encouragement for the widowed family to be involved in church activities. If they're overwhelmed, pitch in and help so they can take part in service, too.

The grief of a lost loved one can at times be almost overwhelming. The enemy of our souls brings the thought to our minds, "God doesn't care about us." Then comes loneliness and no one to confide in, to share the joys and sorrows of life. The thoughts in two verses are felt very keenly when a loved one is missing: *It is not good for man to be alone* (Genesis 2:18). *Thy desire shall be to thine husband* (Genesis 3:16). We as a brotherhood need to be aware of the grieving process. Grief must do its work. That is not the same for everyone, but we need to hold the grieving ones to the throne of grace and let God work. Time does heal. Tears are a part of the healing process. When we see those in tears, we tend to shrink back with a helpless feeling, but the Bible tells us to weep with those that weep.

> Only God can comfort, but there are ways we can be channels for that comfort.

Sometimes in the midst of the grieving process, those who are going through it may tend to think that the way out of this situation is another person, but they fail to realize that they may still be in the grieving process. Feelings and emotions cannot be left to control us at this point. What happens if Mother receives a request for a special friendship? Sometimes children respond quite negatively to this. It needs to be thought through carefully. Should children tell their mother she may not remarry? There are some uncertainties about the future in these situations, but children should think carefully before they say no (Revelation 21:4).

And in those days, when the number of the disciples was multiplied, there arose a murmuring of the Grecians against the Hebrews, because their widows were neglected in the daily ministration (Acts 6:1).

Question 6

Are there times you feel like your ministry is neglecting you? If so, in what way?

Widows answer:

I wish my ministry would

...visit us more often.

... come even when we do not invite them.

...promise to pray for us.

...call us on the phone.

...encourage us to rely on God.

... pay attention to our children...especially the ministers to our boys."

...acknowledge our children's loss and be willing to help them work through it.

...explain what the men's meeting at church is about and ask if we have any concerns. We often feel left out. What was discussed?

.... come to visit together as husband and wife couples. It gives security and stability when the husband comes along.

...have another widow when they have us for a Sunday meal. It is a lonely feeling to sit around a table full of couples.

... be willing to talk with our sons...or, sometimes it means more to them if you simply help them with their work, instead of visiting while the work waits for them to do alone later.

...always make sure someone offers to help with our horse at church... hitch, unhitch, or untie.

...offer to pay for something once in a while, such as the driver when we need to go a distance.

...offer to take me along to school meetings or other church functions.

...make sure we don't feel like we are on our own without help.

Relating to Another's Loss

MR AND MRS DELMAR MARTIN

If you are a widow, you may struggle with how to relate when an acquaintance loses his wife. Should you meet him and extend your sympathy at the viewing or funeral? Will everyone, including the surviving spouse, involuntarily consider a possible future relationship?

Some people might think along that line, but at this stage, the widower still considers himself the husband of the deceased rather than someone else's potential mate. It is important to him that his wife's friends acknowledge her significance in their lives.

A bold presentation would, of course, be offensive. But if you have a relationship with the family, and do not attend, you imply that your feelings about the future are stronger than your feelings about the past. If you can lay aside self-consciousness and enter into the parting ceremonies without hypocrisy, everyone will be blessed. A grieving spouse is especially comforted by someone who has gone through a similar experience, even if that person is of the opposite gender.

Ruth—
Yesterday and Today

PHEBE J MARTIN

Sit still, my daughter: wipe thy falling tear;
The Comfort of the Ages draweth near.
Thy griefs and sorrows, losses and distress
Shall all be swallowed up in joyfulness.

Sit still, my daughter: trust in Israel's God.
Thy fledgling faith which passed beneath the rod
Shall see thy name accepted in the land,
Shall find thy place established by His Hand.

Sit still, my daughter: trust in Israel's Law;
Redemption cometh to thee without flaw.
Thy Kinsman shall procure for thee a rest;
And generations hence shall call thee blest.

Sit still, my daughter: God will undertake,
A place within His congregation make
For thee and thine. And down the stream of time,
The faithful shall rejoice that thou art Mine.

How Can a Widow Serve?

Adapted from a sermon by DARREL MARTIN

One widow wrote, "Widows are only human and sometimes we get very, very weary of accepting another string of fish from the church. We wish we could go catch fish for someone else for a change, but we aren't always sure how."

The following comments on how a widow can "Catch a Fish" are adapted from a sermon preached by Bishop Brother Darrel Martin.

Romans 16:1-2: *I commend unto you Phebe our sister, which is a servant of the church which is at Cenchrea. That ye receive her in the Lord, as becometh saints, and that ye assist her in whatsoever business she hath need of you: for she hath been a succourer of many, and of myself also.*

How can a woman, without a husband, serve? How can she be a sister? You are privileged to provide something to your congregation. Paul, a renowned missionary, acknowledged Phebe as his sister. A sister will relate to others instead of withdrawing, protecting, or defending the unusualness of her loneliness. Do not seek to be independent. God did not create us to be alone.

Give yourself. Lose yourself by relating to others, even if they are not close your age. Romans 16:6 says, *Greet Mary, who bestowed much labour on us.* "Much labour" does not need to be big things. Offer a smile, an encouraging word, a helping hand. These little things pile together and make a big pile.

Do not be dominating, but dedicating. Luke 2:38 tells us that Anna gave thanks and served the brotherhood by coming and going. Be one who can be sent to prepare a place for others to do a greater work, like the disciples prepared the upper room.

Seek other lonely ones. Express appreciation and thanks to others. You can be an encouragement by being a quiet host, or holding a nonthreatening conversation.

Learn something useful and then use it. Beware of unusual crafts that clutter life and serve no purpose. What will neighbors remember you by? Tackle a task. Don't think in terms of "not able, not having." There is something for all to do or give.

John 11:20: *Then Martha, as soon as she heard that Jesus was coming, went and met him: but Mary sat still in the house.* Martha led a meaningful life by laboring in behalf of others. Do things in a personal way. A personal note means more to a sick person than merely a signed card.

Improve something for someone. I Timothy 5:10: *(Widows) are well reported of for good works; if she have brought up children, if she have lodged strangers, if she have washed the saints' feet, if she have relieved the afflicted, if she have diligently followed every good work.* Give careful thought before you make comments; life does not need another voice of complaint. If you have something to offer, give freely. Freely receive, freely give.

Contribute to brotherhood character. Never doubt the significance of your church attendance. Small things matter.

When you feel you are doing without, you can be sure God is bringing about His purposes. God has a place and a purpose for you in the brotherhood.

> Widows tend to lose the identity that they had with their husbands. As time passed, one widow said she began to feel like a marginal person in her congregation. We need to encourage widows that their identity is in Christ and not in any earthly relationship. The Bible tells us that we are complete in Christ. But we also need to do our part in making sure they feel needed in the congregation. *Titus Hofer*

Friends are like angels who lift us to our feet when we have trouble remembering how to fly.

Helping Each Other Swallow the Bitters

Wherefore comfort (console, reassure, encourage) yourselves together, and edify (instruct, inform, teach) one another, even as also ye do. 1 Thess. 5:11

Helping Each Other Swallow the Bitters

SUELLEN J STRITE

Our youngster was down with bronchitis and pneumonia. Among other remedies, the doctor prescribed prednisone. Since prednisone helps to open a person's airways, I am always glad to give it to someone who is having trouble getting enough oxygen.

But it is torture getting that stuff past a child's taste buds. We fill the syringe to three ml, put water in his favorite cup, and hold out a lollipop. We aim the syringe and say, "Get ready, set, go!" One of us holds the child while the other squirts the yucky stuff in his mouth. "Swallow! Swallow! Swallow!" we cry. The little one is choking, and screaming, and gagging, and trying desperately to swallow. Frantically, we command and cajole and comfort. If the stuff comes back up and out, we have to start the process all over again. If it stays down, we pat him on the back and say, "Good boy!" Then we let him suck the lollipop, hoping it eradicates the bad taste in his mouth. Sighing with relief, we all calm down until the next dose. We try to explain to our son that the medicine is what he needs to help him get better, but a two-year-old is too young to comprehend the importance of swallowing such bitter stuff.

I think that all of us in the school of life are too young to comprehend the importance of swallowing bitters. I don't believe any of us ever outgrow the need for a friend to cry, "Swallow! Swallow! Swallow before you choke!" when we are gagging. We are still two-year-olds who need to be commanded and cajoled and comforted. We need one who understands to place her hand on our shoulder and say, "Good girl," and offer us a promise from God to eradicate the bad taste.

Widow's Gift

BRENDA PETRE

It wasn't so much the expense of their gift
    Or the length of the visit they made;
What mattered the most was that somebody cared,
    They thought about us, and they prayed.

So often we keep our two mites to ourselves,
    Afraid of their seeming unworth,
When we could be starting a happiness chain
    That spreads through the rest of the earth.

For certainly God is recording our deeds,
    And though they be ever so small,
He knows with what fervency every breast beats
    And when we have given our all.

Question 7

Do you have any comfort or advice for your fellow widows?

Widows answer:

• You want to know how to cope? Really, we each have different talents and find ourselves in different stages of life, with different numbers of children. But we all serve the same God! *Casting all your care upon Him for He careth for you* (1 Peter 5:7).

• Never give up. Keep on, hand in hand with Jesus. Find someone you can confidentially share struggles with, and unload your feelings of grief and loneliness. Pour out the frustrations you are having with the children. (I unload on my mom.) Yet to a certain extent, we might need to learn to handle our feelings alone. Learn to really pour out to God! A song I sing to try to get my mind to believe is: "Jesus Christ is all I need." Occasionally, I talk with a counselor who used to be a widow and I find that very helpful.

• Take only one day at a time and when you can't take even one day, take only one hour or even one minute at a time. Don't look ahead and fear the unknown. God is already there. *With God all things are possible.* Find a widow friend you can confide in, and do things with her.

• Steer clear of the pit of self-pity! It is easy and human to feel cheated, especially if people around you are living the dream you have now lost. They are raising a family and growing old together. You are struggling to raise your family alone, make a living, and give your children a healthy view of a loving God. At times God feels so far away. Remember, God did not take your husband to punish you. He has a plan and a purpose. We live in a fallen world where bad things will happen, but if you give yourself to God, He can be glorified and your life will be richer than you can imagine. After many, many dark days you will begin to heal, then you will be able to appreciate the better days so much more. Yes, acceptance is a work in progress and can be frustratingly elusive. But fight for it, grab for it, hang on to it, and once again joy will come into your heart and life will seem livable again. You will be able to say, "God is good …even if life isn't."

• If there is anything I would like to stress, it is this: Do not look ahead!! Strength is given at the moment it is needed. Not a minute before. Don't try to carry tomorrow today. I find my strongest desire would be to depart. But, oh! how sweet it is to walk with God! His presence can be felt like never before. Truly, I am now "Alone with God." And He is here. Just ahead, just beside, and just behind me. And underneath are the Everlasting Arms. Deut .33:27: *The eternal God is thy refuge, and underneath are the everlasting arms.* Like never before, I trust the future into His hands, and give every fear to Him. I am drawn to the bruised and wounded, the sick and the dying. God is there.

• There are so many faces to grief. People all go through it differently, but we must all go through. I so wanted to hurry and get it behind me, but instead I sometimes feel that it took me extra long. It has to hurt before it can heal. Avoiding anything that will hurt is not healthy. Having the wound reopened somewhat can help it heal from the inside out… not just over the top. I see couples our age and I wonder how it would be. Then others have their husband not able to think anymore, or they have a lot of serious health problems. My husband was spared that. I have no doubt that God uses a loved one's death to draw us to heaven, but if we really stop and think…our main reason to want to go to heaven should be to see our Lord and Redeemer. It is a bit hard to think that our relationship with our husband will not be the same in heaven. But it will be all right when we get there…it is simply thinking about it now that is a bit hard. There is so much that we can't wrap around our little minds. I resented the widow title. Who was I? Where did I fit in? It is easy to feel left out, even when surrounded by caring people. We have to work on this and accept our lot. It has often been said, "You can accept this situation and make the best of it, or be sad and bitter and make everyone around you that way." A widow wrote something to this effect to me. It hit me hard. Do I want my children to remember a sad childhood, deprived of childish joys? Do I want to be the cause of blemishing others' lives?

• You will find that it helps to reach out to others that are having difficulties. It takes the focus off yourself and your troubles as being worse. Memories are treasures no one can take away, but be careful not to idolize the deceased. Look to those who made it through. See that it is possible. Count your blessings. Help your children count theirs, too. You will need a vibrant relationship with the Lord. You will need strong shoulders. And you certainly need a positive outlook.

• I have a heart for the young mothers that are left with a family to raise, and a living to make. But then when you are alone, the set of challenges is different. Keep a schedule; eat healthy, not just whatever is handy. One does get used to being alone.

• Remember: each soul in this world has a place to fill. You are not the only one with struggles, no matter how much you feel you don't fit in with your friends. Pray for your friends as they continue to learn to know their partners better and enjoy the new bundles that come into their lives. I know it is hard, but there is peace in accepting.

• When you feel you cannot cope, look to others who have a heavier burden. When I became a widow, I had only two children. It helped me to cope when I observed my friend who was left a widow with a big family from fifteen years down to an unborn. I told myself if that dear widow could courageously go on in life without a husband to help her, then surely, by God's help, I could too.

• God always was real to me, but after I became a widow, I experienced an extra special closeness. In thrilling little ways, God answered my prayers. Nighttime was very lonely!! But I used that time for letter writing, reading, and personal things that were not possible or appropriate while the children were up. It passed my time and I often dropped off to sleep without more trouble. This was a blessing from God.

Struggles produce strength when conquered by God's grace. *My grace is sufficient for thee: for my strength is made perfect in weakness.* I think widows understand the feeling of "weakness." When that strong part of our lives is snatched away, we feel so weak and vulnerable. What a blessed promise that God's strength is there to perfect us! If we feel that strength, and depend on it, then it supports us as we face each new day with its responsibilities and blessings.

The journey is a long, slow process for adults and children alike. Each person will react differently, and the path is very unique. Do not measure your progress against someone else's… the Bible plainly says, *For we dare not make ourselves of the number, or compare ourselves with some that commend themselves: but they measuring themselves by themselves, and comparing themselves among themselves, are not wise.* (2 Corinthians 10:12).

• There is no room in a widow's life to say, "I can't." Hebrews 11:11 has blessed my soul and given me strength many times in my widowhood. *Through faith also Sara herself received strength to conceive seed, and was delivered of a child when she was past age, because she judged him faithful who had promised.* God had promised Sara the impossible. She could never have had a child in her old age, of her own strength, and she knew it.

Let us pray one for another as we travel this road alone, and yet not alone. How we look forward to the other side, to see Jesus and be free from this battle and earthly cares! Let us all continue on… Heaven is our goal!

• Reflections after four years…each year came one day at a time. It has been four years of grief, adjustments, and constant changes. Four years of grieving brings healing. Someone termed it "diluting." Perhaps that is the better word. Our grief and loss are diluted with the many joyous moments that have come since the tragedy. It is not the only thing we think of anymore. We can laugh and sing and share precious time together with friends and family. God becomes closer than ever before. I am dependent upon Him, because I have no other. I pour out to Him about my day, my frustrations, my need for wisdom and strength. He has proven Himself faithful. As I face continuing challenges, I remember His care for me in the past four years. Four years. Four long, difficult years— crying to God for daily and hourly strength, coming to the end of myself and finding Him there, growing in faith that He is always good, finding purpose and meaning in life. Four years, but it comes—one—day—at a time. 🌸

Take This

JANICE ETTER

The mixture's made, and you must drink it up,
As all good children do.
See how it follows your averted face;
There is no place
Of refuge, and you close your eyes to brace
For that first gulp, with shudderings and tears,
Held hard by dire, uncomprehending fears—
    Taste! Taste the solace mingled in the cup
    Of sorrow's bitter brew.

Dear Fellow Widows,

I am Mrs James Kilmer. Ruth. How long may I keep on using my husband's name? Last night I dreamed of him again. It felt so complete...then I awoke to the emptiness. It's like the core has been taken out of my life. I keep revolving around that deep empty cavern. I am very busy. I guess that is what keeps me going. I may not look ahead, for the future is gone. My life was so meshed in James's that I don't know where I am going or what I am doing. "Just take one day at a time," I am told.

It will be two years in June...the day my life was changed forever. My oldest son at home is twenty now. Because of him, the farm goes on and we have an income. This is the last summer I really can depend on him. What will I do then? Like I said, I don't look ahead. But it doesn't keep the future from coming! I also have two girls still at home, sixteen and eighteen. We are very close. I must be careful I don't share all with them that I used to share with James. They are still young in the faith, after all. My youngest is twelve. I recognize I am very blessed. Supportive, caring children are all around me. I have fifteen grandchildren, who are very dear...yet...the core is missing. I still don't really belong to anyone anymore. Maybe I was too dependent on James. Now I am so bereft. I don't even want to go to town.

James was sick with cancer for four and a half years. One thing I have gathered is that time will heal. When James passed away, I literally begged the widows for hope that it will get better. They did not give hope. But now, I believe I begin to see how it is. No, we never will get over it, but the pain is not so raw or so constant. It's not there every minute, nor the first waking thought of the morning. But the missing still goes on. That weak, incomplete feeling can still be very intense and painful. But it is spaced out more and the duration is not as long. Without God, I don't know how I would do it. I thought James and I both had a close walk with God, but now...truly He is my husband and helper. I just give everything to Him. How many prayers He has answered! In time. And yet, I am still in the flesh, and I cannot help but long for what was and is no more. Sometimes I rebel. I don't want James to pass out of my life! I don't want the memories to grow dim. *Oh, wretched man that I am! Who shall deliver me?* Jesus Christ.

I just got word that another woman was widowed. A friend of James's had a heart attack. So many widows. Must be God has a big work only widows can do...

May God be your light and guide.

Sincerely

"Lilac"

Don't Cut the Threads

MRS DELMAR MARTIN

I was never a widow, but my husband was a widower before he married me. He has often reinforced this point: You can't thwart grief by cutting off the past relationship too abruptly and tying into a new one. Grief takes time and work.

He tells me of one widow who left her husband's barn coat and hat hanging in the entry for six months. Every time she walked in the door, they hung there. Every time she looked through the window between the kitchen and entry, she saw them. Somehow, they comforted her. She knew it wasn't time to cut the thread that connected her to the old normal.

Memories are a healing balm. Reliving those memories and recording them on paper can bring a comforting, gradual closure to the abbreviated marriage. My husband knew he could not live in the past, but he also knew that he would feel compelled to retell his wife's story often to avoid losing those memories. Consequently, he arranged for the writing of *Transplanted*, the account of his love and loss.

Not every widow or widower will want to be exposed in a book, but what about a notebook full of memories for your children? There are kind words, beautiful thoughts, and tender memories that you can weave together as a blanket of solace. Don't cut out any of those threads.

To Be the Best

Is that your goal in life? To be the best? Maybe you want to be the best wife or the best mom. Maybe you can make the best pies or bread or cakes. Is sewing your thing, and it's important to you to sew the best-looking dresses? I have a friend who makes the best cakes for birthdays. She takes the best parties to school—all the students say so! Or maybe you can write the best stories and the best poems. Or your house always looks at its best with the best furniture.

Recently I was challenged to be the best widow that I can be. Now that was a new thought to me. The best widow? I don't even like being a widow! Why would I put my heart into being the best one?

The writer challenged me to accept widowhood as God's plan, just as I had accepted marriage as God's plan. Okay, so since Plan A failed, I need to accept Plan B. But if God has all my life in His perfect plan, there is no Plan B.

What does God want from me when life is hard? How do I still do my best? When sleep is short and stress is tight, it's hard to care about doing my best. All I want to do is function in survival mode.

I'm so grateful for a God who does not condemn us when survival mode is our best. Sometimes it really is the best we can do, but we should avoid reverting to it for long periods.

Did you know that your thought pattern has much to do with how you view life? Even the Bible tells us to think about things that are lovely, pure, and holy. When I allow my mind to dwell on the things that I don't like, the unfairness of a situation, and all the things I would change if I could, I become very unhappy. God wants me to think wholesome thoughts, to work on being my best to please Him. He wants me to honor Him in the life I live now, even if my circumstances are not the perfect American dream.

But it is hard to be joyful, to love life, and to give it my best when life itself is hard! How is joy even possible?

I need to ask God daily for help. I need to thank Him daily that He loves me, and I need to focus on the blessings that He sends, more than on the disappointments that are in my life.

We encourage our children to do their best when they are nervous about a test at school. The teen who is taking his driver's test needs to hear Mama say, "It will be okay, just do your best." That's all God wants from you and me: just our best. He is not asking for the kind of perfection a seamstress or a cook pursues. He just desires a woman who, with a heart after God, serves her family as the best widow, the best mama—the best servant heart.

We can make many mistakes in life. Our houses may not be spotless, our food may not be served like *Taste of Home,* and our gardens may not be weed-free havens. But if you give your families love and time, they will really think you are the best! Children will forgive many mistakes that mamas make, but when you do not give them your time, you are robbing them of a very important gift. They need you involved in their lives. You need to listen to them and hear their stories and share their hearts. Then, they will view you as the best.

It is important that the local congregation rally around the grieving, especially the ministry in the church. Visit them and invite them over often. Don't be offended if they decline. It is better if the grieving decline invitations because they are too many, than if they wish the telephone would ring on a lonely Sunday, and it never does. Titus Hofer

Say not my soul, From whence can God relieve my care?
Remember that Omnipotence hath servants everywhere.

Twelve Red Roses and a Bucket of Dirt

Now when Job's three friends heard of all this evil that was come upon him, they came everyone from his own place...for they had made an appointment together to come to mourn with him and to comfort him. Job 2:11

Twelve Red Roses and a Bucket of Dirt

SUELLEN J STRITE

In 2011, I lay in the hospital with pancreatitis. All patients with this ailment agree that it is one of the most painful bodily afflictions. In addition to my physical misery was the discouraging knowledge that the specialists could not figure out why I had this problem…and I could get it again at any time. It seemed impossible to find a good reason why I should stay in a sterile bed while my family struggled to keep everything and everyone halfway tidy at home. I counted how many times I had been hospitalized previous to this, and I cried. What was the reason for this? Where was the good?

I had been told before that when something unpleasant comes upon us, we are to look for the roses. Amidst the thorns, there will always be a rose. Well. The rose that comes with pancreatitis must be awfully small; I couldn't find it for looking.

On the second or third morning of my distressing disease, a knock sounded on the metal hospital door, and a nurse entered. Instead of her usual paraphernalia, she carried a bouquet of beautiful red roses. "Someone dropped these off at the front desk, for you," she said, and handed them to me with a pleasant smile. "Enjoy!"

I was dumbfounded. Twelve red roses! I noticed a little note attached to the vase, which I read with interest. "I know you are probably having trouble finding roses in your hospital stay, so here is a whole bouquet so you can stop looking."

Those roses did not take away the pain in my abdomen. They did not diminish the distress in my mind. They did not wipe out the hospital bill.

But they did show me that someone cared! Sometimes the thought of someone's care is all we need to face the next minute…the next hour… the next day of a hard experience.

A bouquet of care does not always look like roses. Sometimes it looks like…a letter, a visit, an encouraging word. Sometimes it looks like…a loaf of bread, a doorknob repaired, a garden weeded.

We should be careful to choose our "gift roses" thoughtfully. I was not allowed any nourishment by mouth while my pancreas healed; what would I have done with a whole loaf of bread in the hospital? Yet bread might be a Godsend to a hungry family who is out of sandwiches.

Sometimes though, no matter how carefully and prayerfully we choose our "rose" we still "miss it." We use our hard-earned money to buy roses, but when we take them, we see five other bouquets of red roses on the hospital tray. In the midst of our busy schedule we bake bread; and when we take it, lo, we see the lady's maid pulling two fresh loaves out of the oven.

Hopefully all recipients are as gracious as my widowed sister. She has said, "It does not matter what someone does for me, it is the thought that counts. Why, you could even bring me a bucket of dirt, and I would appreciate that you cared."

Ah. That was too good. I took her up on it, and one day I took her a bucket of fresh dirt. Plain old garden soil. She was a bit…uh… surprised, shall I say? But amidst our fun, she rose to the occasion and thanked me profusely for caring about her.

See? Even a bucket of dirt can look like roses. Like a bouquet of care.

Question 8

Can you give your friends and neighbors some advice or suggestions on the kind of bouquets that mean the most to you?

Widows answer:

• Share your memories of my husband with me, but don't share too many at first. It takes a while before I can handle even the loveliest memories, because it hurts too much knowing it can be no more. The loss is too great. Don't be surprised if memories bring tears. Weep with me. Don't steer away from the subject of my husband because you are afraid you will remind me of my loss. I think of him all the time anyway and am grateful to feel free to talk about him. I actually fear that people are weary of the subject and wish I would get over it so everyone can go back to normal living. For us, life will never be the same.

• The offer, "Call if you need anything," is too vague at a time when my brain is blanked out. Make specific offers: "I can mow your lawn, pick your peas, clean your strawberry patch, or take you along to visit an invalid."

• If there is no obvious work, now is not the time to come offer to help with extra projects that could wait. It is a burden for me to try to manage a big project.

• Offer to keep my children when I go to town. Know enough about my schedule to know when to reoffer to keep my children. Be sensitive that they may have more favorite places to stay, especially if your place is associated with the happier days of before—!

• Listen, shake hands, or give a friendly "hi" with a smile. Send letters, gifts, or meals. It is meaningful when people remember us after months have passed since the death.

• Remember special holidays or memorable dates with us… Mother's Day, Father's Day, Christmas, anniversaries of our wedding and my husband's death. Visit us—more than once, and even if it has been years since my husband's death. I am still a widow.

• Come visit us, especially on lonely evenings; but find out if we had drop-in visitors all day. One day I had only a half hour that nobody was at our house. The first ones came before breakfast and the last left at seven PM. Having too much company is better than none, but there is a limit.

• I appreciate when you let me share my feelings and keep it confidential. Be sensitive when talking of your anniversary. It is meaningful to visit with a mixed group at times. My husband is no longer here to tell me what the men talked about.

• Sometimes I do not know what I want or need! I used to revel in alone time, but after my husband's death, too much time alone to think overwhelmed me. Yet neither could I handle company every minute. Some family time alone was needed too.

• Maybe some widows prefer losing themselves in managing things. For me, I needed people dropping in and taking on the work that needed to be done, but I also needed someone to sit down and listen to me. I could repeat the story of my husband's last days and hours over and over again. I did not want to weary someone by repeated telling, so I welcomed new faces…people who were interested in hearing. Unless I need help with my work, visiting an hour (more or less) is long enough. And please, don't make us responsible to feed visitors. Rather, bring food in and take care of it. If it is more than we can eat, manage it yourself, if possible. A new widow will not feel like cooking for a long time.

• When you send mail in those first traumatic weeks, I rarely want to hear how much you canned or housecleaned. Grieving people are selfish people. It doesn't harm new widows to reach out to others, but that is something they must decide to do, not you.

• Once when the children and I were invited away for a meal, when we arrived, the host (a widow's son) walked out to my car, took the baby's high chair, and invited us in. I could have managed to carry everything as I had at other places. But a widow's son knew and saw a widow's need! That meant a lot.

• There were outstanding ways people helped us, but I appreciated and never want to minimize the many, many everyday sacrifices people made for us. I often felt like a robot moving here and there, just doing what needed to be done.

• About nine months after my husband's death, a kind mother in our community surprised me with a chrysanthemum flower. We were not the same age; I did not even know I was in her thoughts. That kindness stood out and has not been forgotten.

• I had a widowed aunt who was much older than myself who called me at the year mark for many years to let me know she was remembering. A warm spot. It seems so important to know that someone else is remembering my loved one, too.

• We had lots and lots of mail, which we greatly appreciated. But as the year wore on, it felt like people were forgetting now, or that they thought it was "time to get over it." This is when we received gifts from a family, basically as a gift to each child. Another treasure to tell us someone still cared, and it meant more than dollars and cents.

• Sometimes we need more quiet time, to think and grieve, and have normal family life. The social whirl, while it can be helpful, can quickly become suffocating. It is very hard for me to decline an invitation or say "no" to company, because I don't want to offend anyone and we really do enjoy the exchange…if it has not become too much of a good thing.

• Bits and pieces

An unexpected gift goes a long way to show you care.

It is okay to eat with us once in a while, but we need time to ourselves, too. Things can be overdone.

Find out what job is dragging me down, and help with it; washing dishes, folding laundry, sweeping.

I especially appreciate when you include me in gatherings where we would have been if my husband was still here.

Include me in trips, picnics, and Sunday dinner invitations!

Listen without being judgmental.

Make consideration when charging for services performed.

Lend a helping hand.

We appreciate when you make sure we have wood during the winter and have the money we need to live.

Once I took something to a grieving lady, and she said, "Oh, I knew you would come." It almost gave me a tingling feeling...what if I would not have gone? The Spirit does lead, and I sure don't know how to follow sometimes, so I blindly stumble on. *Mary Petre*

Dear Widow Friends,

I love writing letters. Today I chose to write to you because I want to let you know that I think of you often and include you in my prayers. It refreshed my spirit when I saw you flash a smile to someone on Sunday morning at church. It was like a shining dewdrop glistening on a summer rose. I am not a widow, so I cannot say like some people do, "I share your experiences." I do hope to be a widow someday, though. (I will explain why later in this letter.)

You are a unique person; not because you are a widow, but because you are you. I will not tell you that God chose you especially for this, or that it is God's will that you are a widow, because I am sure you already know that...somebody probably told you that when you stood in the viewing line back then when the tragedy shocked the community. We all wanted to help at the moment. I remember going through the visitation line myself and I felt speechless when I held your hand. Maybe I told you that I was praying for you, which I certainly was. I don't remember how I said it, but I felt like wrapping my arms around you and telling you that someday you will smile again. A rainbow comes after the storm.

Time heals, but it does not erase the memory. Really, it is not time that heals, but God. He plans circumstances for each one of us. We are not all widows, but we are all unique. We all have our tests and trials. My life has not been a life of trauma or tragedy but a life of change. I was single until I was thirty-seven, lived in three different states and two different countries, changed churches three different times, taught school for twenty years, then married a widower with five children. Since I have no relatives in this church circle, I admit that sometimes I feel alone in a crowd too. Then I remind myself that I am here because this is where God wants me to be—in this unique situation.

I must admit (I hope you are not offended when I say this) that when I was single, I thought, "What is the difference between a widow and a single lady?" Now I am married and see a big difference. God takes special notice of the widows and fatherless. Isn't it comforting to know that He has asked His people to visit the widows? Probably nobody else ever thought of this on their wedding day, but I remember thinking the first evening of our married life, "Now I could be a widow." And even after being married only for a few hours I knew there was a big difference between a widow and a single lady. Before I was married, I called myself an old maid and didn't care.

I was not living in gloom or despair when I was single but enjoyed the freedom I had. I had the liberty to travel and I had the opportunity to do it. I enjoyed hiking over desert hills alone with God. Often, I was surrounded by people and not at all lonesome. Maybe I thought I lost some freedom when I got married because I married a widower with five children. Did you ever think of how difficult the situation would be for a widower, especially a younger one with five children? That is why I want to be a widow, if it is God's will, rather than have him experience the loss of a wife for the second time.

I have been watching your children grow up, and I know they silently suffer with you when they think of a father, but I am so glad you have children. As you get older, and they get older, you will appreciate them even more. They will be ready to care for you, just like you care for them now. A single person does not anticipate this. Maybe someday you will have fun being a grandma. You will be so happy to see your children in their own homes with their married partners. I remember being extra thankful for our girls when they got married. Somehow, I felt like they deserved a home of their own after they had experienced the loss of their mother. Because children add much to life, I was so glad God added children in my package deal.

I know a lady who is totally blind and lives by herself, holds a job, and makes her own living. She cheerfully told me that being blind is not the worst thing in life. What is the worst thing in life? I am not blind, and I am not a widow, and I am certainly glad I am not a blind widow! But how dare we compare one difficulty with another if God allowed it all? Didn't all of us promise in our marriage vows that we would be faithful until death does part? From this statement, we infer that someday death will be the cause of separation, but we do not know when, and I am sure you did not anticipate it so soon. There are many widows in the church—you are not the only one. One time I counted all the older single ladies, the widows, and the unmarried on the three benches in front of me at church and I counted eight. All those ladies have a story to tell and a life to live. Wouldn't the worst thing in life be a life without Jesus?

My husband, as a widower, was a good example of looking ahead and moving forward. It did not at all mean that he forgot his first partner. (I bristle a little when someone implies that marrying a second time indicates this.) Time does not stop. Nor would we want it to, when our life is disrupted, but time just leads us gently on and shows us new passages to follow. I know that you look ahead and trust the Lord, and that is why your face lights up in a smile!

I just wanted to encourage you to keep on smiling, because you are an inspiration to others, and especially to me.

I read this quote somewhere and it applies to all of us. "Life can only be understood backwards, but it needs to be lived forwards."

Sincerely,

"Lily"

109

Blessed to Receive

M L

We want to do all we can for our widow friends, but many times we wonder, "What is the best thing to do for them?" One gray Sunday afternoon in November, we talked of going to visit Widow Edith along with two other couples. After the other two couples backed out, my husband and I tossed the idea back and forth, "Should we go today anyway by ourselves?"

The cozy woodstove and dry house invited us to stay at home and relax. Edith is the type who makes it appear she is fine without company. But our children begged to go, and finally we decided to dress up in our Sunday best, harness the horse, and go. My husband and I were melancholy, and we questioned ourselves the whole way there, "Why are we doing this? Does Edith even want us to come?"

Edith welcomed us warmly, and our children were soon playing together. My husband, Marvin, and I and Edith discussed the weather, community news, her new clock. Then Edith went on talking. She shared the cares of raising her children alone, the woes and joys of her schoolchildren, the mother-heart worries about her children. Edith is yet young, but her husband is not here to talk out these things with in the evenings after the children are in bed.

Edith shared with us how her husband was taken from this earth in the blink of an eye, and while she was still numb with grief, here came men. Three men, all in that first year, asked for her friendship. It was a double pain to her grieving heart. All she could feel was their thoughtlessness. She told us how her first year she grieved in sadness, and the second year bitterness came knocking at her door. She told us how a minister once remarked that widows are very special people…like they have been tried by fire and come forth shining like gold. Edith said, "I don't think I came forth shining as gold, but I do feel Jesus' presence about me." Marvin and I concluded that it is Jesus we see shining through the widows.

But what hit Marvin and me that afternoon, as the rain drizzled down, was the encouragement Edith had for us. I doubt she had any clue that our marriage was going through a period of struggling with self-first. We thought if our marriage bond was stronger, then it would be easier to be strong in the Lord. We were forgetting the value of first being strong in the Lord so as to forget the importance of self, and to let God's love flow freely through me, not my spouse.

But there Edith sat looking us in the eyes and telling us how much a man really does for a woman by loving her, just her, for who she is, no matter what she does, no matter how she looks, no matter what mood she is in. Just loving her. Edith's mind was traveling back memory lane, rehearsing in her mind the glories of marriage, of a husband's love, and the security of a spouse. Of knowing the other is there even when others wonder about you. How often I take those things for granted. But coming from a widow's heart, it hit deep down in my heart.

It was past suppertime when we left Edith's home. Our hearts were full of awe and inspired by God. Our conversations had reached a deepness that she needed, and we needed. We were grateful to be there to listen for her, but as much as we like to give, God put us on the receiving end. Reality struck. God had something for us. Encouragement to better ourselves, to love while life is granted, to take hold of those vows of nine years prior and with God's help live them out. It is easier to give than to receive, but that Sunday we were blessed to receive. 🌹

The Cold Cottage

SUELLEN J STRITE

As I was journeying through life, I walked upon a certain road. And it came to pass as I walked, that I neared the cottage of a very young widow. And I found myself entering her driveway with the hidden hope that I could be of some encouragement to her, although I was doubtful of my ability to accomplish this.

Now it was a very warm day, and I was perspiring greatly as I neared her door. I rapped but once and the great door tumbled open instantly by two or maybe by three of the very small boys. The terrible blast of cold air that poured from the cottage was shocking. It very nearly chilled away the warm smile that I had prepared to present to the inhabitants.

The very young widow appeared then, and I noticed that her head was bowed low with her recent and heavy grief, and when she grasped my hand in greeting, it was a very cold hand. I felt the need to hold this hand awhile and warm it, but it did not seem to be the appropriate thing to do at the moment, since the baby in her arms was fussing, and another toddler was pulling at her black skirts and begging to be lifted up.

There were six children in all, and I noticed that every one of them was dressed in warm fur coats. And I wondered much at the cause of the coldness in the cottage. Although I did notice that after I had visited awhile, maybe one hour, and listened to the young widow's sorrow, and spoke a few words of God's comfort to her, that a small portion of the dampness left the room. And a bit later, when the godly pastor and his wife came, it warmed up in that cottage to the extent that the oldest child and maybe the second one shed their fur coats.

I rose to leave then, and the young widow grasped my hand to thank me for coming. And later, as I walked toward home, the thought came to my mind that her hand was much warmer at my going than at my coming. And I pondered this much, and asked my good husband when I arrived hom, what could be the meaning of it all.

Then that good man lifted up his eyes and put a smile upon his face and told me that he is not wise enough to have a ready answer for all of my perplexing questions, but this time the answer seems obvious to him at once. He said I should go and visit the young widow many more times until I have figured out the answer for myself. Then he would say no more, but he did smile at me in a very kind way.

And so, on a particular day, the very next week, I hastened myself and prepared a great kettle of hot soup. I bade my good man farewell, and carrying my kettle I walked directly to the bakers where I ordered a large loaf of wheat bread, warm from the oven. And I asked the head baker to wrap it, and after he did so, I placed it on the lid of my kettle. Then I paid him his dues and left that place and headed for the cottage of the very young widow.

Now as I neared her cottage, I met two gentle ladies, and they informed me that they had just been to see the young widow. Moreover, they told me that they too were widows, and had been for many years. Then I knew that these benevolent old souls must have been an inspiration and an encouragement to the young widow and I prayed that God would bless them.

As we went our separate ways, I thought of something, and I called back to them and asked if the young widow's cottage had been cold or warm that morning.

"Cool, at first," they answered. "Very cool and damp. But much warmer when we took our leave."

Then they saw my great perplexity over this matter and they drew quite near and told me one or two things about grief. And to these things

I listened attentively, and when they said that grief is hard and cold, I understood. And when they further said that only God's love can penetrate that coldness, then I nodded my head and bade them good-bye and I hastened my steps toward that lukewarm cottage with my kettle of hot soup and warm bread.

And at noon when I returned to my home, I had much to tell my own good husband of all I had learned. And that night when we knelt together to pray to our Father, we asked Him to touch many other hearts with a desire to go and help to warm up that widow's cottage.

Moreover, before we rose from our knees, we pled also that our Father would guide us and that He would put only His words in our mouths to speak to the very young widow so that we would never be the cause of making her cottage colder instead of warmer.

And what we prayed that night, we prayed many other nights also. 🌹

Kindness is the velvet of social fellowship. Kindness is the oil in the cogs of life's machinery. Kindness is the controlling spring which holds back the slamming door. Kindness is the burlap in the packing case of every day's merchandise. Kindness is the color in the cathedral window which, woven into beautiful characters, shuts out the hideous sights of a world which is all too practical. Kindness is the satin lining of the silver casket. Kindness is the plush on the chair. Kindness is the touch of an angel's hand. *Author Unknown*

The home should be a lighthouse that has the lamp of God on the table and the light of
Christ in the window, to give guidance to those who wander in sorrow. Rische

One Little Scratch

God setteth the solitary in families... Psalm 68:6
And I will very gladly spend and be spent for you. 2 Corinthians 12:15

One Little Scratch

SUELLEN J STRITE

My parents had seven children, and they spent a lot of breath trying to teach us how to take care of things. Today, a special dish slips from my hands and I can hear my mother's voice, "Careful with that china! It was my great-grandmother's and I would feel bad if it went to pieces." This afternoon, I see my child bump his truck into the wooden table leg, and I can hear my father, "Mother gave that desk to me for a wedding gift! Please don't scratch it all up."

Ours were the parents who punished us when we recklessly gouged the baseboard paint or tore paper off the parlor wall. They were the type who taught us not to ruin the little chair, given us by our first cousin twice removed. They were ones who made us dip into Mr Piggy and pay for the window we accidentally broke at the house down the lane. I am thankful that due to their persistence, none of us children grew up to be destructive savages. But once, long ago, my parents did not make a squeak when I damaged something valuable. And for that, I appreciate them.

It happened soon after I got my driver's license, and I was still a nervous wreck on the road. My mother sent me to get something at the little country store just two or three miles from where we lived. I managed to wiggle safely out our lane, turn right onto the dangerous highway, and creep up the road while trying to keep my wheels between the white line to my right and the yellow line to my left. My eyes glued to the road, I put on my left blinker and eased onto a little byroad, skirted the stones and weeds at my right, and made it to the stop sign. I sat there and surveyed the store right across the road.

Where would I park? That was the big question. A road bordered the store on two sides and the store did not boast much of a parking lot. I did not want to pull in and then back out onto the road, for fear I would back into a vehicle. I did not want to pull in alongside a vehicle for fear I would sideswipe it. The longer I sat, the more scared I became. There was no empty space!

Then I noticed a small space beside a little red car. Could I fit there? I had to try. Gulping down my nerves, I inched forward past the stop sign, crossed the road, and pulled in beside the red car. And you guessed it…I did it. I slid right into that car. Not much. Not bad. Just scratched alongside it. But my heart and stomach slithered south. I could not figure out how to go forwards or backwards without making the scratch much worse than it was. What could I do?

I walked into the store and meandered around not knowing what to do. I looked at each shopper and wondered which one owned the little red car. I glanced at the clerks and wondered which one could help me out. I searched in vain for another Mennonite. Finally, I decided there was nothing to do but to solicit the manager's help to find the owner of the red Mustang. He announced over the loudspeaker that the owner of the red car was wanted at the cash register.

My heart and stomach felt as if they were crawling with a thousand insects. The car owner was a lady, but she was a hot-cross bun. Suffice it to say, it did not turn out to be a good day. I do not remember all the details, but I do know she got my personal information, pulled her car away from mine, and left.

There were a lot of things I would have rather done than face my parents that day. I knew they would think I had made a heap out of nothing. And why wouldn't I have stayed a half inch away from that car? And was the scratch even big enough to worry about? And…

But my strict don't-scratch-that parents did something amazing. Other than asking to hear my story, they said very little. I fought my own way through my muddle of feelings and gradually became brave enough to drive the car again. Although I never enjoyed going to the store for my mother after that, I heroically went when she requested it. As time went by, the incident dulled in my mind, and though we didn't talk about it, I was often grateful my parents had not lectured me that hard, hard day.

Not until years later did I learn how costly that scratch was. The owner of the little red car certainly was not as silent about the matter as my parents were. She had worked and fussed until she squeezed several thousand dollars out of my father's thin wallet. When I received this knowledge, I was stunned. And doubly grateful. Would I ever have gained enough courage to drive on the road again if I had known? A scolding would have been devastating.

Parents of a widowed daughter have a difficult job. Their daughter left them to cleave to her husband. She loved him, cherished him, and submitted to him. Suddenly he is gone. Now who is she responsible to? Her parents may automatically feel responsible for her. But is it fair to expect her to give up the home (new patterns, new habits of doing things, new ways of thinking) she has created with her husband?

This is an area where there needs to be a lot of give and take. And the parents need trainloads of wisdom. Wisdom to know when to warn their daughter, "Watch out! You might break that dish!" And wisdom to know when to quietly go and pay the bill for one little scratch.

> They who have loved together have been drawn close; they who have struggled together are forever linked; but they who have suffered together have known the most sacred bond of all. Anonymous

Question 9

How do your parents support you; or not support you?

Widows answer:

My parents:

...come to visit often. They listen with care to our struggles and joys, then give advice in a way that gives us courage to go on.

...support me so-so. They do special things for me, like buying things we need and helping with financial decisions. They make monthly donations, but they almost never visit, even though they live only one mile from here. Sometimes I need mental support more than money.

...scheduled the first three months (after my husband's death) so the friends were spread out over the weeks, because everyone wanted to do something.

...fixed up the second house on their farm for me to live in. They willingly feed us supper every evening. They help out in major decisions, such as what vehicle to buy, if the lawn mower is worth fixing, etc.

...take a keen interest in the family, and especially the spiritual standing of the children.

...were very caring. They brought a meal and shared with us one evening a week for a long time. My mom played games with the children and they loved it. Dad was a very good financial counselor. I always felt loved and prayed for!

...helped put up the gravestone. I appreciated that very much.

...help with monetary donations. I hope to become self-supportive to relieve their load.

...thought I should be done grieving after one year. They pushed me to make decisions that could only be made after more time had elapsed.

...did much in making the first years easier. Even the care of the children's physical needs were often supplied by them, since we lived together.

...let me be in charge of the bank account....we were amazingly provided for!

...lent a listening ear, and gave advice when I wasn't sure how to proceed...especially where the children are concerned. They have helped in the greenhouse and garden and with lawn mowing and general upkeep around the house/barn.

…support me mainly by phone calls since they do not live nearby. And I feel their prayers.

…read stories to the children, let them ride along in the tractor or combine, and take them along to the shop. They really like Grandpa, and it seems to work out well. He even occasionally helps discipline the boys, ages 3 and 5, which works out okay and is helpful and appreciated.

…let us live with them quite a bit the first few months after the funeral. And we still occasionally spend the night there and frequently have meals at their house. Daddy kindly helps with business dealings, sometimes dealing with men so I don't need to, or just listening to my concerns, questions, apprehensions…and offers his advice. Mom will babysit when necessary or sometimes just for anyhow to give me quiet time at home alone. I appreciate that.

…took care of all packing and sorting of household items for moving after the funeral. They also helped with painting at my new house.

…spoke highly of my husband, his personality, his work, and how much they missed him. This meant a lot to me.

…gave encouragement when my husband's father informed me that the financial side was going to be bleak. (My father helped me through our visit to the Register of Wills and things were much brighter. The Register of Wills was very considerate.)

…would do anything for me and the children. They come to visit and help as often as needed. 🌹

Lord, give us eyes that we may see, lest we as people will,
Should pass our daughter's Calvary, and think it just a hill. Unknown

Dear Mothers of Widows,

To those mothers who have lost a son-in-law, keep in mind that life has changed for your daughter. Don't pick at her choices if either way could be a right way. Sometimes the situations can be awkward to deal with, but our daughter has a way of making others feel comfortable. Keep in mind, dear widows, that your visitors will feel at ease if you do.

Our daughter loved having others bringing in food. Even if she had plenty and maybe even had the same thing the day before, she was grateful and did not complain to the kind soul who brought it. She thrived in their love, which made them want to come back again. Always accept others' offerings to you as manna from heaven and don't complain as the Israelites did when they were tired of God's manna.

Pity the widow who receives company that sits there and tells her how busy her husband is, and how rarely he is home. Remember that many a widow would just love to have her husband be alive and busy. Our daughter accepted such company, and smiled and went on, realizing the company didn't think how their words might hurt. So, enjoy your visitors and they will come back again.

Our daughter also enjoyed gifts whether small or large and accepted them so graciously that the giver left feeling blessed for giving. Once I heard someone say, "I got three of those and I don't even use that kind." I feel that is being ungrateful. Our daughter used every gift in one way or another. You know, dear widow, the giver can soon see if it was appreciated.

Our daughter talked to her children about "Daddy" and what they used to do together. It made Daddy seem like a real person in their life. If you clam up and want the past forgotten, just don't talk. But be assured, your children will not talk to you either. Then you will wonder why.

Our daughter showed appreciation to us as her parents for anything we did for her. She thanked us even if it was a small thing like cutting her boys' hair or washing her dishes. She did not like to ask for help, but generally the needs were obvious. So, open your eyes, mothers, and you will see where to help out. The love our daughter showered upon us for all we did was worth a lot. To the widows on the same path as our daughter: show love to your parents even if you would have done it a different way.

None of us would ask to walk this path of grief, but as we help and encourage each other, God will help us through.

Sincerely,

"Marigold"

121

Question 10

How do your husband's parents relate to you and your children?

Widows answer:

• My mother-in-law came on work bee days and took over the meal. Sometimes I appreciated it, and sometimes I didn't! My father-in law does many odd tinker jobs for me and I appreciate it.

• My in-laws will do whatever it takes to help. They say, "If you need anything we will be here." "We understand you are struggling today." "Do you need anything in town, as I am on the way?" If something needs fixed, they go ahead and do it.

• My mother-in-law was not supportive because she was old and only thought of her many health issues.

• My husband's parents were very supportive. My son was happy to sit with his grandfather at church.

• My husband's mom calls me regularly and his dad gives needed advice at times.

• My in-laws include me. They say, "Just keep on doing what you're doing." They come to visit and spend quality time with the children. They respect my wishes and encourage us to keep on.

• My mother-in-law insisted on wearing black as long as I planned to; it made me feel like she thought she was just as, or more important, to my husband as I was. But I didn't want to wear black longer because I knew my husband wouldn't have wanted me to. "Get over it and on with life" was his philosophy.

• My mother-in-law told me I would still be part of the family. She included me in her will. I appreciated being included.

• My in-laws accept me as if I were blood family. They thanked me for taking care of their son/brother. They grieve with me. His mother gave me a Mother's Day card, "To a dear daughter-in-law." They visit and write. They gave me a memory scrapbook of my husband.

• My in-laws probably never meant to, but I got the feeling they felt my husband's passing was as much a loss to them as to me. You just need someone to listen and weep with you. 🌸

Don't Turn Bitter

A WIDOW'S MOTHER

Our daughter never became bitter, therefore she reached out to anyone who cared. She is very precious. It hurt very much to see her agony. I just wished I could pick her up and hold her awhile. Advice: don't turn bitter. You will hurt yourself and your loved ones. It will make them feel helpless and they can only watch as you make selfish choices. We don't understand, but we submit and don't blame God. Walk close to the Lord. Make sure each step is according to His will, which is through praying and reading His Word. Appreciate your church. 🌸

Question **11**

Do your in-laws have any thoughts to share?

Widows' in laws answer:

• Be consistent in child-training. There may be times when you feel you haven't the energy to discipline your child, but the child will feel more secure in his shattered world if you are firm but loving at all times. By all means, keep up church attendance even if you don't feel like attending social events. Everyone assumes since I am a widow, I should really be able to feel for my daughter-in-law. But everyone grieves differently, and since she moved closer to her parents since my son's death, it seems we aren't as close to her in relationship anymore, either. It seems I never really got to know her well before my son died. While he was still here, he was always the bridge between us. Then when he was gone, that connection was severed.

• We loved the family dearly and we miss our son, too. We want to help, but don't want to be overbearing or a nuisance or pry into her business. But we still would like to know how she is getting along. I am afraid I stir up memories too hard to face again. And should I talk such in front of the innocent, carefree children and stir up more sorrow? I think our daughter-in-law has very good management. Her children all seem to respect her as Mother. They all miss Daddy a whole lot and I believe this draws the ties to Mother. Our prayers are our daily help in these years, since we live so far away.

• The children help us stay connected. I think we should do more for widows. Her mom is closer, and they do so well at babysitting and taking her places. Many people plan things for our daughter-in-law, and sometimes it is too much. We are too far away to babysit much. I am always glad to know about her meeting other widows, and if she is going on a trip. Also, we don't go to the same church, so we don't see each other there, and are not able to take one of the children. It is hard to see her have to discipline a misbehaving five-year-old, when children come tattling on him…she can't go tell Daddy or send him to Daddy. There were times I felt her mother tried to shield her too much, especially the first six months. But with a six-month-old baby and two other children, she did need some assistance. Her mother got burned out trying to help her. They lived at her parents' place for six months or so.

I sought my soul–but my soul I could not see;
I sought my God–but my God eluded me;
I sought my brother–and I found all three.
Anonymous

One Piece of Toast

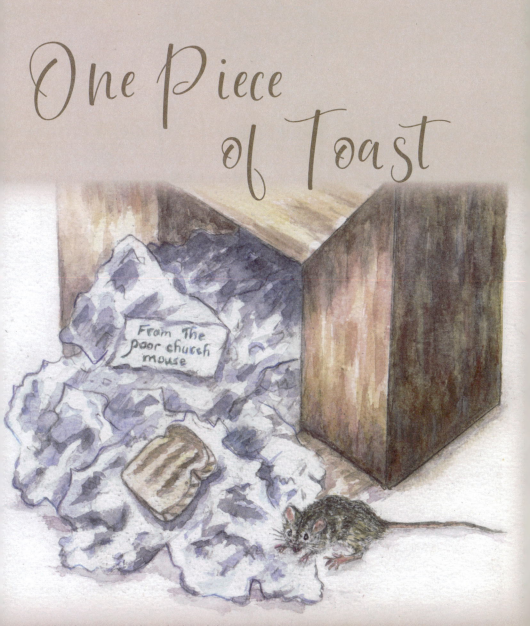

If a brother or sister be naked, and destitute of daily food, and one of you say unto them,
Depart in peace, be ye warmed and filled; notwithstanding ye give them not those things
which are needful to the body; what doth it profit? James 2:15-16.

One Piece of Toast

SUELLEN J STRITE

One snowy day, as I wondered if I would survive a vicious infection without losing my sanity, my brother knocked on our door. We had spent the winter away from church and social functions, nursing anything from strep throat to wrenched stomachs. I was beginning to feel deprived and disheartened. But here! My brother was handing me a present. Oh, joy! Don't I love presents! And to think, he actually cared enough about us to go to all this bother. It was a cardboard box, unwrapped, but that was fine; the box was big.

I opened the box and peered in. Ah. Lots of paper on top. How kind! He had wrapped up lots of small presents, I thought. Excitedly I dug under the paper...and found...nothing. This couldn't be real. I dug deeper. This time I found...one small hard crust of bread.

One slice of toast. That was all, except for a little note explaining that he was the poor church mouse kindly giving us what he could in our time of need.

Since then, my brother has learned a little about the art of giving, for he has blessed us with kind words and free parts for our broken stove. Recently, he even wrapped up a box with ice-cream mix, and books, and toy airplanes to cheer us when my husband had surgery.

Today my brother and I laugh when the subject of the cardboard box comes up. I remind him that he should not play that trick on anyone else. But sometimes…sometimes I feel a little sorry for him. He had intended to cheer me with a good laugh when I pulled out that crust of bread. He had never expected it to push me farther over the edge.

Really, on certain days, at certain times and places, it would have been a good joke. On a day when I was well and happy, just slightly bored, a visit from my brother and a gift of one crust of bread would have put me in a jolly mood. We could have laughed about the poor church mouse, and I could have offered him jelly and let him eat the toast himself since he was "destitute."

Most siblings intend to be kind to their widowed sister. But at times their words are ill-timed, their gifts inappropriate. Sometimes when they try to cheer her up, they end up pushing her over the hill instead. Then everyone feels bad, because guess who gets to help pull her back up? The siblings.

Of course, we need to remember again, that what lifts up one widow's spirit could be the very thing that pulls another's down. We must keep our ears and eyes open to be sensitive to what is really a help.

And always be careful what we put in that cardboard box.

We are used to things happening fast nowadays. We have fast food, high-speed internet, fast speed limits, and so on. With such a lifestyle we might be tempted to push people through their grief. "You cannot grieve forever; it's time to get hold of yourself." The truth is that sometimes we are just tired of being comforters, and we wish that the grieving would stop being a drag on our energies.

People who try to hurry others through their grief are usually those who have not yet experienced the loss of a family member. The Bible says there is a time to mourn, and we must give people that time. Grief has an important healing work to do in the lives of God's children. That healing simply takes longer for some than for others. Titus Hofer

Question 12

What level of care do your siblings show you?

Widows answer:

My siblings:

...walk beside me and cry with me. My sister's husband helped my oldest son on the farm many times. They shared memories freely and acknowledged the hole and loss in our home. They often called with, "How are you today?"

...are very helpful. They came once a week to do projects for me the first summer. They gave me much needed incentive to get at least one small job done a week, so they didn't think I was a freeloader. They are still only a phone call away. "Let us know if you need anything." I try not to abuse that generous statement, but I use it often."

...built a greenhouse for me where I raise tomatoes. It is a stay-at-home job which I appreciate."

...call quite frequently and are very understanding. They always have a listening ear. None of them live close by. They come to visit and help with lots of projects around the house. They give words of affirmation, which goes a long way.

...spent many nights sleeping in my spare room, just so I was not alone.

...see after needs around the farm. In a kind way, they suggest that we may want to do this or that, to make it more handy or practical.

...include my boys in projects. They always welcome us with their Sunday afternoon plans, so our day doesn't get too long.

...all come once a year to help with mulching, cutting firewood, or whatever man-jobs need doing. My sisters do well at having us for a meal, or keeping children to give me a break.

...take care of the fences, pastures, and field work, along with furnishing feed for the animals—cows, chickens, and pigs. They frequently supply things free of charge, and all my siblings are helping with mortgage payments.

...are sympathetic and caring. I can go to my younger brother for advice on "man things." He fixes things free of charge and files my income taxes. My oldest brother helps with legal work.

...hold our children, love them, and read to them. My brothers take my son fishing or hunting... doing things that his father would do if he would be here. They remind my children when they misbehave.

...say they really care. They pray for me. They offer to do work that a woman cannot easily do. They take my children to the zoo with their family. They take me to visit distant relatives, and take me shopping for my store.

...offer to help with the work. They think ahead to our ongoing needs....someone to sit with at weddings/reunions, etc. They accepted my children into normal family life, not as company.

...take my one-year-old along in church. Another brother boards at our house and tolerates the bedlam.

...are always ready to listen to my worries and fears. Money was sent, help donated, and improvements were made on the barn, by my siblings.

...are not exactly sensitive to my needs, but one brother has helped me a little.

...seem to expect more of me at times than I can do. We lost our father when I was two. I felt they thought I should relate to my husband's death like they did when my father died. To me, it was a big difference.

...became a real support. I could go to my brother for advice. He was also the deacon in our church. He had always cared for my widowed mother after my father died.

...all left our church fellowship except one couple, so I felt like I had to stand alone. But I am glad for my church family and appreciate it."

...care, even though my one brother wears a tough exterior. He calls me occasionally just to talk.

...are not especially supportive. The one brother who is appointed to be my main standby is usually too busy to come, and when he does, he's dozing off while I'm trying to share my deeper concerns.

Charity sees the need, not the cause. *German Proverb*

Dear Siblings of Widows,

Are you the sibling of a new widow? If so, you have a challenging role. The death of my sister's husband was the most shocking, devastating thing that had ever happened in our family. Every one of us was affected, and not one of us knew exactly what to do or say.

Even though my sister and I had always been close, when her husband's life was so suddenly snuffed out, we hardly knew how to relate to each other. I felt trapped and uncomfortable when I was alone with her. The air between us was tense, charged with unbelief that this had happened. I had never been in a situation like this, and I had no idea what was expected of me.

Although I could not have known it that day, there would be hundreds more times in the days and years to come when my siblings and I would have no idea what to do or say. Should we drop everything and go fix her leaking kitchen spigot right now, six hours after it broke, without telling her that water has been dripping into our bathtub steadily for six months, and we haven't had time to fix it yet? Should we all sit together at a family gathering so she can hear the men's conversation sometimes, or should we sit separate so we aren't rubbing in the fact that we still have our companions? Should we offer her a ride to church so she doesn't have to drive, or should we let her go herself so she doesn't feel like extra baggage in our vehicle?

I have a distant friend whose sibling became a widow about eight years before my sister did. In those first awful months after my sister's bereavement, this friend wrote to me, "We wish you all could be where we are now." I didn't understand. What good would eight years do? Even if we could jump ahead twenty years, my sister's husband will still be gone. But today, ten years later, I understand what that friend meant. No, I do not fully understand what it is like to be a widow, and my sister does not understand how it is to be a widow's sibling. But we siblings are slowly learning what feels like "crust" to my sister. Thankfully, she is usually open with us, so we have an idea when to bring on the Apple Butter.

So, I say to you who are new to this situation, "I wish you could be where we are now." And perhaps ten years from today, you will understand the encouragement those words carry.

Sincerely,

"Pansy"

Question 13

Do you have any thoughts you would like to share in relation to your widowed sister?

Widows' siblings answer:

• People grieve as individually as their personality. Don't expect the grieving one to react as you would. Your shoulder might be all padded, ready to receive her tears. But that is not her way. She'd rather keep that part of her grief private. Accept that. It is all right.

Bear with it if your imperfect brother-in-law is suddenly faultless. Not that anyone would claim that he was perfect, but be patient with the intensity of bereavement that magnifies the good traits of husband/son/brother.

Could a mother try to be so brave that her children don't have enough chance to grieve openly?

Too many sunshine boxes and random gifts carry their own stress of what-to-do and thank-you's. Not that people shouldn't be generous. It's just one of the added stresses.

Ministry should be thoughtful to inform widows/singles of matters that would be communicated among heads of homes. Ministry should think twice about low-maintenance widows. Maybe there is an area of need not so obvious. Be sure to give her a chance to express it, not just float on in life.

A widow can so dutifully live out her husband's wishes and ideals, that she can become undiscerning of how those positions/decisions fit in the changing of his view as well. That's where a widow needs to trust others to take up where her husband can't.

Kenneth and Virginia Kreider

• We shared the grief and sorrow. At first, visiting my widowed sister was very hard because it was a fresh reminder of reality. I felt guilty that I still had my husband and she didn't. We still struggle to know when to voice our opinion on decisions that need to be made concerning her livelihood/farm and how and when to pitch in and help.

• My brother-in-law's death has really pulled our family together, especially us sisters. These circumstances give us the opportunity to support a family close to our hearts instead of someone unknown from a far country. It is hard to find a subject that does not involve husbands. We laid away a four-month-old baby, so we have also experienced grief. But losing a life partner goes much deeper. We wish to help, but we do not want to add to the burden by saying hurtful things or giving them more unneeded items.

• It has been my experience that grief can easily turn to self-pity. I like to see other people rise above their circumstances as Joseph in the Bible did. Maybe they are brought to "such a place as this" as Queen Esther. Healing comes by spurts, sometimes two steps backward for every step forward. But there is light at the end of the tunnel. There are brighter days ahead.

• We had a good relationship before, but now we relate on a closer level. Sometimes it is hard to find enough time to reach around, as I also have a family to provide for. At times, it is a challenge to know what decisions are best at her farm. We seek to reach decisions that rest well with her and her oldest children. The greatest challenges were during the first and second year, when the grief and loss were keen. It can be a real challenge for widows to be firm enough with the children. Young children especially need firm training. When we notice needy areas in the children, such as being overbearing and demanding, we long to be a help but do not wish to overburden the widow. She has a heavy load of responsibility. Allow time for the grieving process. Do not act like you understand it all, if you haven't been through it yourself. Be encouraging. Take time for her children. Take an interest in their life and what they are doing. Listen patiently when the widow wants to talk.

• My sister and I both had a trying and growing experience through her husband's death. As an older brother, it is hard to know how much to ask her, such as whether her finances are reaching around, or if someone is taking advantage of her. It is difficult to know how much advice I

132

should offer in areas I see that need attention. From my perspective with my sister, her children are candidates for having a welfare attitude. The community reaches out to them so well that the children are showing signs of expecting handouts. Some things we had to bear in mind when offering support: we did not experience the loss she had, and different personalities work at grief in different ways. We need to learn to have patience and forbearance to know when to take over and when to *back off*. This takes continual guidance from above and a willingness to learn.

• My sister and I are closer in some ways since the death, but it has brought challenges that can be stressful at times. Probably my biggest problem is knowing how and when and how much to help. We do want to help, but we also see what it can do to the children if everything is just handed to them. They can get the idea that they should receive everything, and resent if other people also receive packages. I notice a rut my sister falls into, in becoming so dependent on others that she seems to have the idea she cannot do certain jobs anymore, like baking bread and canning vegetables. I realize the widow is the one that needs the most encouragement and help. Sometimes I wish the widow's relatives would also have some teaching on what to do that is best for her and her children.

• We communicate more. I needed to accept the fact that I could not be the most understanding or the best comforter to her, because I do not fully understand. But I can still be her sister. Advice to widows: Please forgive us if we talk about our husbands too much, or if our children want to talk about what Daddy did. Sometimes you must let our well-meant advice go in one ear and out the other, because we don't always understand the situation.

• My sister and I share a deeper relationship than before. A challenge I face is that whenever she and I part from a time of being together, I go home to a husband and she doesn't. There is nothing I can do to change that. We should look out for her children, offer to babysit, and offer to help with men's work around her place.

• My sister and I discuss things on a deeper level since she is a widow, because I know she does not have another adult in the house to talk to. We feel helpless to know how we can help or what she needs when she is going through a dark time. I know I cannot fully relate to widowhood; I still have my dear husband. Sometimes I am not sure if I should be relating our special family trips and Daddy times to them, since I know they are missing their father figure. It seemed my sister was so overwhelmed with grief and loss, and new decisions and more responsibilities, that it was hard for her to focus on her children, to give them the needed training and discipline. I don't know what she could have done differently, though, that first year or two. I can tell it has improved now. My sister was told to focus on being a good mom instead of trying to be Mom and Dad. She said that was helpful and encouraging to her. She is usually quite open about how she is doing, and I think that makes it easier for the rest of us. I think it is really nice when her neighbors take the fatherless boys along on the tractor or to the sale barn.

• At first I was afraid of saying the wrong thing. I so much did not want to be the bad person that makes her mad. But I came to realize that I can't be perfect, and I can't stay away either. Since expressing frustration is a release of emotion, I decided I will do my best. If I in my ignorance make her mad, well, maybe I helped her by letting her vent her steam all over me! Satan does not want us to encourage each other, and almost every time I was preparing to go visit my sister, I experienced all kinds of setbacks and doubts about my plans. But I chose to go out of obedience to God's command to visit the widows, and things always worked out in the end. Weeping with those that weep does not feel good to our flesh. We can't expect to go and have a good time, but we can have a blessed time. I think it is good if a grieving person can recognize how impossible she is to please. It is good if she can see that what is all wrong today may be okay tomorrow. I would tell the widow that we as brother and sister feel so helpless. We would so gladly bring your loved one back to you. But since we cannot, we resort to doing things for you. Don't accuse your supporters of thinking that having this work done replaces your husband. We know it doesn't, but it is *all we can do*. I would encourage the widow to make up her mind not to allow herself or her children get caught in a victim attitude. I want to bless my sister for the wonderful way in which she seeks to accept this as part of God's will for her life. We know that God makes no mistakes, but man does. And because of sin, bad things happen that are not God's perfect will. But we serve an all-powerful God, He is able to make all things work together for good (Romans 8:28). In helping my sister I came to understand that to be a help to her, I need to be careful not to be too quick to share advice and solutions. Often, she only needs an ear to listen to her problems and frustrations…the unloading she used to do to her husband. If we want to be a listening ear, I think we need to be very careful not to turn her talk into gossip. Don't take sides or form opinions on what happened. Just let her pour out, knowing that you will listen and not pass on. In one situation, my sister kept referring to this one person that so aggravated her. I finally asked my sister if we should say something to our friend, since I know she doesn't want to be a hindrance. But my sister said she thinks the problem is her own self; this person is a faithful friend, one she can get riled up about, but she is still there. It is so much easier to process our own grief and adjustments because of my sister's openness and acceptance of it. I really appreciate that she shares as openly as she does about the elephant in the room. Although I would so much like to send it back to Africa once and for all.

• How do you help them move beyond? How much is too much dwelling on the loss and memorializing their lives? Don't idealize your lost loved ones at the expense of the ones you still have. Embrace the new normal. 🌷

> "Fear not" is used 366 times in the Bible: one for each day of the year, and one to spare.

Question 14

While your husband's siblings are grieving the loss of their brother, how do they make things easier or harder for you?

Widows answer:

My in-laws:

...share memories about my husband, especially of when he was growing up. They have helped with fixing things, and are helping with mortgage payments. I know they care about us.

...visit often and supply us with food that our small garden has no room to grow. Only one in-law had some problems in relating, but my mother had taught me from little up not to hold grudges. "Rather forgive and forget." To this day I thank God for a wonderful godly mother who learned as a stepmother to love even when it hurt. I personally think it an injustice to pass on hurtful things. Christ taught us to love and so as a child of God, we too must forgive and forget.

...want me to keep in touch with them as usual. A sister-in-law doesn't mind if I go over to her place often to visit for a day with her and her little ones, which brightens my day. They think of me as a sister, no matter what.

...mention my husband, instead of pretending he never existed.

...treat me okay, except one sister-in-law had a problem feeling jealous if too much attention was directed to me and my children. She would sometimes say something degrading about my husband.

...once remarked that my husband did not have an easy life. (Yes, I do realize I often didn't respond right, or do my best! But the past is past, and everything was apologized for and forgiven and we had a clean slate when he passed away!) So please, don't put anyone on a guilt trip.

...were more compassionate than I expected.

...tell me memories they have of their brother, my husband. They take time to visit or play with my children. It is special to have them interact with their daddy's brothers. I appreciate the couples who are comfortable visiting with me, even without another man present. At family gatherings, I sometimes prefer that the others sit in couples to eat so I can hear the men's conversation.

…love to have us with them and we love being with them too. That's as close as we get to dear Daddy and husband. They like to come and visit us for a weekend.

…help me not feel like an oddball.

…intervened and corrected info with family members. Tried to keep me in touch when they had siblings-only meetings concerning caring for their parents.

…started rumors, especially about finances. Almost never mention their brother, and especially do not acknowledge their loss…they seem to feel it would hurt me. Did not offer to help with the overwhelming farm work, and at times made excuses when asked to help. 🌷

The Lord never wastes suffering in the lives of His children.

Question **15**

How do you deal with relating to the widow, while missing your brother?

Widows' in laws answer:

• We talk more. I find it a challenge to chat without mentioning my own husband and his merits too much, so as not to appear to be better off somehow. A rut widows should watch for…in reverting to being in their own little corner too much. Getting out and doing things for others is wonderful therapy, as my sister-in-law does! I want to remind everyone that grief is an individual journey—*they who compare themselves among themselves are not wise.*

• We like to invite her and her children here because Grandpa is here with us. It seems like she feels comfortable with us. If she wouldn't, I would see that being a challenge. About every time they go past here, they blow their horn. That brings smiles to Grandpa. I am sure going to weddings is hard. Lots of the family would love to help out in taking her, and seeing that she is okay.

• Our relationship has changed since my brother is absent; he was the one to whom I related directly. But I appreciate the respectful way in which we can relate together as families. I feel like we too often forget about her needs, or fail to think about occasions we could be reaching out to her. I hope she can feel free to call on us if and when she needs us, even if we failed to think about what we could have done. The following comments need to allow for the difference in what each person appreciates in how they relate to their need. This is not a widow-only observation. But no matter what our unique situation may be, we all need help to relate as a brother among brethren or sister among sisters seeing that our varying struggles are a need we share in common, rather than to have a lot of ado made over the uniqueness of our trial. Family has an important place in including the widow in the routines of life, rather than constantly reminding them that they are victims of misfortune.

• I hesitate to speak of my husband and his activities, yet we can still enjoy visiting on women's interests and activities. I do not want to say anything that makes her wound deeper, yet my life does so much include my husband that little things do come out at times.

• We are closer since we have shared the bond of grief. Our observation has been that the degree of closeness will be in proportion to the relationship that the family members had with her husband before death. Our sister-in-law has been very open to accept the help of others. This makes it very easy to relate to her. As a result, her children also seem to appreciate their uncles and aunts. They need to be careful that while they are grieving, they do not draw into a shell or neglect their parental duties. This is not easy, but it will help to avoid more grief later. For the first number of years, anniversaries and birthdays are understandably very difficult times. But if someone else forgets these dates after several years, she should not be offended. It is right and good to continue to respect the deceased husband and father. But we don't want to idolize them. Both the widow and her family need help to accept that life will never quite be the same again. But with time and support of others this is possible.

• Sometimes we didn't know where to fit in since she relied heavily on her family rather than her deceased husband's family. We wanted to help, but didn't know where we fit. It would have been good for her to respect her husband's families' input to the family farm that so suddenly fell on her shoulders. Their experience with farming would have gone a long way, rather than advice from inexperienced people whom she may have respected more. Drastic changes were taking place on the farm, and we, as her husband's family, found out through the grapevine that she was seeking counsel and advice from others rather than the family. So we stayed aloof because it seemed we were not wanted, and yet, we wanted to contact and help where we could. Appreciation for family must be there strongly before death, so it can be there after death. Share with your husband's family! Do not think they are grieving, so you won't share. Part of healing is the respect you show for them.

• It is a challenge to know how to mention things my husband did for me or the children, because her husband is no longer here to do things for her. How do we most appropriately visit them as a complete family? We would not want them to feel no one cares about them. Without the stability and encouragement of a husband, the widow may need to be extra careful not to become too lenient in child-training areas, and in relating to young people. The in-laws should be available to help with maintenance projects. At family gatherings and other events, other men in the family should take an interest in the children and help to monitor their activities, especially the boys. 🌹

Perspectives

S W

Rather go Home in the throb of youth
Than age under God-sworn woes.
Rather be plucked a perfect bud
Than linger a blasted rose!
Rather die young under cancer's sword,
Pardoned and free within,
Than live long years in the devil's employ,
Chained by the vice of sin.
Rather find rest in the quiet earth
Near to the bosom of God,
Than live with the tumult that haunts the streets
Rebels have always trod.
Rather be snatched by the tide of death
And sweep through the heavenly gates,
Than live to the fullest of life's wild mirth
And know that a hell awaits.
O, grief is real when the righteous die,
And the grave has a mournful toll…
But it's harder by far to have loved ones live
And know there is death in the soul.

A Bereaved Sister Looking On

DZ

I saw them as they dated.
They seemed so fresh and young.
Life offered many roses sweet;
Their love was growing strong.

I heard them plan their wedding,
And dream of future bright,
And love's anticipation glowed
Like early morning light.

I watched—they stood before us,
Joined hearts and hands for life.
The minister so solemnly
Pronounced them man and wife.

"I promise I shall cherish you
Till death should part," they said.
With hearts entwined, they turned about
To face their life ahead.

I saw him four months later.
He still looked young and strong,
But oh—so deathly silent.
His life—their vows—were gone.

I saw her weep beside him.
His hand in hers was cold.
No longer could they share their dreams,
Together growing old.

I saw the teardrops falling,
As she knelt beside his grave.
She cried to God Who took him Home,
And grace and strength He gave.

I see her smile in spite of
The heartache in her way.
She has a strength that's not her own
It carries her each day.

And in her eyes a longing
As she gazes toward the sky.
She's living for the day when she
Can join him there on high.

When Grief Comes Calling

Helpful advice is not the focus of this article. It is only a heart cry from one grieving heart to others walking this same lonely trial.

Weariness engulfs me as I settle into my easy chair. I am weary beyond words—a weariness that no amount of physical exertion could produce. It is a weariness that arises from heaviness of the heart and sorrow of the soul.

Once more death has come knocking at the door of my heart. This time it has taken a beloved brother. Hearing those fateful words from the messenger standing at our door, I stare in disbelief, my mind and heart numb at the sudden shock. Too soon comes the pain. The stabbing, searing pain.

Why, God, why? He was too young, he was needed, he was loved. I knew he had been ill, but dead, God? Surely there's some mistake! His wife still needed him, his children needed him, his whole family needed him. Why, God? No answer comes...

I feel almost guilty for still having my husband and my children, when another home has been torn asunder. I grieve with them, and for them, and for all of us whose lives have been affected by this death. How it has

142

shattered the placidness that was in my life right now!

Like beads on a chain, I let the thought of each of my remaining siblings slip through my mind. Then comes the hole where a bead is now missing. Such a large hole, God! Why us again? Our family has gone through this so often—and this time death snatched the one closest to me in age. We had shared so much in life, and surely a part of my heart has been torn away by the cruel hand of death. The large chain that had been my family circle keeps shrinking, as one by one, God's call comes for each of them. How terrible the rending of a family chain, and yet it seems as each one is torn away, the remaining links become stronger.

But why did it have to be our family again? I think of families I know, generation upon generation intact. The hand of death has never plucked even one from their midst, nor the winds of sorrow blown cold and harsh across bleeding hearts. Then, there are families who are not close in heart, whose only kinship seems to be in the name they share, and the parents who gave them life. Why none of them? And yet I know I would rather grieve in love, than to have a family where it hurts but little if one would die.

Fresh tears course down my face as I think of the last time I saw my brother alive. I try to recall each word, each look. How little I realized that day that I would never see him alive again! What would I have said or done differently had I known it was our last meeting on earth? Did he know that I loved him, that I considered him a very special part of our family? Ah, surely he would have been embarrassed had I heaped him with flowery phrases.

How hard it was to go to his home today and see his grief-stricken wife and children! How hard it will be to go tomorrow and view that once-vibrant body now cold in death! I shrink from the thought as fresh "whys" course through my mind. No answers come, but that does not keep our human minds and hearts from questioning God's wisdom. I trust God understands.

I have traveled through this black vale of sorrow before, and disjointed phrases that meant much to me in times past flit in and out of my jumbled thoughts. "Grief has its rhythm; first the swift, wild tide of dark despair, the time of bleak aloneness, when even God's not there…" (Forgive me,

143

Lord, for finding those words so fitting. I know You are here with me, but in my first blinding grief I often feel as if You must have abandoned me, and the unknown poet surely shared those same feelings.)

The words that come most often, though, are only one line from a poem, the rest having slipped into oblivion in my mind. "Give me strength for each tomorrow..." Yes, Lord, through all these hard tomorrows. How I will need Thy strength, God, as we go through the viewing, the funeral... and then those difficult times of going to visit my brother's family and finding the house so empty. How can only one person leave so large a hole?

God, why? Why? Why? No answers come; I know from experience no answers will come. But I have traveled this pathway of pain before, and so I know that while I can never understand, I can accept. It will not be tonight or tomorrow; it might not be next week or next month; but someday, with God's help.

Someday, bright sunshine will no longer make a mockery of the dark pain in my heart. Someday, I can smile on the outside and not be shedding tears inside. Someday, I can sing with my heart rising in praise with the notes of the song. Someday... But for now, Lord, just hold me close, and let me cry.

Comforters come in all ways, shapes, sizes, ages, and personalities. But the one thing that any true comforter will do is walk "with" you into the valley of the shadow of death. True comforters realize that the only way to healing is to go through the pain. You cannot go around it, nor over it. They do not try to "take away" your hurt, or "fix it." True comforters will be beside you in your grief, anticipating possible hard spots, forgiving when you stumble with anger or frustration, listening when groaning with the heaviness of the load, always pointing to the light of healing. Through the hands and heart of a true comforter, God's love and goodness will shine brightly into the darkest hours of His grieving children.

Courage doesn't always roar; sometimes it is a still small voice at the end of the day that says, I will try again tomorrow.

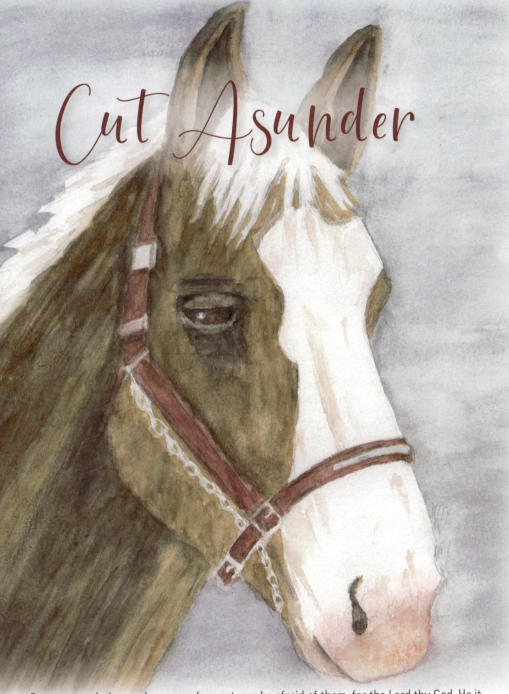

Cut Asunder

Be strong and of a good courage, fear not, nor be afraid of them, for the Lord thy God, He it is that doth go before thee. He will not fail thee nor forsake thee. Deut. 31:6

Cut Asunder

GRACE SHIRK'S STORY *Grace Shirk with Suellen J Strite*

Thursday, May 21, 2015:

Oh. The awfulness cannot be described. The awfulness of receiving a message that my best friend...my confidant...my lover...my husband! is in the hospital, critically ill.

A horrible foreboding stole over my being, telling me he won't come back home. This was not what I had biked to the phone booth to hear. Samuel was several hours away in Kentucky, boarding with his sister Lucy and working on a job, and I wanted to find out when he was coming home. Instead I got the awful tidings that he would hardly wake up this morning. When Lucy asked him our children's names, he could only name three of our eight children. Imagine! My husband, our children's daddy, the man who loved his children up and down and around, could no longer name all of them. Samuel's nephew rushed with him to the ER in Russell Springs, KY, where he was given IV antibiotics. Tests showed high liver enzymes, low white blood cells, and severe dehydration; but he was given no concrete diagnosis.

A terror overtook me. I tried to contact a driver to take me to the hospital, but I couldn't get plans to work out. I heaped all my troubles on my friend Norma, and she stepped under my hands that hung down and made all the arrangements. Wearily I left the phone booth, and biked the

1½ miles home. My knees were so weak I wondered how I would ever make it. My eyes were so dimmed by tears that it was hard to see the road. Landis (10) and Geneva (5) ran out the driveway to meet me. Geneva collapsed crying into my arms, while Landis asked for more details. I staggered onto the couch, held my seven-week-old baby, and told my children and our maid the terrible news. The children were probably more alarmed by their upset and tearful mom than they were about their daddy being in the hospital.

I pulled myself to my feet and feverishly packed an overnight bag. I would take baby Wesley along with me, and I tried to make my numbed brain think what all he would need. My mind raced across the reoccurring infections that have been invading Samuel's body, with MRSA boils being his latest infection. We had recently moved to Tennessee, and others told us, "Yes, I was depressed, too, and low on energy when we moved. Be tough." But my husband *was* resilient. I knew something was physically wrong; I was sure. I threw clean clothes for Samuel into my bag and hoped desperately that he would need them.

The children convinced me they had to go to Wilma's house. Since they get along famously with Wilma, I decided to let them go with her. My maid agreed to take the children to Wilma's house. I hugged or touched each child good-bye with tears streaming down my cheeks and theirs. Then, taking baby Wesley along with me, Sue and I drove over to Samuel's parents to see if his mom would please go with me. "Yes, I want to," she said, and stuffed clothes in a backpack and finally we were Kentucky bound.

It was a long, lonely ride to the hospital, five hours from home. I thought back over the past week. Samuel had been feeling extra tired and weak. I felt helpless. Exactly a week ago today, Ascension Day, he began running a fever. But he is a resilient man. Four days later, on Monday, we bade each other good-bye and he went to work a job he had promised to finish in Lexington, KY. He is a man of his word. He always was. I had learned that back when we were dating. I had made plans to stop by his home one afternoon and he said it would suit; he would be home. Later, I inconsiderately decided to stop by in the evening instead. When I arrived, Samuel was about to leave, because he had other arrangements to do for someone that evening. Even though he hated to miss seeing me, he planned to keep his promise. I thought of this as we silently drove toward Kentucky. Part of me is upset that he thought he had to finish the job he promised. The other part of me feels only respect for him, the man of his word.

Partway to the hospital I borrowed a cell phone and called Samuel. How wonderful to hear his voice, even though his comprehension was slow. He told me they were preparing an ambulance to transfer him from Russel Springs Hospital to the UK Hospital in Lexington, so we headed straight for UK. One of his cousins was with him. I was glad he wasn't alone, but I wanted to be by his side!

Finally, we were in Lexington. My sister Faith called and asked, "Are you close to the hospital?"

Something in her tone of voice made me ask, "Do you think he will die before I get there?"

"Well, I hope not," she stalled, "but he is not getting better."

I asked to talk to Samuel again. "Where are you?" he wondered.

"We are crossing Man-o-War Boulevard."

"Oh, then you are almost here." He sounded relieved.

We neared the ER entrance and I began unstrapping seat buckles. I grabbed baby Wesley's car seat and my bag. Thankfully my mother-in-law had the presence of mind to pay the driver. I hurried to the doors and was met by Faith. She went with me to the front desk. The receptionist was not as much in a hurry as I was. She methodically looked at Samuel's records. "He is only allowed two visitors at a time," she informed us in a dry voice.

I was appalled! "But I am his wife!" I felt frantic! Here my husband was almost dying and this lady wouldn't allow me back to see him.

Then she did show a kind bone and looked at Faith. "Give her your sticker pass. He is only allowed two visitors. Go through that door and to…"

I grabbed the sticker, waiting for no more instructions. I ran to the door and was there before the automatic door opened. I raced back the hall. I don't know how I even knew where to go, but there on the bedside stand was Samuel's hat and I knew I had found him.

It was a comfort to be together. But oh! It was awful to watch Samuel labor for every breath, while he concentrated on talking to me, his wife. I shuddered. I was watching my husband deteriorate before my eyes! He had seen a doctor close to Lucy's house four days ago, on Monday evening. That doctor had given him a prescription along with the words, "If you do not feel like a new man by Thursday, come see me again." Today was Thursday, and my husband neither looked nor felt like a new man.

Far from it. My handsome Samuel was deteriorating! It cannot be true. To me, he was the most handsome man in the world! His black hair and dark brown eyes only added to the appeal of his caring heart. We grew up in the same community and he was always a part of my life. I was honored when he chose me to be his girlfriend! His thoughtfulness made me feel so special. One Sunday we were both at his parents for a family gathering. I had a splitting headache and told Samuel that I planned to take a nap in the afternoon. Children were playing a noisy game outside the window where I was napping, and later I discovered that Samuel had gone out and told them they had to play elsewhere so I could rest. See? Already then, I could tell he would be a considerate husband.

And even now...he considerately tried to talk to me...for my sake! Even though he was laboring for every breath, he talked with me for about an hour and a half. His comprehension was good, but his speech was slow. He was looking forward to the relief of the breathing machine. The doctors told us that they would need to sedate Samuel before they put him on the breathing machine. "So, if you have anything you want to say to each other, now is the time." Oh! How terrible. I thought it could not be happening. We still have years and *years* of things to say; how could it all be said in sixty minutes?

Instead, we prayed together. Then Samuel whispered to me, "It's okay to use life support to try to help me." His dark chocolate eyes were full of care for me, even while he was fighting for life. Deep inside, we both knew he was dying and that he only allowed life support for my sake.

And then the doctor came and said I must leave the room while Samuel was sedated for the breathing machine, and moved to MICU. The doctors described my husband as a very sick man. His liver, lungs, and kidneys are being attacked by something powerful, but the doctors couldn't figure out what. They started him on a broad range of antibiotics, since his symptoms do not point conclusively to any certain disease.

An intern came and showed us the way to the MICU waiting room. We gathered our belongings and staggered after him. We sank down on the nearest island of blue and white striped chairs under a glaring light. Across the room is a coffee station. Greenery is placed strategically to provide some privacy.

We waited and waited. Two kind ladies appeared. "Oh, hi! Who are you? Are you new here? Why are you here?" They listened sympathetically to our stories and we listened to theirs. They suggested we move farther back into the waiting room where the lights are dimmed, since by this time evening had approached. So, we chose another island, where we settled down and claimed this section for our campsite.

After a long time, I was allowed to go back to Samuel. I was eager to be with him, even though he was sedated. Surely now he will start getting better.

My parents arrived at 2:00 AM. Never have I been so glad to see my mom! And just knowing my dad is here to help with decisions is such a comfort. God orchestrated their travels home from Wisconsin perfectly. A blessing in the midst of our nightmare.

Friday, May 22, 2015:

I found it a comfort to be with Samuel, but after a while it overwhelmed me and I was glad to go out to the waiting room and care for baby Wesley. There were lots of family members in the waiting room…both Samuel's family and mine. As the day progressed, Samuel's friends and cousins arrived. It was nice to see them, but after a while that was overwhelming, too, and I was glad to escape back to Samuel. Each time I was with Samuel I talked to him, telling him what I was doing every time I came or went.

The cafeteria is just across the hall from the MICU, so we go there to get food. The first time I burst into tears just seeing the cafeteria. Our daughter Geneva needed an ultrasound here at UK, about a year ago. Samuel and I ate in this very place, enjoying the day together. Now, what a stark contrast.

Evening approached and the visitors went home. My parents, Samuel's parents, and our bishop prepared to spend the night in the waiting room. They draped themselves over chairs or curled up on short sofas. After they were tired and cramped enough, they no longer cared how awkward it looked. At 9:00 PM, the hospital provides blankets and pillows for the waiting family. I am privileged to have a nice recliner in Samuel's room and the nurses provide all the pillows I need.

Saturday, May 23, 2015:

Today I rode a nightmarish roller coaster. The doctors decided to start Samuel on steroids to combat the most likely, but unconfirmed disease, HLH. This is a case of an overactive immune system, which is attacking his organs. The lead doctor gave his chance of survival at 50/50. That is an awful estimate for a wife to hear about her companion. The doctors describe their efforts as putting on Band-Aids to buy time for the test results to come in. The problems now include: low blood pressure, low heart rate, uncontrollable blood seepage at IV port, low kidney function, continuous high liver enzymes, low white blood cell count, and low blood oxygen level.

Ten of my brothers and sisters and some of Samuel's family came to visit us. I am so touched that they made the effort to travel all those miles for our sake. As one of my brothers was leaving, he shook my hand in farewell. Tears splashed onto my hand; I was so touched by his empathy that it made my pain a bit more bearable.

I talked to the children this afternoon. Uncle Jasons (Wilma's parents) are doing a great job caring for our children. They took them on a drive to the fire tower and then visited an elderly neighbor where they used the phone to call me. Each child asked hopefully in turn, "Is Daddy getting better?" I could not bear to tell them across all these miles that their daddy is dying, but neither did I want to create false hopes. I told them Daddy is very sick and that they can pray and ask God to heal him. Surely God will answer a child's heartfelt prayer!

Sunday, May 24, 2015:

Today there was a bit of hope for my husband. I thought the Lord was answering our children's prayers. When the blood clotting was under control, a continuous dialysis machine was connected and things looked better than they have for a while. The medical team was upbeat and hopeful. I thought maybe, just maybe, he would get to wear the clean clothes I packed for him to go home.

As I sat beside Samuel's bedside recoiling from the reality of the past couple days, my mind wandered back to our courtship. Back to those days when our relationship was on the shoals, and it seemed that we would need to part ways. I remember the prayer I prayed, the gist of it: "Lord, I understand that it may not be Your will for Samuel and me to continue our friendship. I resign my right to him. I give our friendship to You. In Jesus' Name." Then to my sweet surprise, that is when God gave Samuel back to me, and our relationship flourished.

As I mused over that past miracle, there seemed to be a striking likeness to that far-off time and the here and now. I realized anew that the only restful place to be is in the center of God's will. Now it seems the Lord is asking me to give Samuel back to Him again. This time my prayer ran something like this: "Lord, thank you for giving Samuel to me these happy years. I do not want You to extend Samuel's days beyond Your will. (Visions of King Hezekiah flashed through my mind.) I give our relationship back to You. I pray for Samuel's healing, but I am resigned to Your will."

I sat back to watch the miracle. But God answered my prayer in a different way this time. Samuel, from that moment of resignation, began rapidly to die.

Monday, May 25, 2015:
Things kept falling apart. The medical team worked frantically to make adjustments. They started new medicine and made last desperate efforts to support Samuel's blood pressure. His lungs filled up with fluid which could not be removed by the dialysis system because of the deterioration of his body. At this point, the doctors received a positive test result for a tick-borne disease called Ehrlichiosis, which was already being treated for by some of the antibiotics being given him.

I thought 50/50 was a terrible thing to hear. Today the lead doctor gave a 10/90 or less chance of survival. No. No. It cannot be. Oxygen was increased to 100% from an earlier 40%. Still Samuel's blood oxygen levels slipped below acceptable limits. Time was running out for my husband! Nitrous oxide was added to the air to increase the body's ability to retain oxygen. I felt frantic! "Help us, Lord."

Yet more horror awaited me. Samuel's oxygen drop...drop...dropped. When we asked the lead doctor if Samuel still had a viable body, he replied, "Samuel's kidneys are not working, his heart is not working, his liver is not working, his lungs are not working, his blood is not clotting..."

This morning more family and ministry came to visit. We waited while they went back two or three at a time to see Samuel. Everyone had the same heart-stricken look when they came back out. I was sitting under the TV and could effortlessly block out the noise. Until the lyrics of "You Are My Sunshine," began to play. How cruel. How ill-timed. Many times, Samuel sang that song to me. That will be nevermore. For even then I was facing the awful task of meeting with my family and Samuel's family to decide to take him off the maximum life support.

We sat in the warm stuffy cramped family room with the doctor and her assistant. Poor Daddy got the job of telling them of our decision. The doctor looked sternly at us over the top of her black glasses. "You understand we have not given up on Samuel?" she asked. "Samuel is still so young. If he survives, he will not have much quality of life. But we have not given up. Are you sure you want to unhook him?"

Horrors, I don't want to be a widow, but about the only thing worse would be having a vegetable husband. And Samuel would hate to be an invalid. I was actually very relieved when Samuel's dad said with an authoritative tone, "The decision is made." I hated the limelight and hugged Wesley close for support.

The doctor slid the forms across the table to me. NO! NO! NO! Oh! I needed to sign a paper that said it was okay for my husband to die! But it is not okay. I need him. Eight children need him. Yet underlying was the calmness that I had given Samuel back to God and this was the Lord's doings.

We discussed who would go back with me to Samuel's room while they removed life support. I chose both sets of parents. I wanted some support, but not so much that I would need to hide my feelings. The doctors explained that they would leave the ventilator on so Samuel wouldn't choke to death, but that they would turn down his heart medicine and other stimulants. Then the assistant led us out of that stuffy room. I handed Wesley to my sister Anita, and followed the doctor on the most awful march of my life.

Imagine my devastation when I walked into that now-familiar room to discover the nurses had invited all those in the waiting room to come in! Those who were a support in the waiting room now formed a bank of eyes all along the left side of Samuel's bed. I didn't like the publicity at all. Samuel and I were joined together in front of a crowd of witnesses. Now I guess we had to also be cut asunder in a crowd of witnesses. Now I had to keep my feelings in check because how I reacted would be spread in the highways and byways.

The nurse provided a chair for me on the right side of my husband's bed, and I sank into it. My parents and Samuel's parents stood beside and behind me. We waited and waited and waited as Samuel's body shut down. It was a tense time for everyone. Someone suggested that we sing, which was okay with me, but it seemed no one could think of all the words to songs. Samuel's father requested the song, "Have Thine Own Way." We sang it, and then other suggestions were made with discussion about which song would be best and I felt awful. I didn't even want this whole crowd of witnesses in here, let alone all the discussion about songs.

And then the blip, blip, blip…stopped. The machine went black. My lover's heart stopped. I was overwhelmed with sadness and loneliness.

At that moment I became a widow. I became a widow with eight children and the youngest is only seven weeks old.

I felt very, very sad. My sister put her arm around my shoulders and whispered, "This is precious in the sight of the Lord." I felt like I needed comfort; yet I didn't want comfort. I just wanted to be very, very sad.

The hospital staff offered that we could go back in to see Samuel after they removed life support hoses and all those other wires. That was such a nice gift. Without all the gadgets Samuel looked like himself. Before he died, he looked tortured and in pain, as the breathing machine breathed for him. Now he looked relaxed, calm, and at peace. I could see his whole face and rub his cheek and feel his whiskers. His whiskers were always such a special part of him, so it was touching that though the rest of his body struggled to function he still grew whiskers.

I said good-bye to him in that room, where he still looked so much like himself. It was an awful, awful good-bye. The worst good-bye of my life.

The doctor asked to do an autopsy since the medical team still does not understand exactly what he died from. I agreed, because Samuel always wanted to help anyone he could. I remember once watching Samuel and one of the children eating an M&M. Samuel had the last piece, so he bit it in half, so he could share. He would have given you his last five dollars if he thought you needed it worse than he did. So, if this autopsy would help one person recover it would be worth it. But...why did such a kind generous husband and daddy need to die?

The job ahead of me looked enormous...going home and telling Samuel's eight beloved children that their daddy had died. How do you explain death to a three-year-old? Or a ten-year-old? How do you tell them that their best friend, supporter, advocate, and encourager just died? "Oh, God, help me with my impossible task"

My family arranged for me to meet my children at my parents' house for the awful task of telling them of their father's death. The hospital no longer had any pull because Samuel was no longer there. As we were loading the van at the hospital entrance, one of the ladies who had helped us find a better place in the waiting room on our first night here, saw us leaving. She said, "I am sorry..."

It was a lonely ride back to my parents' house in a van full of people. My mind went numb as I thought of trying to break the news to my children. I pictured each of them as happy and carefree as they were on the Monday before Samuel left for his Kentucky job. Landis (10) is an energetic lad with unruly hair and a thousand questions. He is such a help around the house. Brenda (9) is dark complexioned with dark hair, reminding people of Samuel's sisters and aunts. She is outgoing and makes many friends. Eric (8) is ever cheerful and a willing worker. He loves the outdoors and anything to do with horses. I have to remind him not to shoulder the whole world's burdens. Kenneth (6) is a happy-go-lucky, lovable little chap. He can entertain himself for hours. One day I found him on the pony cart with no pony. He had makeshift lines rigged up, and I asked him, "Where are you going?" He had a ready reply: "Around the whole world!" Geneva (5) is an affectionate girl after Samuel's own heart. She laughs easily and cries easily and sucks her thumb. Samuel told her not to suck her thumb when she is holding baby Wesley, or next he will start too. Loretta (3) is quieter. Sometimes she is pouty and Samuel would tell her, "A little bird could sit on your pout." That always brought a smile. Elaine (21 months) has not started to talk. She can't even say Daddy yet, but that doesn't mean he isn't important to her! She is only a little girlie and doesn't even have enough hair to pull together into ponytails. And then there is baby Wesley (only seven weeks old). Of course, I won't have to tell him the news, but my heart breaks to think of him growing up never knowing his daddy.

Even as we were headed south, my brother Timothys were bringing my children north to meet me at my parents' house. God timed it so that our van drove in the lane only minutes after the Tennessee van did. I watched my precious children get out of that van. Within minutes I would tell these children that the daddy they love and still need is not living.

The others kindly stepped aside while I shattered my children's world with the heart-breaking news of the death of their father. Listening to their anguished weeping was terrible to my mother heart. Loretta asked again and again, "But where is Daddy?"

The children's Aunt Lavina shared an illustration with them. "Remember on the way up here we saw a curly slide? And Brenda told us that one time she had a chance to slide down one of those, but she was too scared. Then Daddy spoke up from the bottom and told her to come on down, he is waiting at the end. That is how it is since Daddy died. He is waiting for you on the other side."

The grownups had planned we would travel back to Tennessee yet that evening. But the children protested; they did not want to get back in that van already. Plans were changed slightly and we stayed at my parents' place for the night. It was nice to be somewhere that I didn't have to work anything and I had help with the children. But I longed to go home to *our* house…what used to be *our* home.

Even as I wept, the angels rejoiced with happy cries, "Samuel is home. His day has just begun." But on this side of eternity, it feels like inky night. The climax of each day had always been the moment when the children rejoiced with happy cries, "Daddy's home!" This was never news to me, because from the time Samuel left for work in the morning until he returned, my ears were tuned for the familiar throb of the pickup. I always heard him coming long before the children noticed! Our day had begun, Samuel was home!

Now…now I am back to waiting. Not waiting until Samuel comes home, but waiting until I can go Home to Samuel. At this point, I need Samuel so much. Samuel is much more tangible than God. As I longed for Samuel to come home, so I long to go Home to him. He was my shield against the harsh world, and now when I need him most, he is gone, and I have to face the world alone. (Eventually I would learn to replace my need for Samuel with fellowship with God, but that came much later.)

Even so, Lord, come quickly!

Tuesday, May 26, 2015:

As we traveled from my parents' house in Kentucky to our house in Tennessee this morning, I asked Mom what I need to do when I get home. She said, "Nothing. You may just sit on the couch." That was the most comforting thing she could have said. She understood that my world had stopped and it was okay to act that way.

Our church community came together to help plan my husband's funeral. I sat on the couch in shock and overwhelming sorrow. Then I happened to see Landis out on the porch sitting on a chair looking lost and dejected. I went out and told him he may come sit on the couch beside me. I needed someone to sit in that great empty place as much as Landis needed to sit with someone.

I looked around our living room and thought back three short months ago. How happily we had placed our furniture in February, looking forward to settling into our new farm. Now, so soon, the furniture will all be moved for Samuel's visitation. It is awful to think how different the two circumstances are.

I let my mind linger on memories of our life when we still lived in Kentucky, where Samuel's roots were deeply entwined. He loved the soil, the people, the roads, and the countryside. For over 20 years he built silos in a 200-mile radius on the farms in Kentucky's hills and hollers. His customers from far-flung areas were not just customers to Samuel. They were his friends.

Then God asked Samuel to do something way out of his comfort zone. Our church as a whole had agreed to all relocate to Tennessee. Samuel couldn't move his business because where we were relocating there is almost no farming. Very little farming means very few silos need to be built. Samuel was losing his job, his customer friends, his Kentucky… for stump land. It was almost more than he could do, but his first commitment was to God and His church.

Our stress level was high as we endeavored to follow God's plan. Selling our property and sorting and packing all our worldly goods was a mammoth undertaking. Samuel was also working at building our new house in Tennessee. He had three hours each way, so sometimes he would stay over three or four days at a time. Is it any wonder Samuel was run down and ill?

Only three months, I think, and another wave of overwhelming clouds my being. In three short months, I moved, had a new baby, and am burying my husband. I wonder, how much can one woman take?

Thursday, May 28, 2015:
The most terrible ordeal arrived this morning…the hearse that pulled in. Everyone was drawn toward it to observe and help. I felt near to losing my mind. How could this be happening to me, this last time that Samuel comes home, he comes in a coffin? Oh, God, why? Why? I was tempted to run away. Far, far away. But instead, I hid in the bathroom to pray and gather strength. God gave me the strength and calmness to go out and face the multitude of eyes, and to face the cruelness of seeing my husband in a coffin.

The undertaker had combed his hair back over his head, unlike Samuel always combed it. Mom suggested that we comb it in his normal fashion. I tried, but I just could not. The comb scraped awkwardly on his hard scalp. His hair was stiff, not soft like it used to be. Mom kindly finished it for me.

I was in awe over how many people come for Samuel's viewing. His friends, co-workers, and neighbors. Then there were people I didn't even know, who came because they care about some of our siblings. I was grateful for each person.

But the sweetest of all were the caring handshakes and words of comfort from widows and widowers. One told me, "We wonder how we will ever get the children through this...then it is the children who get us through."

Others gently shook my hand and clasped it in both theirs. "Time goes on," they said softly, "and it drags you along."

The children were crowded in around and behind me. They are very social and most people who went through the line took time to shake their hands.

Elaine stood on a chair at the head of the coffin and leaned on it with her arm inside. She loved her daddy! It was so sweet and heartbreaking at the same time.

Landis seemed to mind the publicity the most. So when someone slipped me a wad of cash, I handed it to him to count and keep for me. My sister commented, "I am surprised you trust Landis with that money." I didn't even try to explain to her how money is of absolutely no value to me right now. No amount of money can buy for me what I desperately want. By the end of the funeral day, I have more hard cash than ever before in my life. But I also have a newfound realization that money really does not buy happiness!

Friday, May 29, 2015:
Today they buried my best friend while my daughter asked, "Why are they putting Daddy in that hole?"
Yes. Why?

Sunday, May 31, 2015:
Today I went to church without Samuel. I was so torn up that I had to concentrate just to breathe. To think I have to drive Samuel's horse to church without Samuel. Samuel possessed the charming ability to drive horses that preferred not being driven, and I often felt like Laura Ingalls

Wilder when her ma accused her of liking his horses better than Almanzo. And like Laura, I could say, "I wouldn't have one without the other."

Others commented on appreciating the good sermon. I was so torn up that I retained very little. I was touched that Minister Joe commented in his sermon that at our last communion he admonished that this could well be the last communion for some members, but that he never thought it would be Samuel. It felt good to know others are thinking of my loss.

After we were home, Geneva commented, "I know you were thinking about Daddy in church."

"Oh, how do you know?"

"Because you cried."

In the afternoon we looked at the cards folks had given me at church. Then I looked at the clock and it was only 1:00! I nearly panicked. How would I make it through this whole long afternoon? Sunday afternoons used to be good times spent with Samuel. Now all I have for company is a raw, aching wound. Thankfully, Dad and Mom came to sit out the afternoon with me. We didn't talk much, but at least I was no longer alone with that huge hole.

As soon as our babies were one year old, they started sitting with Samuel in church. And too bad for me…all the other children wanted to sit with Samuel, too. He was their best friend! Now…now Samuel is not here. I am glad I let them sit with him when they could. I get weepy just remembering the beautiful sight of Samuel with his little "row of Shirks."

Friday, June 5, 2015:

Do not ask me how I am doing, because I do not know. Some days are not too bad; others are hardly bearable. Someone told me after the funeral that it will get worse before it gets better. How can it be worse?

Today I was struggling with my thoughts. I wonder, what would I have asked Samuel if I had known it was my last chance? Probably nothing. I think we both *did* know that he was dying and it was not something we wanted to talk about.

I just wish Samuel would not have pushed himself to go put in Mr. Colson's silo unloader. We knew he was not feeling well. If only we had not been too busy and too poor to run to the doctor more often.

Samuel sometimes contracted jobs for the next summer, his silo building business being a summer job. And there seemed to be no job opportunities in Tennessee. Moving, building, and providing for eight children creates a financial vacuum. So, going back to Kentucky to finish silos was the practical thing to do. Samuel was a man of his word. So, he went to put in Mr. Colson's unloader despite being sick.

If only I had gone with him that fateful Monday morning. Maybe the consequences would not have been different, but at least I would have been with him. But our baby was only seven weeks old and someone had to care for the animals here, so could I really have gone?

If only I would have realized just how sick Samuel was, I would have taken him to the ER here in Tennessee. If only the Kentucky doctor would have known how sick he was on Monday. Isn't diagnosing sick people the doctor's job?

I feel so badly that baby Wesley will never know his daddy. Samuel had been so pleased with his fourth little son! By some feat only he could manage, he would hold Elaine (20 months) and Wesley (7 weeks) while sitting on the couch to shave, and he was humming besides! Even though the babies won't remember, I comfort myself with that memory from our last morning together.

Saturday, June 6, 2015:

Mom and Dad encouraged me to plant some garden stuff to have something to do with the children. Lucinda offered that we may come to her greenhouse and pick out plants. The children enjoyed doing that, but I walked after them feeling like a dazed observer, detached from the world. I had no energy to help plant those plants, so I tried to encourage the children to do it while I sat on the porch swing. Then Landis said, "I wish you would come out to the garden. It is gloomy out here without you." That warmed my heart to the point that I had strength to go out and help for a while.

This morning Geneva was sitting on the couch holding Wesley. I said, "Oh, Geneva, look what Wesley is doing!" Geneva looked down and saw that Wesley was sucking his thumb. Remembering her daddy's admonishment, she quickly said, "I didn't teach him."

I stand in fear and trembling to help these children through their grief, then they unexpectedly warm my heart and make me smile above my grief.

Thursday, June 11, 2015:
Today neighbor James Kilmer passed from this life. Now his battle with cancer is over, but his family suffers a tremendous loss of husband, father, and grandfather. "God," I wonder, "do You know what You are doing? We need our husbands!" Can my family and I go to another viewing and funeral already? It looks overwhelming.

Sunday, June 14, 2015:
James's widow needed to go to the funeral home on Friday. The funeral director asked her to bring Samuel's death certificate to me. She brought it to me at church. All that legal stuff "fulates" me. (Would give anything to avoid it.) His certificate says:

> Disease resulting in death: Multi-organ Failure
> Due to: Disseminated Intravascular Coagulation
> Underlying Cause: Ehrlichiosis

Now, at least I know what to say when people ask what Samuel died from. But such a mouthful. He worked at dangerous heights building all those silos. Why couldn't he have just fallen off one of those and broke his neck? Much simpler to explain and the end results would all be the same.

Monday, July 6, 2015:
I walked to the neighbors this morning, and on the way home stopped and picked a half-gallon of blackberries beside the trail. I came home and promptly made a cobbler for supper. It felt so good to actually be able to function normally for an hour or two.

Tuesday, July 7, 2015:
"Widow!
That's what they call me now.
But I am not a widow.
I am married.
I have a husband.

He is just away for a while." Dorothy Hsu, in her book, *Mending*, has captured my sentiments exactly.

The two youngest children are on my bed looking so relaxed. Elaine is slipped under the sheet with her head on her daddy's pillow, her favorite place to sleep. She is finally not so clingy. She had not yet adjusted to Wesley's birth before Samuel died. She reacted strongly to her collapsed world. She is a strong-natured child. A child of variables. Very happy. Very cross.

I am also a child of variables. Very sad that Samuel is not here. Very grateful for all the discipline he got done before he died. He showed me, by example, that consistency is the key to correcting Elaine's strong will.

This little one who was not talking two months ago has started speaking sentences. She takes such good care of her doll, even disciplining her at times. Yesterday I watched her look very sternly at her doll, then smack her mouth!

Today I received very special mail. Samuel's aunt sent a card and letter. She shared memories of Samuel's boyhood days. Some people thought Samuel's parents spoiled him because he had such nice clothes. But no, it was because he was a neat boy and took good care of his clothes. Hmmm…that sounds like one of his sons who can't stand wearing patched pants!

Samuel did not like picking pickles. He thought he could make more money picking up pop cans along the roadside and recycling them. Hmmm…so his sons came by that trait honestly! Samuel grew up to enjoy work, so that gives me hope for his boys.

As much as I enjoy hearing memories and, "I appreciated Samuel because…," I have to think of the song, "Give me the roses while I live, trying to cheer me on." Samuel had discouraging times and could have used that cheer. He doesn't need it anymore; now I do.

Thursday, July 16, 2015:
This week was rough. My brother Tim and others were tearing down a barn for us to reconstruct on our farm. Samuel had started the job; now the financial ends needed to be settled. I had to dig into records to see what I could find. We are poor record keepers; Samuel had an amazing

memory and kept track of such records. So, I missed him terribly. Going through papers that he had handled last, covered with his writing…the papers even smelled like Samuel!

Then Tim brought me the undertaker's bill and the bill for the coffin. That is one of a wife's worst nightmares. So of course, I was weary and weepier, and my girlies have very good radars and pick that up, reacting accordingly. When one is on my lap, suddenly two more need to sit on my lap. Right now.

"How can the days be so long and the years be so short?" someone asks. And I answer, "How can the days be so long and the Sundays come around so fast?" Sundays go slightly better than before. Sometimes I find something to talk about other than *that*.

Thursday, July 23, 2015:

My sister Lucy sent me mail and wrote how she felt it could not be true that Samuel died. When she first heard the news, she called a friend and wailed, "My sister is a widow!"

My sister Anita called a friend in Canada and cried, "My sister is a widow!"

They echo my own heartthrobs of, "Oh, no! A widow. At thirty-one. Thirty-one is too young."

Wednesday, September 23, 2015:

Today was a bad day. I had no energy to work. I feel overwhelmed with work; every room except the kitchen is in shambles. The sink is terribly disorganized. I don't get anything done except the daily little duties.

School has only been in session for two weeks, and already the teacher has sent a note home. Now I have a decision to make. All by myself. Samuel is not here to ask for advice.

Neighbor Nevin built a silo this week and we could watch it go up from our house. That hurt. Samuel enjoyed building silos. How special it would have been to be able to watch him work from home at this project. Then Nevin came for silo parts and I had to price them…

Everyone says I am supposed to take one day at a time. I want to balk, rebel, and throw a fit. I am tired of hurting. Tired of being strong. Tired of being the only disciplinarian. Tired of managing. Tired of putting on a good front. May I stop now?

God provided a lighter moment for us through Landis this evening. Landis got up from the supper table and went to the sink to fill a glass of water. He was in the middle of telling us a good story while he filled his glass. Absentmindedly, he walked over to Brenda, talking all the while. Brenda took his glass of water and drank it all up. Only when Brenda returned the glass, did Landis's story end and he realized what had happened. Landis laughed the hardest. He enjoys a good joke even if it is on himself. Thank you, God. Thank you that we can still laugh, even when most of our life is not funny at all.

Monday, October 26, 2015:
I keep being hurtled through more firsts. In the fourteen years since I was baptized, this fall is the first time I took communion and Samuel didn't. I was a teary mess the whole forenoon!

Yesterday I had visitors from church. One asked, "Is it possible to go on without a husband?"

I quietly replied, "Almost."

"Are you happy again?"

"No," I answer hesitantly. "Peaceful, maybe, but not happy. Resting in the fact that I am in God's will is the only way I can go on."

Heads nodded in mute agreement.

What would I do without a faithful brotherhood? It still comforts me to think how many people showed up to offer their services and help plan the funeral. I was in a daze, but when I was asked if I had any preferences for the service, I was able to recall Samuel's favorite song, "Shall We Gather at the River?" The whole process ran smoothly and kindly. It was soothing to know that here were the people that would stand under my arms.

Thursday, October 29, 2015:
Five months can seem like a lifetime longer than the 11½ years we had together. Yet it seems just like yesterday that I stood beside Samuel's deathbed and watched the heart monitor say "zero." I no longer walk

through the day, screaming underneath, "It can't be true, I can't believe it." But a new sort of hollow loneliness fills my soul. This is for *always*.

Yesterday the children brought home report cards. I struggled with tears. Samuel always signed them, and looked over them with each child, encouraging them to do their best. Our oldest child in school is ten.

He was born less than a year after our wedding. Samuel was pleased and loved to take his son everywhere I allowed him to. In closer intervals than I felt ready we had seven more children. Samuel enjoyed them and welcomed each one. As soon as they could sit well enough, he'd take them along to the barn, giving them his signature shoulder rides.

In the last year before Samuel died, we often had leisurely Sundays. Sometimes we'd hitch two horses and go for drives. The children were old enough to enjoy nature drives. Sometimes we stayed cozily at home. Occasionally Samuel would join the children and me in our games. The children were amazed when Samuel sat down and played Dutch Blitz with us, and then he was the best player.

After supper, Samuel would often lie on the floor and the toddlers would lie with him or crawl over him.

Samuel took the children along anywhere possible. We have many happy memories of going with him to the feed mill, to haul hay, and to auctions. One time Loretta went along to milk the cow and fell asleep while leaning on Samuel's knee.

Thursday, October 29, 2015:

Why do so many people ask how the children are coping? Inside I scream, "How? Yes! How? How are children supposed to cope with the terrible, traumatic loss of a loving daddy?"

The scary part is that sometimes it seems they have accepted it and just go on. I fear they are not processing it right, and will be mentally impaired their entire adult life.

Today I unloaded these worries on my mom. She kindly said, "If you accept and adjust to it, the children will too."

That makes so much sense. But it does put so much responsibility on me!

The bottom line is this: God allowed this situation and He has grace available for us. Will we take His offer and grasp His promises?

Friday, December 4, 2015:
God will take care of us. I didn't want to go shopping this morning, but we needed so many things. Mom agreed to go with me. When we returned, I was overwhelmed! Some friends had dropped off a grocery shower at my house. It was a direct reminder that God will take care of us over and beyond what we think or ask. Everything that had been on my grocery list was in those bags, plus much more besides. I needed laundry soap, and God sent me eight different kinds!

Saturday, December 12, 2015:
Incredible! It's been a wild week with lots of plans. I had company every day. Thursday beat all with company from my morning visitors until after the youth girls left from singing in the evening. Till I had my little ones settled, I felt like saying, "Never again." But what would we do without friends?

Now it is Saturday and already Ammon came to fix the dumpster; when he left, Lavina and her girls came; while they were here, Isaac and Marlin stopped in; Henrys dropped by; and Elva Mae came to help for the day! Probably this afternoon Melinda, Jesses, and Daudy (Grandpa) Shirks will come. Around here you never know! Certainly, we have not been alone in our grief since the day Samuel was hospitalized.

Those days at the hospital were swamped with visitors. I stood in awe. Samuel had a compassionate heart which gained him many friends. I could hardly wait to tell him the outpouring of love that was shown, but I never could.

Wednesday, February 10, 2016:
I had fun sewing three girlie dresses and bonnets to match. But now I feel guilty and confused. Is it okay to still enjoy sewing? Shouldn't we just wear mission barrel clothes since we now have no breadwinner in our family? I feel like I should be able to stretch every dollar twice as far and patch every piece of clothing patch upon patch since we are a financial burden to our extended families. Yet, somehow, I can't handle that stress

on top of all my other grief, stress, and responsibilities. It seems I can no longer handle penny-pinching like I could when Samuel was still alive. Then we were partners in rags, and after all, "Home is where your Honey is." Samuel decided which corners to cut; now it is all my responsibility and I feel like I cannot handle it.

Sunday, March 6, 2016:
I knew that someday I would have to take the plunge and start singing in church again. But every Sunday I put it off. Today Loretta (4) whispered to me, "Why don't you sing?"

I tred it, shaky at first, but guess what! I could sing. What a relief.

We got to hear our newly ordained minister preach his first sermon. He spoke of accepting God's call to preach. He went on to mention that we are vessels to perform God's plan whether we are willing or not. I almost smiled, because it is so true!

Tuesday, March 22, 2016:
Somewhere I read about how many changes a child faces when he loses a parent. Not only does he lose the one to death, the other he loses to change. Sometimes I feel so changed. I used to enjoy writing; now I don't know how or what to write. I used to like cooking; now my favorite person is not here to cook for. I don't even feel like making our favorite kind of cake anymore. Our children all inherited Samuel's chocolate brown eyes. He was fond of saying that their eyes were brown because we eat so much chocolate cake. When the chocolate cake pan was empty, he would dump milk into it and he and the toddler and whoever else would scrape it clean. I used to like sewing; now I feel sad and guilty when I sew. I think I feel that way because I really do still enjoy sewing, yet it feels wrong to enjoy something in this terrible grief.

Wednesday, March 30, 2016:
Two friends stopped in and offered to help plant tomatoes in my hi-tunnel. How thoughtful. They told me of their plans for having a ladies' day in the near future. That sent my thoughts spinning. A ladies day! Such news would have been exciting in the past. Now…the other ladies will bring their babies while their husbands stay home and care for

the preschoolers…the other ladies' husbands will hitch their horse for them…the other ladies will leave the ladies' day and go home to their husband and tell him all about it…

I don't want to throw my widowhood into their faces. I don't want everyone to feel they need to change the subject when I walk into the room. But why is a conversation more interesting if it is about me and my loss? I am conceited. Will I ever again be interested in other people's lives?

Friday, April 1, 2016:
Only three and one half more weeks of school. So far, all the children except Eric have perfect attendance. Surely God was with us. At the onset of this term, I thought the year looked long and impossible.

Wesley cannot walk yet, but he can open the door and go outside. He is *boy*. He cheers when he sees the pony and cart, and roars when they don't take him along. He likes to sit on Geneva's lap, and they'll cozy up and both suck their thumbs. Today Samuel's baby is a year and a day old.

Sunday, May 8, 2016:
There is a great big problem coming toward me. It is enough to make my stomach churn. My sister-in-law asked me if we have plans for lunch next Sunday.

I began to freeze inside, but I answered hesitantly, "No…"

"We want to invite all the Shirks for lunch next Sunday," she stated sweetly.

I mumbled some reply. But my heart was screaming! "No, no! I don't want to go. I can't. I can't go. I can't face it. Not there. Not now. Not with all the other Shirks. Not in this memorable month of May."

Last year the Shirks were all together for supper on Ascension Day. Samuel was already sick, though we didn't know how sick. It was the last time Samuel and I went away together.

Now this gathering will be exactly at the same place, exactly one year and a day later. Will I be rude not to go?

I am not ready to tell the children that Aunt Martha is inviting the Shirks next Sunday.

But joyfully the children tell me on the way home, "Mom! Daryl said they are having Shirk family gathering next Sunday." Oh, my.

Thursday, May 12, 2016:

It's done now! Finally. My parents and Samuel's parents, and Amos the gravestone-maker, met me at the graveyard to erect Samuel's gravestone.

I dreaded this for so long. A few weeks after Samuel's death, Amos approached me about a stone. It hurt so bad, I didn't even want to think about it. I tried to decide on an epitaph. I asked for advice and got no answers. What do you put on your husband's gravestone? I wanted to put something on besides his name and dates. Finally, one night I came up with the idea of putting Father along the top curve, and then his name and dates. Underneath, would say, "Resting in the Lord." Amos finished making the stone. Then the stone waited. And waited. Finally, I realized that to continue on my healing journey, that stone had to go up.

So today we did it. Dad thought we each should take a shovel of dirt out when we dug the foundation. It felt so harsh and cruel. And healing. Now it is there. No more dreading it. Now I can move on. I feel relieved.

Sunday, May 17, 2016:

Cast your burden upon the Lord and he shall sustain thee (Psalm 55:22). All week I repeatedly cast my burden on the Lord. Now this morning our horse was lame. Now what? Let's just stay home. But the children wouldn't hear of it, so we borrowed a horse from my brother.

It is awkward in every sense of the word to have to drive into a farmyard without a man. Now we even had a strange horse.

After church, my brother Sidney told me how he thought the day would be hard for me and he wishes he would have thought to offer that they could come past our place and provide our transportation.

"You should have! That would have taken care of so many problems!"

Since we need to pass our place on the way to the family gathering anyway, Sidney offered that if we go put away the horse, they will still give us a ride.

God sustained me. He sent help. To me it seemed late, but His schedule is different than mine.

It was so nice to sit in the back of Sidney's carriage and just be a nobody. No longer did I need to be the strong one. I didn't need to drive into the farmyard without Samuel. I didn't need to find a place to park and unhitch my horse. I didn't need to *hope* someone would come take my horse to the barn while I screamed inside that it should not be this way.

I suffered through the afternoon. There was a stone in my stomach and a walnut in my throat. I was with Samuel's family, the same as last year on Ascension Day. But this year I was here without Samuel. I was thankful that I made it without self-igniting. We were all missing Samuel so much. Why didn't we talk about it? Finally, I was safe back in Sidney's carriage, where neither he nor his wife would need any feedback from me.

Jesse came and thanked me for coming and said he realizes it is probably a hard day for me. I was surprised. But. Why did I forget that Samuel was a part of this family long before I was? Of course, they are all missing him. I appreciated both his words of sympathy and Sidney's soothing help.

Wednesday, May 25, 2016:
I can't believe it is a year already. And only a year. Time to quit wearing black. Ready or not.

Actually, Ascension Day, and the day that marked one year since I last talked to Samuel, were harder than this fateful day: 5/25.

This morning at breakfast, all was quiet, then Landis asked, "Why doesn't metal grow like wood does?" Oh my, how am I supposed to know answers to questions like that? Brenda is baking black-bottom cupcakes. Geneva is washing breakfast dishes and we are all looking forward to Mom and Dad bringing supper tonight. If Samuel was here, we would be a normal happy family.

Last evening when Elaine crawled into my bed, she wanted to talk about her daddy. I was pleased, yet saddened to think that she just does not remember him.

On Sunday someone complimented me that I never fuss. Hmm. If they only knew how fussy I feel at times. I was grateful for the encouragement. I do unload a lot on my sisters. But I do not want to dishonor God's Name by complaining, looking slovenly, etc., though I fail often.

Wednesday, July 20, 2016:
God did not plan it thus. He created the family to be a circle…with one daddy and one mom. How then can one frail woman keep the family from falling apart?

Without even considering the spiritual welfare of our children, the task is daunting…just the daily grind of chores, meals, dishes, laundry, gardening, cleaning, organizing, and discipline. It is like trying to run in so many circles at once and none of the revolutions match!

Some days just the general hubbub of eight children under thirteen years old is about to render me like a turtle on its back. Even though my children are all jolly and good natured, I am still the boss. I constantly need to be on guard and never allow myself to relax completely, because I am the boss.

So how do I cope? Some days I don't. Some days I just do nothing. My circuit breaker snaps and I must stop to rejuvenate and reevaluate my priorities. Then it is back on the treadmill where I have to keep walking to keep from being dumped off the back.

One way I cope: All the children are assigned chores, and they are responsible to me for negligence. I do not do any jobs the children can do.

Since Samuel died, I have kept a fairly tight schedule of mealtimes and bedtimes. Our life was spinning out of control, but here was one place that I could enforce routine.

Sunday, July 24, 2016:
Loretta (4) is processing her loss of her daddy. Recently, out of the blue, she asked, "Mom, do you wish we had a daddy?"
"Yes."
"Why?" she wondered.
Today she asked, "Mom, did you cry when Daddy died?"
"Yes."
"That's okay," she comforted. "Moms may cry when their daddies die."

Thursday, October 20, 2016:
God answers prayer! God has answered so many prayers in the months since Samuel's death that I feel surprised that I still feel surprised when I marvel over answered prayers. I must be hard to teach.

We needed to clean up around the barn for the landscaper crew. Some were little trashy things that the children and I could handle. But there also were piles of lumber that I wished for help to move. I hoped someone would offer to help, but no one did. I get tired of asking, and besides how do I decide when we can handle a job and when to ask for assistance?

This morning I brought this burden to the Lord. I asked Him to send someone to help us. But I doubted. I figured no one really cares about our work, which was really a roundabout way of figuring God didn't care either.

After breakfast I dispatched Landis to find out if we could borrow a team of horses from one of his uncles. And maybe a few sets of muscles, schoolboy-sized ones.

I was scurrying around in the house doing things that needed to be done, when the cry arose, "Davids are here!"

Oh, no! I don't have time to entertain company. "The whole family?"

"No, just David and the boys. And they plan to stay and help the whole forenoon."

Really. Really? "Thank you, God! That was a custom-made answer to prayer."

Who would fit the situation better than David? He is so good with the boys.

Two of my nephews also came. With their good help we were finished by lunchtime. It looks much better. I feel especially satisfied because I helped instead of simply asking my brothers to do it for me, which really is the lazy way out. But what makes me feel the most peace is that God heard, God cares. Before they cry, He shall answer…

Saturday, February 4, 2017:

Today I filled out the information sheet for Samuel's second cousin who is putting together a relationship book for Samuel's great-grandparents. One of the blanks to fill out was Occupation. I felt like writing: "Widow—it is a full-time job."

I am invited to Samuel's nephew's wedding in Ohio. Do I go? I have more than one hundred nieces and nephews and I was looking forward to attending the weddings of the ones we were invited to. But in those dreams, Samuel and I were both invited. It is so *different* now.

Samuel thrived on traveling and I enjoyed going with him. Can I survive the pain of going without him?

I decided to go. If Samuel were here, I am sure we would attend. But weddings are so hard for widows. Later Samuel's parents stopped in. Of course, we talked of the wedding, and Samuel's mom wondered if I am going. When I said I plan to, she exclaimed, "Oh, I am so glad. Having you along is like having half of Samuel along!"

I was surprised and pleased. I had told myself that Samuel's family is glad when I am not along because I am a grim reminder that it really is true that Samuel died. If I am not there, they can pretend it didn't happen, and they don't have to feel guilty that they still have their companions.

But…now Samuel's mom makes me feel like I am not just a widow. I am half of Samuel. I like that! I'll cheer myself with that many a blue day. That was a very nice thing to say, Mom!

Friday, May 5, 2017:
In our small group sharing at Penn Valley, we were sharing how our husbands died. One widow shared, "Our husbands die in the way that God knows is best for us." I quit listening and wrapped my mind around that idea. Indeed, God gave me just enough time to resign my will to His. He knew I would not have made a great nurse, and He did not allow a long convalescence, or bedside vigil, or whatever.

On the other hand, sickness and accidents are the result of the curse of sin on this earth. I don't want to argue with the Penn Valley lady, but I would rather say that God *allowed* my husband to die in the way he did. Then He gave me grace to go on one step at a time.

Saturday, October 7, 2017:
Family gatherings are still hard. It is a place where families go… husbands, wives, children, grandchildren. Complete family units; except for the widow's family. Her heart thump-thumps as she hops on one leg and tries to serve herself and her children lunch with one hand. Some sort of emotion erupts from the half of her heart that she has left. She either talks incessantly, or wipes a never-drying stream of tears.

Two days ago was my brother's wedding. I prayed a lot about it and felt with two and one-half years of widowhood behind me, I should be about ready to handle the joy. Some of the traveling relations were staying at my parents place for supper. I was not wise enough to decline the invitation to stay, too. Last year, at my other brother's wedding, I declined, realizing my nerves were too frail for a wedding plus a family gathering all in one day.

But this year…we are all a year older and more healed. So, we went to Dad's. The children were behaving and I was actually enjoying it. Until Dad dropped a bombshell. One of the travelers wanted to see Dad's grandchildren, so before we ate supper, we were supposed to go up front for introductions. If it would have been feasible, I would have gathered my children and run home. How could I go up on stage without Samuel? I managed to walk woodenly forward, squeak out our introductions, and then I escaped to the back of the crowd and collapsed on a chair in a flood of tears.

It is always worse when I think I have everything under control, then something unexpected happens and I feel like I am socked in the stomach. *Let him that thinketh he standeth, take heed lest he fall…*

Friday, November 3, 2017:

At a funeral I shook hands with a remarried widower. He asked, "How are you?" I replied, "I am slowly dying from the inside out." He nodded. "I remember just how that feels." We discussed the hardness of going on, to be the only parent, the only disciplinarian, and the only encourager. How much we miss the camaraderie of our spouses. Someone just to bounce ideas back and forth with. I said, "There are people that really care about me, and I can share with them, ask advice, and such. But in the end, they really don't care if I paint my kitchen blue or green. I am the only one responsible for the end results of my decisions." He nodded his head in agreement and added thoughts of his own. It was very encouraging to hear his words of comfort. But what counted the most was the understanding that there was no need to explain myself so he didn't think I was crazy!

Sunday, November 26, 2017:

Today the minister had Luke 5 for his text. That is the chapter where Jesus preached from Peter's boat and then told the disciples to go out in the deep and cast out their nets.

Peter said, "We fished all night and got nothing. But for You I will."

The minister expounded it this way: "When the fishermen were trying to catch fish by their own strength, they got nothing. So it is with us if we try to do things by our own strength…we cannot. When the fishermen took Jesus with them on the boat the nets were so full that they broke. So God will bless our efforts if we take Jesus with us."

Peter went fishing for Jesus. I need to think about fishing when it is time to get up in the morning. Getting out of bed is still hard. Who cares if I stay in bed all day? Samuel isn't here to fix breakfast for, to wave off to work, to look for at day's end. I tend to argue with God about why I need to get up. There is nothing to get up for. Instead, I need to think, "Even though there is no one special to get up for today, I will get up for Your sake. Please go with me through this day."

After church, we were invited to my brother's place for lunch along with some other families. We sang a song before eating. The singing sounded nice, but suddenly I was crying. Why? I noticed all the other dads sitting around the table with their toddlers beside them. Will I ever get used to it?

Monday, March 12, 2018:

I awoke at 2:00 AM and my mind was going in the well-worn circle. "Why? Why did Samuel have to die when we still need him so badly?" It seems so senseless. Our eight children need his nurturing. How will I ever raise them alone? I am weary of plodding on alone. Weary of being lonely. Weary of trying to keep myself from the pit of despair.

I got out of bed and sat at the sewing machine. When I sew, my mind can only run at half-speed. I felt a sense of accomplishment that I had a dress finished by the time I usually rise at 4:30. I picked up my Bible and headed for the couch with a sigh. Lately my time of devotions have been dull, my prayers have seemed unheard, and the Scriptures incomprehensible. Listlessly I found my place to read—John 9. This is the chapter about Jesus healing the blind man. The disciples asked Jesus, *"Who sinned, this man, or his parents, that he was born blind?"*

My heart echoed, "Whose fault is it that Samuel died? Did I love him too much or not enough? Did we have too good a marriage to last? Did he die as a punishment because I didn't love God enough? Why? Why? Why did we only have eleven years of marriage, when some couples have 30 or more years of marital strife?"

If we had done things differently, would Samuel have lived? What if we had gone to the doctor sooner? Maybe we should have tried the Roto-Prone bed sooner. Maybe we should not have taken him off life support when we did. Maybe we should have prayed more. Why are some people's prayers answered with a "yes" and ours was answered with a "no"? Does God love them more?

Jesus' answer is still true after all these years. It applies to me, Grace Shirk, today! *"Neither hath sinned, but that the works of God should be made manifest in him."* There. I must rest in that answer. God wants to make His works manifest in our lives. Am I allowing Him to?

Thursday, April 12, 2018:

Today I attended yet another wedding. Weddings are such a couple affair! I enjoyed weddings when Samuel and I were a couple. Today I tried to focus on visiting friends, instead of thinking of *me*. As we sang together in the afternoon, the clock edged toward 4:00. People had been leaving for the last hour…husband after husband came to find his wife to leave together. I didn't pay much attention; after all, this was a wedding. But suddenly it was one husband too many and I felt suffocated! I had a terrible fear that I would fall to pieces in a puddle of tears. This was so unexpected. I managed to brace myself, because I knew if I let go there would be no stopping. I quickly left.

I think of my aunt's question at lunchtime. "It's now almost three years. You were told that the first one to two years would be the worst. Can you say it is going any better?"

Oh, what a tall question! There is so much involved in such a question. Am I used to being a single parent? Am I used to being a widow? Am I used to attending events as a single parent in a couple world? Am I used to the loneliness, the decisions, the disciplining, the financial responsibility? How can I answer all that in one sentence? Finally, I told my aunt, "I don't know. I haven't pondered it lately."

But on my way home and throughout the evening, I pondered her question. Is it going any better? Yes, I have finally resigned myself to the title "widow," but I hate the life and the stigma it brings. Ever notice what a conversation killer the introduction, "I am a widow," is? What are people supposed to say? Some say, "Oh, you are Grace…" and I feel like telling them, "Yeah, I still look human! Did you think I only have one arm and one leg now? Well, it sure feels that way!"

Yet, I decide being a widow is easier since time has elapsed. It is sort of like this: Many times, I have heard married people say, "Oh, we might be married ten years, but we are still newlyweds." Or… "We are the first newlyweds with three children in school." So it is with us widows. We are so busy trying to live, that the days slip by and now it is almost three years of widowhood. But the loss is still there. I am just as much a widow as I was two years ago, just as a bride is still a bride after ten years of marriage. Widowhood isn't enjoyable like being a bride is, though.

Four years ago, I would have thought a widow of three years should in all rights be well-adjusted and refocused. But though my wound is not so raw, my loss still has the same magnitude.

Thursday, April 26, 2018:

I stopped at the harness shop to have our horse's harness repaired. The carriage maker, Edward, stepped in and I told him that our carriage leans badly to one side. Edward went out to look at it and soon pronounced the verdict, "Your fifth wheel is broken in two places!" He peered under the carriage and gasped, "Your cross tie is broken! One of these times you'll be braking while your horse is backing and your cross tie will fold up."

"Help! Is it still safe to drive home?"

"Yes," Edward tried to assure me. "Sometimes this goes on a long time before something worse happens."

Oh, but I already feel I am on the verge of making a dunce of myself every time I go out in public, let alone knowing I am driving a vehicle containing a time bomb! We scheduled the repair for Tuesday, and I came home on prayers.

Friday, April 27, 2018:

Landis took the carriage to the shop, and my brother Matthew stopped in here. Was I ever grateful! My wash machine refused to start, so here was my repairman. While he was here, Landis returned with a borrowed carriage: and bad news. Our carriage has major issues. "Another decision," I groaned aloud. Matthew leaped into the breech, offered to go to the carriage shop, evaluate the situation, and make the decision for me.

Praise God! His hand was so evident in this whole situation. Without His help I would *not* make it! I thank Him for all the times others have responded to His promptings to be at the right place at the right time to come to my assistance. God really does care about details.

Wednesday, June 27, 2018:

Does time heal the gaping wound that's left when a marriage union is cut asunder? Yes, I am glad to discover time heals, albeit slowly. No longer do I feel family gatherings are the worst thing ever invented. It seemed a bit thick to have two family gatherings in a row, and I dreaded each of them with equal dread.

The first family gathering was with Samuel's family again. I actually was able to enjoy it. Now I can talk and think of things other than *it*. We all have healed to the point that we are able to talk of Samuel's death and the following pain. It is special to discuss Samuel with his family. The men in the family do so well to remember to help with my horse. It is such a blessing and gives me a chance to converse, very briefly, with one of Samuel's brothers.

The second gathering was with my family. We were all at church together and our children fetched rides with their uncles to the family gathering. I was left to drive over all by myself. And I didn't fall to pieces! At the lunch line I didn't have to hide my eyes when I saw the other daddies helping their toddlers. Instead, I encouraged my three-year-old to go ask his uncle to help him with his food. We had a pleasant visit afterwards, and the afternoon waxed old as the men continued to visit. I have made a few awkward mistakes before I learned it is best to wait till the rest of the people start to leave, and then go with the flow. This time it continued to get later, and finally I decided there was no reason I needed to wait on the men. There is a back door to the barn and I had no problem getting my horse out of my brother's barn. We started for home and I didn't have the grumps. That is improvement! It gives me hope for dark days.

In Conclusion:

I have taken myself on many guilt trips during my widowhood. Why didn't I realize Samuel was so sick? Why didn't I cancel his job and take him to the Chattanooga ER? Why didn't I go with him to Kentucky, then I would have known sooner how sick he was and made him go to the doctor sooner? Why didn't the doctor see on Monday that he is a dying man? Aren't doctors in the business of healing people? Why? If only… If only…

God finally got through to me that I am not God. God is fully capable of filling in where I fall short. He could have done any of those things that I thought I should have done but didn't. I am not in control. God is. It took me two and a half years to come to this level of acceptance. So when I become frustrated, depressed, angry, sad, uptight, or upset, it helps to remember this is not about me. This is about God.

Disclaimer:

To my family and friends: If you feel I wrote about you in a negative way, remember, this is not about you. This is about my journey through grief. Every time I am in public, every time I read a letter, I deal with my widowhood. Thank you for all you have done and will do for me.

If you are a sister, friend, mom, daughter, father, son, or brother of a widow and have read this, please do not go to the widow in your life and say, "Now I know how you feel." You really don't know. This is an abridged version of how I feel. There are many subjects I have not touched, and I have picked out only the tidiest entries.

If you are a widow and you feel that I made too rosy a conclusion, making it sound like I have learned all the lessons, please change your opinion. I have learned these truths, but I am very forgetful, and need to learn them again and again. Even though I had some sunny days to record, I still have cloudy, lonely days.

But remember, God goes before and it is all about Him anyway.

The friend who can be silent with us in a moment of confusion or despair; who can stay with us in an hour of grief and bereavement; who can tolerate not knowing, not healing, nor curing; that is a *friend* indeed.

B&W Ointment and Burdock Leaves

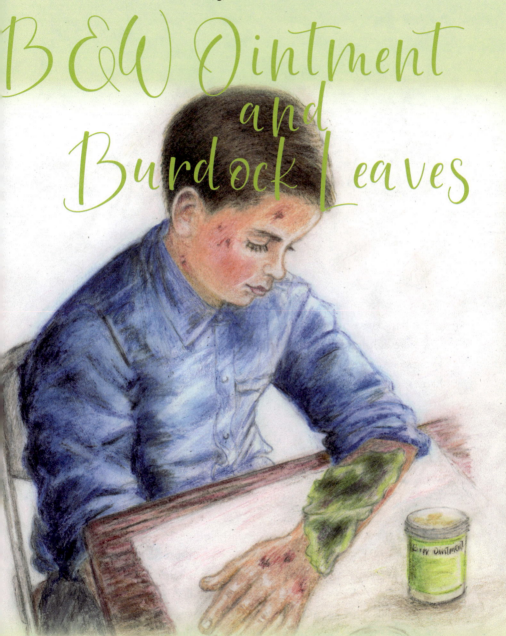

...But I would strengthen you with my mouth, and the moving of my lips should assuage your grief. Job 16:5
Wherefore comfort one another with these words... 1 Thessalonians 4:18

B&W Ointment and Burdock Leaves

SUELLEN J STRITE

It happened on a windless evening in early summer. Our friends were lighting up a brush pile when paint thinner ignited…and poof! Kraig's eleven-year-old face and arms lit up, too. Kraig rushed from the flames, groaning and wailing in pain. Large red patches appeared on his arms and face, his hair was singed, and his lips were charred. This was not what anyone wanted.

"Just take me to the hospital so someone can make me stop hurting," Kraig begged. Everyone's first impulse was to head to the ER. But wait. Who wants to postpone help for pain while waiting for a doctor? So, Kraig's knowledgeable Aunt Brenda was called in to treat the burns with B&W ointment and burdock leaves.

"Cool the burns with cold, wet washcloths," she instructed over the phone, "and I will be there as soon as possible." When Aunt Brenda arrived, everyone sighed with relief. She put the anxious family to work. She asked Kraig's mother to heat water in the electric skillet. Aunt Brenda cut the thick veins out of the huge burdock leaves, and dropped them into the boiling water. "It is important to make the leaves soft and pliable," she instructed, as she flipped the leaves and let them scald on the other side.

The properly scalded leaves were laid on a towel to cool and smeared with B&W salve. Then Aunt Brenda gently arranged the soothing leaves over Kraig's burns and wrapped them tightly with fluorescent gauze to keep them in place. Kraig actually smiled a little through his cracked lips when he looked at his colorfully wrapped skin.

However, smiling was not something Kraig did a lot in the following days. The dressing needed to be changed every morning and evening. Pain, irritability, and boredom stalked him constantly. But, little by little, the B&W ointment and burdock leaves soothed his raw flesh, and coaxed Kraig's body into making new pink skin. Within a month of being burned, Kraig's face and arms looked much better. In six months, not a scar remained, and Aunt Brenda proclaimed him healed. "Keep away from brush fires," she warned Kraig, shaking her forefinger at him. "B&W and burdock leaves kept you out of the hospital this time, but if you ever burn yourself worse, you might need medical assistance."

When the poof! of death burns holes in a family, our words can be B&W salve…soothing and helping assuage the tremendous pain. Or our remarks can be a horde of wasps, stinging again and again. Let's remember to soften our words in the skillet of God's Word, smear them liberally with the soothing ointment of love, and wrap them all in the leaves of prayer. 🌸

Do all the good you can, to all the people you can, in all the ways you can, as often as ever you can, as long as you can. Spurgeon

Question **16**

What are the most soothing words you have heard?

Widows answer:

"I am praying for you and your children."

"Is there anything specific you wish I would pray for?"

"I appreciated your husband, and I miss him."

"Your child is doing well in school."

"We will take you along to _____ if you want us to."

"Do you have any fix-it jobs you would like us to help with?"

"My father died when I was young, and I remember what it felt like."

"You are doing a good job. Keep up the good work."

"I can see you are putting forth your best effort."

"Your husband was an encouragement to me."

"Your husband did a good deed for me."

"It will get better."

"It is okay to cry and grieve and miss your husband; this is part of the healing."

"You work through grief; you don't get over it."

"Your husband would be pleased with the direction your family is taking."

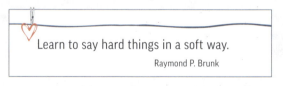

Learn to say hard things in a soft way.

Raymond P. Brunk

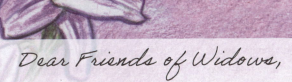

Dear Friends of Widows,

It is not pity we want; don't tiptoe around us. Yet, in many ways our grief is compounded when we feel totally forgotten by everyone whose lives are going on as normal. Not that we need flowers and gifts regularly; just the caring comments from those who think of us amid their own busy schedules. That is the most blessed encouragement I know. And in case you wonder what some of these comments are, I will give you a few examples.

• A sister from church commented, "When my husband comes home from work, then I especially think of you. The children and I are so eager to see him and I look forward to the relief of letting him carry some of the parenting responsibility for the evening. Then I pray for you and ask God to help you through your lonely evening."

• My sister-in-law mentioned that she felt for me the day we were all together. The rest were there with their husbands and I was there alone. I had missed my husband so much that day, but I did not want to be a kill joy. Her comment helped me realize someone remembered my sorrow.

• Several friends said they know it is a hard time for me, at a wedding, a funeral, council and communion services, after the sermon that enlarged on the father's role in the home, the first death in our congregation after my husband's. No one said much, but just the small comments that let me know they care go a long way.

• My pen pal added a personal note on the end of her form letter that said, "Surely it hurts to receive mail like this and yet it would hurt even worse to be excluded. So, I am sending this with a prayer that God will bless you especially today." It was special to feel understood, when I hardly understood myself why it hurt to read letters from friends who were enjoying normal family life. I didn't think I was jealous when I read of husbands doing home improvements, beginning new family ventures, or plans to take over the family farm; yet my own emptiness and longings did hurt in comparison.

• A sister who I don't even know well sent me a note the week of our congregation's ordination to say she is praying that I can find someone to share with during this emotionally draining week when I long to talk to my husband.

• A grandmother in our congregation told me she feels I am doing so well with the children; they seem so calm and happy when she sees them. I will assure you she is an older lady and did not see everything! Yet we hunger for those validating encouragements now that we do not have our husband's reassurance. And to hear it from a grandmother who had raised a large, fine family, a grandmother whom I had supposed had been looking critically at everything I am not reaching around to, well, it strengthened and blessed me many a day.

• A friend gave me a sincere compliment on my new dress, saying, "That dress looks becoming on you. I think your husband would like it." That affirmation means a lot when we are feeling lost and insecure, having lost our better half.

• A sister from church sent a card and gift bag home from church two to three years after my husband's death. The gift? A new nightgown! So sweet and practical. I was touched by her thoughtfulness, because though she had no idea, I really did need one—and what widow feels inspired to sew herself a new nightgown?

• Some friends take time to listen and care when I am not sure what to say in response to a cheery, "How are you doing?" I don't always need to unload everything then and there, but if they understand that it is a hard time and I am struggling, and they promise to pray for me, the burden of feeling alone is halved and I feel supported.

One week, discouragement threatened and I struggled with thoughts that everyone else is used to our loss by now and they think we are too, when in reality I still couldn't believe this had happened to me, and the longer it went, the bigger it felt. In just three days' time three different friends asked me how it is going for us by now. I could tell they asked out of genuine care, not superficial sympathy or curiosity. It brought relief to be able to share, to admit that I have been told the second year is the hardest and that while I would not say the second year is harder, it is certainly *not* easier! The reminder that others still cared made the load feel lighter and brighter.

Sincerely,

"Petunia"

186

Comforting Comforters

A WIDOW

Caring Carrie: Carrie is sensitive to your needs. She notices that you are alone at a wedding or family reunion, and asks if you want to join her and her husband at the table. She makes sure to invite you and your family along when they visit other church families. She asks if you need the garden plowed or if there is something her husband could fix in the house.

Encouraging Edna: There are many precious promises from God in His Word and Edna knows you need to be reminded of them at times. She does not quote them glibly or use them to preach at you. She realizes that a pained and hurting heart can only absorb small tidbits at a time, therefore she spreads her encouragement over weeks…a short poem, a verse, an "I am thinking of and praying for you today." She remembers your birthday, the year mark, your anniversary, Father's Day, and other difficult days and she sends a card or gives a short phone call. Even though her gestures of kindness may cause tears, they are healing tears for the grieving.

Fatherly Frank: Frank has a heart for the hurting fatherless sons. Even though he knows he will never take their father's place, he does what he can to fill the hole in their lives. He will ask them to sit with him in church. He will ask them to help him with his work within their age and ability, or take them along to a farm sale. He will fix their bikes, help them build a simple wood project, show them how to start the weed-eater, explain how an engine works. His comfort is spelled T-I-M-E, not just once, but for years!

Friendly Fred: Fred is up in age, but he still loves children. He does not single out the "unusual" from the group but makes sure to meet all the boys and shake their hand. He looks them in the eyes, and encourages them to do the same. He asks them about any special interests they may have—rabbits, puppy, or school. He loves children and they love him.

Listening Lena: Lena always has time to listen. She knows that healing comes when the grieving are allowed to share their grief with others. She will listen to your story for the second or third time when she already knows it. She knows that sharing memories of happy times is healing and will listen and ask questions to help you share. She will ask about specific struggles that you have shared with her before.

Memory Menno: Menno has many good memories of times shared with your husband and he shares them freely. He feels not only your loss, but his as well. He tells you he missed the presence of his brother or friend in a circle of company. He is not afraid to acknowledge that he is grieving too.

Counseling Conrad: Conrad sees the struggles of the older sons and encourages them to open their hearts. He asks questions like: "What do you miss most about your father?" or "What is your favorite memory of Daddy?" He is not too busy to listen, and he knows it will take more than one visit to reach into their soul. He also knows he may be privy to some inner conflicts, and will be judicious in what he shares with others.

Praying Pauline: Pauline is an elderly, quiet-natured sister in the Lord. She knows there is not much she can do to lighten your load—but she can pray! She understands that prayer is what moves the hand of an Almighty God in behalf of His people. She intercedes for the suffering saints and pleads for God's mercy and loving kindness to be shown for them. She reminds Him of His promise to be a Father of the fatherless. She mentions any specific needs she knows of. Her comfort is not public or noticed, but is felt in the heart of those who are receiving the answers to her prayers. It is not the *only* thing she can do—it is the *most important* thing of all!

Sharing Sherri: Sherri enters into your pain, especially if she has experienced a similar pain. Her eyes fill with tears when yours do, and she is not ashamed. She puts her hand on your shoulder or squeezes your hand in sympathy. She does not have a lot of advice, only the encouragement that she will pray for you. Then she does it.

What Can I Say?

Usually less is best. There is no way to sugarcoat grief. There are no perfect words. The compassion we show is more important than the words we say. Neither should you tell them, "I simply don't know what to say." If God does not give you the words, say nothing. Your presence is enough. Words hardly register at such a time anyway.

Be very careful about saying, "I know how you feel," even if you have had a similar experience. You are not the other person and you don't necessarily know what she is feeling. Every situation is different, and every individual grieves differently. It is best to just say, "We care about you, and we are praying that God will comfort and strengthen you as He did for us when we went through a similar experience."

Unwise condolences can add to grief instead of lessening it. One thing we need to guard against is to start condolences with the words, "at least." "At least he isn't suffering anymore." "At least you knew it was coming." To the one who is bereaved, there is nothing "at least" about the heart-wrenching experience. Let's avoid that phrase.

The time of a family's grieving is usually not the time to unload a rebuke for shortcomings that we have seen in any of their lives. If we knew that admonition was necessary, we should have given it before the family was crushed by sorrow.

Grieving people sometimes say things that we know should not be said. Here are some: "Out of all the families in our church, why were we singled out?" "Why was my brother taken? He never hurt anyone." "Some nights when I am so lonely and discouraged, I have no desire to read my Bible and pray." "It's so hard sometimes to reach out for comfort to the very One who allowed the situation in the first place."

How do we answer such remarks? Do we say, "Hold on there; that's not true; you are getting off track; you need to repent"? If it becomes obvious that repentance is necessary, there may be a time for saying that. But if we listen with compassion, most times we'll know that we are hearing a heart that loves the Lord and wants to accept His will, but is struggling to come to terms with an overwhelming loss.

It is mildly surprising that after all the questions and doubts that Job expressed, God said to Eliphaz, *My wrath is kindled against thee, and against thy two friends: for ye have not spoken of me the thing that is right, as my servant Job hath* (Job 42:7). God said this because He knew Job's perfect and upright heart. Likewise, if we believe that the hearts of the grieving are right, we can listen to them compassionately as they sort through their sorrows.

All the most beautiful influences are quiet; only the destructive agencies, the stormy winds, the heavy rains, are noisy. Love of the deepest sort is wordless; the sunshine steals down silently; the dew falls noiselessly. And the communion of spirit with spirit is calmer than anything else in the world; quiet as the spontaneous turning of the sunflower to the sun when the heavy clouds have passed away, and the light and warmth reveal themselves. Ada Allen Bayla

Question 17

What are some of the most hurtful things you have been told?

Widows answer:

"You are still young and can get married again."

"God must really love you."

"It would be worse to have an unfaithful husband."

"God knew you could handle it."

"You will get over it."

"You are too young to be a widow."

"Now you will have to be Dad and Mom."

"This must be God's will, so count your blessings and move on."

"It will get worse before it gets better."

"You must be a very strong person."

"Have you had the opportunity to get married again?"

"I pity you."

"I am glad you got a break from having babies."

"We would rather not have you along."

"Are you having a pity party with your widow friends?"

"My husband went on a hunting trip, and I am terribly lonely without him. It has been three whole days since I saw or talked to him."

"You have it better than those who lost a child because you could have another husband, but I can never have another child."

"I had a hard time appreciating your husband when he lived."

"Children who don't have a dad do not turn out right."

"I have a hard time appreciating my husband."

"We are glad you can *all* be here at the family gathering…" (When I am sadly missing my husband.) 🌹

> Affliction's sons are brothers in distress:
> A brother to relieve—how exquisite the bliss!
> Robert Burns

191

Miserable Comforters

A WIDOW

Calloused Catherine: "When are you going to get over it?" Catherine wonders. She does not realize that a widow never "gets over it." The loss never goes away. The hurt heals, the pain lessens, but it is a journey into the valley of the shadow of death. One needs to go through it, not over or around it.

Distant Daniel: Daniel does not notice the widow. He hides around the corner, or behind his wife. He does not want to be seen as a softy. He finds it hard to know how to relate, so he makes it his wife's job and he keeps out of it.

Embarrassed Emma: Emma does not like to see your tears. Perhaps she will need to cry too! When a song like "Take What Thou Wilt, Shall I Repine" brings tears in church, Emma sings louder than ever. She is not grieving!

Ignoring Irma: Irma ignores your loss completely. She talks about the weather, the garden, and her children. She doesn't see the weariness on your face or the droop of your shoulders. To her, life is going on as usual and yours should be too.

Joking Joan: Joan feels it is her duty to make you laugh again. She is unwilling to allow pain to enter her own heart, and it hurts her to see you in pain. So, she laughs and jokes and tells funny stories. She knows a merry heart is medicine, but she does not know how to weep with those that weep.

Pitying Patty: Patty can hardly cope with your loss. "How do you do it? I could never do that! Oh, it must be so lonely," and on and on she goes. At times it seems she is the one needing the comfort for your loss!

Whining Wilma: Wilma wants you to know that she has problems too. She wants you to know that it is hard for her when her husband is gone so much for church work. Her children always misbehave then and she can barely cope. Her washer needs fixed and her husband is busy…

> One minister mentioned that when a death occurs, the husband just about becomes perfect in the eyes of the widow. His faults are all buried with him, and the good just becomes better and better. That was an eye-opener for me, as that is how I found it for myself. *A Widow*

Tread Softly

ELEANOR MARTIN

Tread softly, friend,
Tread softly.
This is my heart. Tread softly.
You'd never mean to hurt me, friend—
How well I trust and know;
You have sometimes come rather near it, though.
Tread softly.
You cannot comprehend how fragile
Is my trust, my confidence, my heart—
Restoring it, how intricate,
How painful, and how slow.
This is my heart.
It is, and lies within your reach.
And so—
Tread softly—
Tread softly.

Someone Said Grief Is a Virus

SHEILA J PETRE

If grief is a virus, these tears are a symptom,
a rash, if you will, or a scab
that won't go away, though I dress it with ointment—
or does go away, but comes back.

Courage has no banners,
Courage has no drums;
But softly when the heart asks God,
Courage always comes.

Juggling All the Balls Alone

...but His mother kept all these sayings in her heart. Luke 2:51

Juggling All the Balls Alone

SUELLEN J STRITE

Juggling balls is an art that must be learned through practice. No proficient juggler got up one morning, ran to town, purchased seven rubber balls, went home, stood on his back porch, and easily tossed seven colorful balls toward the clouds, and kept them in the air for five minutes.

He did not even purchase balls on his first trip to town, if he used the Jugglebug method to learn. Instead, he bought nylon scarves which are soft and slow-moving. Not until he could successfully juggle three scarves, did he go for the balls. Then he began with juggling just one. Once he mastered the skill of keeping one ball up, he added more, one at a time. Finally, after enough time and experience, he is considered a successful ball juggler.

Parents spend the better part of their life teaching, training, and guiding their children in the ways of right. Most parents feel overwhelmed at times. They wonder how it can be possible to juggle the material, emotional, and spiritual needs of each child. How can they keep it all from crashing to the dirt? But they look to God for wisdom, and they work through the tough spots together.

When the father in the home dies, the new widow is suddenly left alone with all these balls to juggle! How can she do it? Her husband led their home as God ordained, made decisions, and encouraged her when she thought a ball was dropping. Now, in the throes of her grief, when her mind is numb, she is responsible to juggle all by herself with not much previous experience. True, she juggled alone while her husband was at work or away on a business trip or sick with the flu. But always, he had come home eventually or got better. Always, even those times when she felt alone, she was comforted with the relief she would feel when the children's daddy walked in the door. Now she knows he will never walk in again.

So here she is, with her beautiful God-given balls. How will she keep them out of the dirt of fussing and bickering? Out of the wickedness of this world?

Jugglebug instructors want the potential juggler to keep several things in mind as he begins learning to juggle. Here are a few pointers paraphrased:

If you keep making the same mistakes, stop. Figure out what you are doing wrong, and how to correct it. If you find yourself irritated at everything three-year-old Jack says and does, consider whether this is your problem or Jack's problem. Then search till you find a solution.

Don't keep jumping around from one method to the next. Consistent discipline works best.

Don't let your friends talk you into seeing how far out you can throw your balls. Keep them in the confines you can manage best. If someone from two hours away invites you to their home for a meal and you know you will be totally stressed till you get there and your children will be out of control, politely decline the invitation.

Don't just doggedly juggle until everything falls apart. Get help before all the children are unmanageable.

Find another juggling friend and learn together. Among other friends, be sure to find fellow widows for tips and encouragement for mothering alone.

Set goals for yourself and keep practicing. Don't give up. Ever.

God makes a way. He delights in providing possible solutions to impossible problems.

Question 18

How does mothering alone make you feel?

Widows answer:

• When I was alone with the children, I sometimes felt like I was trying to bob apples, keeping them all under water at the same time. As soon as I felt I had everything under control, another trouble would pop up.

• It seems mothering alone as a single parent is described in one word: *trust.* How do I cope when there are endless squabbles, and I am getting tired? When there are decisions to be made and I don't know which one would be the best? Or when the older ones wonder, "Why, Mom? Why can't I do this?" "O God have mercy! And give me wisdom and grace," is the feeble heart cry of the widow. Just do what is the most important thing to do right now and give the rest to God and trust. He has not failed me yet, and He will not now. If I cannot decide on a decision that needs to be made, I give it more time. Time will, in itself with God's help, bring the right answers. *Waiting* is often the answer God has for us right now.

• Mothering alone, and yet not alone. We often feel alone, but we don't have to. There are so many that are also facing this journey toward heaven as a single parent. We have God first of all to be our constant companion and friend. We also have friends, church brethren, parents, brothers and sisters, and extended family members. They all care about us and want to lighten the loads. We just couldn't go on alone and so we depend on God and others to help us. Yet the one we loved so dearly is still missed so much. It will be like this as long as we live. God provides grace for this, but it takes the widow's grace. A special kind of grace that God saves for His widows. He gives it as we need it, daily. And it never runs dry or goes empty. He is our Provider!

• Don't think I don't love my children, but my husband just loved them up and down and around and around. He took them in church and was patient with them, held them, sang to them, played with them, disciplined them, let them dunk cookies into his coffee (when he hated having crumbs in the bottom), and broke his last M&M in half with them. So, when they are tired and fussy, it helps to remember they lost their best friend, too.

• Five months after my husband's death, our dear little daughter was born. That evening my ten-year-old said, "This is the best day we had for a long time." Many people told me she would be sunshine for me, and I agreed. I would not go tell others that having eight fatherless children to raise, one from baby on, looked very overwhelming. But God only asks us to take one day at a time, or…one moment at times. That was so often a relief when the mountain looked high and the path rocky.

• We live on a dairy and the boys did well, but not without bumps. I often felt I should be in the barn more, but was also needed in the house. I felt at times I was only halfways in the middle, and not a help anywhere. Somehow God helped me get the family raised and kept the family together. And most times, happy to be together!

• The load of raising the children was most overwhelming. We had all the support I needed, but no one takes the place of a father. I often wondered why God allows such a thing and how it brings glory to Him. One person pointed out to me the many Scriptures that especially have promises for the widow. God does care! One widow mentioned how the fact that her husband will never return just nearly overwhelms her. Isn't that so true? If we were only expected to be a widow for one or two years that would be awful; but at least it would have an end, and we could look forward to his return. But we do the best we can and just pray for the Lord's return, don't we?

• As I think over the years, I sometimes wonder how I ever made it through those times when the children were all small. But God was with me through it all. I am now a grandma.

• Never ever forget that we are not truly alone. Our Lord is present each moment and is a constant source of strength, comfort, and help.

Dear Fellow Widow Friends,

I think every widow knows that a wedding day is a day of many stirred long-ings and emotions. When we see a young couple being joined together, we think back to our own special day, that weighty, yet precious moment. And throughout the day, the singing is always so stirring for me. The tears fall for what was and is no more. And only a deep ache and loneliness is in the heart.

When I attended my thirteenth wedding (in nine years' time) as a widow, I came home late, tired, and full of longings. It was a peaceful evening and the nearly full moon shed its rays across the quiet landscape. I stopped a moment before stepping in the door, lifting my longing eyes to the heavens, a wordless plea for strength.

Upon entering, I saw my only child, my nine-year-old daughter, still had a light on in her room. I knew she would be waiting for me, so I stepped into her room and she was so glad to see me! She said she made a card for me tonight. After tucking her in and a goodnight I went to my room. There on my dresser was the card she had made. On one side she had printed the words: *Jesus wept, and I love you.* I sat on my bed and thought for a long time about those precious words, "Jesus wept." It just brought tears to my eyes as I again realized God knows so well what I need. It must have been Him that put it in my daughter's heart write those words, as I did not even know that she knows that verse, and how else would she have known to write them on the card that evening. It brought a com-forting feeling to my heart and reassured me—Jesus wept too. He understands my tears and sorrow. He knows it all. Oh, comforting thought! He has promised to be the widow's Husband, and a Father to the fatherless. He is true to His promises! Sometimes He sends His love and encouragement in such small ways that it is easy to miss them. Let us keep our eyes and hearts open to receive the sunbeams He sends on our path here and there as we journey on.

Sincerely,

"Rose"

Raise Them Alone?

A WIDOW

When I realized my husband had so suddenly left us behind, one of the first overwhelming thoughts was of our children, and my heart failed within me. Raise them without him? The idea couldn't even register in my mind; it was too impossible.

That first year, my hardest struggle was not accepting the loss to me personally, but the loss of my children's daddy. I am an adult, and if God willed that I live the rest of my life single, I could accept that. But children are not meant to grow up without a daddy. *My* children most of all! I am not a strong woman; marriage was a step of faith. Having a family was an even bigger step. So, it was overwhelming to find myself suddenly a single mother. My responsibilities doubled—no, tripled! —at the same time my main support was taken out from under me.

Not only were my children deprived of their wonderful daddy, death had robbed them of childhood innocence and security. While we sometimes say that children adjust easier than adults, the trauma takes its toll on them. I found that the older two became high-needs children overnight. While I longed for quiet time and space to think and grieve, my little ones needed me more than ever before. Those first months, bedtime was a taxing ordeal with tears and fears and hours of tossing and turning before they could relax into sleep. And the four-year-old child's daily behavior became hyperactive, with discipline helping only marginally.

I remember thinking one of those first days that if I am the only parent now, I must be firm and consistent right from the start. Yet I found that in those first weeks I was too weak and my children too unsettled. Others' support and advice was a blessing as we struggled to function without our husband and daddy.

I used to struggle more with the feeling that I must be both father and mother for my children. I have come to rest in the fact that if God allowed my children's father to be taken from them, then He will need to fill that lack for them. Of course, I want to do my part, but I just realize more and more that I cannot be everything to them, and God will have to meet those needs. Then, like one of my widow friends reminds me, we need to be ready to accept however He chooses to do that…perhaps it is not always the way we would hope.

Mothering alone? Not one of us would have chosen this calling. Yet the Bible is full of examples of God enabling His children in the severest of trials and the heaviest of burdens. The extremities of life are our opportunity to trust His promises and find His strength made perfect in our weakness. *He is faithful that promised* (Hebrews 10:23).

> God can mend a broken heart if we give Him all the pieces.
>
> Raymond P Brunk

202

Bedtime for Widows

ANONYMOUS

It was bedtime.
I took my small son by the hand.
We went upstairs to bed.
His brothers were not home and he must sleep alone.
He looked at me with troubled eyes and said,
"It's dark and I am scared. Can bears come
Through the door when it is locked?"
We knelt beside his bed.
I put my arm around him and he snuggled close.
"Dear God," I prayed. "Keep Danny safe tonight.
Help him to be brave and to sleep good. Amen."
He climbed into bed and I pulled the blankets up.
I tucked them under his chin and gave him a kiss.
I pointed out the window, where he looked
Up, up, up to see the stars.
He smiled and slept.
I went away and knelt beside my bed.
My husband was gone and I must sleep alone.
"Dear God," I prayed. "It's dark and I am scared.
The doors are locked, but what about the bears?"
Then God put His arm about me and drew me close.
I snuggled up to Him and He said,
"Under the shadow of My wing, make thy refuge
Till these calamities be past."
I climbed into bed and looked out the window—
Up, up, up to the stars.
Then I fell asleep in the shadow of His wings.

Mothering Alone, Yet Not Alone

KAREN CARPENTER

When our husbands are taken from this life, it falls to us as mothers to assume the role of leading out at home, whether we wish to or not.

I think for the boys to know, even when they are older teens, that they are just the boys in the home underscores their accountability to us as mothers. They need that.

I took the lead in family worship, and in asking visitors to lead us in prayer at mealtime, even when the boys were in their upper teens/low twenties and still home. They could have been the spokesmen for me, but I wanted them to be boys while they were in our home; they would have the responsibility of being the leader later in their own homes, Lord willing. I always appreciated when other fathers led out in prayer when we were the company and my oldest boy was 14, 16, and even 18, instead of asking my boy to lead out. It was so good for us to hear the father pray—so restful, so secure…

Do not lean too heavily too soon on the children's advice. It would be easy to. Know their thoughts and consider them. But lean more on other mature people.

It is most helpful to have a few trustworthy people to be your advisors. People who share your convictions, and who will guide and support you in decisions that must be made. It gives the children security to know that you confer (even when they don't want you to sometimes) with Uncle Pauls or Brother Johns whenever you want to. Not too large a circle, or you'll still end up not knowing what to do.

Honor your husband's convictions, and implement his ideals as much as you are able. To tell the children, "I know this is what Daddy would want us to do," gives validity to your decisions. Seeing you honor Daddy's direction will help them honor yours.

By all means possible, we should strive to teach our children the joy of submission. Teach by precept, by example, by discipline. No matter what our circumstances in life, I think this is perhaps the most crucial lesson to be learned.

Nurture your relationship with each child. You are the only parent they can hear and see now. They *need* you. Guide their thinking; never scorn it. Be sensitive, thoughtful, and wise. Build the kind of relationship they will still want to draw from in twenty years.

We are not to be pitied because of being bereft. The same God who allowed death comforts the sore spots with extra special tenderness. Teach the children that the thoughtful deeds of others prove God's love to us. We are loved and cared for. Pity is weak, and weakens. True comfort strengthens. We look for comfort but not pity.

"Keep your chin up," my uncle said. God hears our pleas for courage and wisdom. We look *up* for God's help and *beyond* to the comfort and joy that awaits us over there. That's what keeps us going, and we want to do all we can to bring our children with us. 🌸

> God doesn't always smooth the path, but sometimes He puts springs in the wagon. Lucas

205

Question 19

Do you have any tips or child-training advice for other widows?

Widows answer:

• Your children become what you live for after your spouse is gone. They also have the most needs and can be demanding at times when you feel you have no more left to give. The disciplining is very tiresome if you end up always having to do it. Consistency is a key even in the worst times. Show them that you love them, but demand respect. Be open to them; their world has broken in hundreds of pieces and the only one left is a shattered mom, looking lost and hopeless most days. Speak to them; tell them it is not because of them. Tell them you are just having a sad day and things will be okay. Talk about the missing parent if you can. Show healthy grieving skills; they live what they see. Finally, take time alone for yourself. Remember, you are only human. Take time alone to be with God. Talk to God. Tell Him how much it hurts, and how tired and angry you feel; He knows it anyway. Tell Him how frustrated and overwhelmed you are, and before you leave, ask Him for eyes to see and ears to hear the blessings He is trying to bring you. Thank Him for something every day no matter how small. Make it a family thing to ask the children to help you find something to thank Him for. He will open your eyes and small things become miracles. The journey is a long, slow process for adults and children alike. Each person will react differently and the path is very unique. Do not measure your progress against someone else's. The Bible plainly says, *Those who compare themselves among themselves are not wise* (2 Corinthians 10:12).

• When there are squabbles to settle, I have discovered if Mom stays calm, and talks quietly but firmly, it will do much better than to become impatient with a rebuke. Even with no daddy around, children will respect Mother if discipline is used in love. Children soon learn whether they can sway Mom...or if Mom means what she says.

• Soon after my husband passed on, I nicely told the children that I'm not going to call them in the morning; they have alarms and they need to depend on them. We need to rise and shine, and start butchering chickens early in the morning.

• I have found keeping a schedule to be a lifesaver. Our life was spinning out of control; small tasks that were neglected looked like insurmountable mountains. I felt everything would avalanche on me, and I had no extra energy. Having a certain time to rise, eat, brush teeth, and go to bed gave us a feeling of control and security when everything familiar was gone. Of course, we had to be flexible because we got lots of visitors, but sometimes we just kept our schedule, because after the visitors left, everyone was cross.

• Try to keep your connection with each child. You need to earn their respect. But with no husband to back you up, you are the one who needs to make your children respect you and not talk back. Try to keep each one involved as much as you can in family devotions. Be very specific in bringing out the spiritual points, because you are the one responsible to teach. We are using a book from CLP for youth and I really like it. It gives stories with the Bible reading to bring out the point and that makes an impression.

• Don't let your children compare themselves with others who are rich, but teach them to count their blessings. Name a number of your blessings and help them understand this is where God wants us and we can be happy with our many rich blessings.

• If you are feeling overwhelmed by the older ones nearly running over you, have a heart-to-heart talk and tell them you are depending on them. Tell them that you cannot do it yourself and you need their cooperation. Ask them to pray for you to have the strength and wisdom to handle things.

• Talk about Dad. Show them pictures. Make a memory wall. Put clear plastic over your table for mealtime conversation. Make a corner for all the memories of Dad.

• Teach your children to give. My daughter thought it was fun to receive mail and packages. She loved to get, but there is a ditch to thinking you must always be given something. We worked at giving baby gifts, or putting a balloon in a birthday card for one of her little friends. Here we moms must be careful. We do have ends to meet, too. Seriously, we are the ones in charge of our money. How it gets spent, and how we save it. Where children are involved, there will always be bills. But just the thought of giving even something homemade can be a real blessing.

• It is very important to talk about your loved one. Have family time and face your boys when they face problems. Talk it out with them even if you break down and don't know what to say next. Now, looking back, I believe that breaking down may have spoken the loudest. Praise to God, for so far all our children are happily married, church members, and they are all very caring to their lonely mother who lives by herself.

• Make special effort to play with your children or just do something to make them happy. We won't be throwing them up in the air and giving piggy-back rides like Daddy did, but we can hold them on our lap, read them stories, play pitch and catch, or bat balls for them. Some of those things don't take a lot of time, but it helps to insure and build a parent/child relationship with them. This is very important since you are now the only parent. But give yourself time. In the early stages of grief, giving your children a happy time can be the last thing you feel like doing! It might go quite a while before you are really playing with your child with your whole heart instead of forcing yourself to do it.

• Be even more firm with discipline than before.

• Accept offers for babysitters to keep your children for a day to give you a break alone at home. Then take the time to refresh yourself by doing some reading, writing, or whatever. We used to get short breaks when the children were out with Daddy or when Daddy took a turn holding the baby. Needing a break is not a sign of weakness. If no one ever offers to babysit, gather a bunch of courage and *ask*. Easier said than done! It is not fun to always feel like the needy one.

• Converse daily with your Lord. With your children, be firm, yet gentle. Do your best to not go back on your word. Say what you mean and mean what you say.

• A gem from my mom: The children are...whining, talking back, disobeying, whatever....*because you let them!* Have a sense of humor. Laughter lightens many a tense moment. Play with the children. Let them know you love them and enjoy them even when you are burdened with grief or the added responsibilities.

• Remember Daddy together....the pleasant, the funny, the serious. Miss him together, but do not have a pity party together. Honor your husband's wishes and convictions. Telling the children, "Daddy would want it this way, or Daddy did not allow that," carries a lot of weight. Just sitting down and holding an uncooperative child, and calmly talking of things unrelated to the situation has worked wonders. Keep in mind that we are not always in the present situation. Life is constantly changing.... albeit very slowly at times.

• Make mealtimes cheerful and full of friendly conversation even though the empty chair at the head of the table is cutting a hole in your already hurting heart.

• Lead the family in daily worship, even though it should be Daddy's role. More than ever your family needs to be taught to find comfort in God and the promises in His Word. Teach them verses like Ps. 68:5, and remind them often that they have *two* fathers in heaven. Pray aloud for each family member by name. Pray for your own needs also so they can understand that you too depend on God as your Father. Thank God for the gift of memories and the years of happy times you had together. Thank Him for the contribution their father was to their lives, his example of godliness, and the confidence that we can meet him in heaven.

• Sing as a family, even though the bass voice is missing. Though it may cause tears in your own eyes, and pain in your own heart, your children should not get the message from you that singing is no longer approved of because of the grief in our hearts.

• Remember to be calm during scary times such as severe summer thunderstorms. Our children are very aware, by their personal experience, that God does *not* always keep us safe from physical harm! Your example of trust can become their security.

• Make the evenings a time of pleasant family togetherness, even though you don't feel like a family anymore. The first winter after my husband was gone, we needed to have a project of some kind for each evening we were home ...playing together with Play-Doh, puzzles, games, paint by number, sorting change and rolling into tubes, simple cross-stitching, simple wood projects, baking cookies, making casseroles for busy mothers. Even though it is the last thing you feel like doing after a weary day, you need to focus on the family members you still have with you.

• Review memories of happier days with your children. One of the first things I bought after the death of my husband and sons was a notebook to write down memories. When someone you love becomes a memory, those memories are precious indeed.

• Don't keep saying, "Daddy wouldn't like you to do that." That has its place; it is appropriate depending on the situation, but in general help them to know what Daddy stood for at other times rather than correction times.

• Talk about Daddy as you work. Children want to know about Daddy. Shed the bulk of your tears in private. Try to keep an orderly schedule.

• Correct your children as you would if Daddy were here. They are simply being children. Never make excuses or let wrong actions go unpunished. Be firm, speak to and treat a child as a real person. Then drop the offense after it is tended and use diversion. Change the job, if possible. Move on; don't let it smolder. This works if they are from a "perfect" home, or "half" a home (widow's home).

• Don't forget or push off disciplining your children if they need it. At first, I didn't punish them when they were naughty, as I thought they were hurting enough and were just being naughty as a cover-up. But I saw they'd soon be out of my control. So stay on top of it. Sometimes they need to be held and talked to. Other times they need to be punished. Make them help with the work. Give them something to do to help them feel needed. They want life to go on as close to usual as it can.

• Talk often of their daddy and how he would tell them things when he was here. Add something special on his birthday or Christmas. Read them stories of other people's experiences of losing their father or mother. Visit other widows and widowers. Visit people who are worse off than you are. Or write to them. Don't feel too sorry for yourself and your children. There are a lot of sad people. We all have our own cross to bear. We can do this with God by our side.

• It is not easy for a widow to have company. But for the children's sake, she should. It helps the children to see whole families interacting. It is a help to our sons to be with men and learn from them. It also helps our families see that we are reaching out to others, instead of us doing all the receiving.

• Go to weddings and family gatherings even if it brings tears and acute loneliness. I still firmly believe it helps our children to see that life goes on.

• This is a touchy subject, but I believe widows can and do rely too heavily on older and younger children in the home. Without being conscious of it, they are being used as substitute companions. We tend to share too much (things we would have told our husbands) and that stifles their growing-up, carefree years by carrying our burdens, loneliness, and cares.

• Don't make your children take your husband's place, by doing things that are distinctly for the man or the husband, such as welcoming in visitors, meeting authorities, paying dues, sleeping with you, etc. Let them stay in their place and be children.

• Each day, whisper all your children's names in prayer, that God would help them, correct them, and encourage them. Reach out…send mail; write to unknown, hurting people; it brings healing. Let the children know that God takes care of the fatherless, and only if it is His will, will He send a new daddy. Always lean thine arms on the windowsill of heaven and turn strong to meet the day. God desires that we bless others as He has repeatedly blessed us. We experience inner joy because we have cared about and blessed others.

• Be flexible with your teenagers. They have ideas and thoughts that are not quite your own. It is okay. Let go and let God. Help them become who they should be. Trust Him; He is able.

• Allow your children to live a normal life. Have friends over. We tend to be overprotective. We have lost so much and we don't want to lose anyone else!

• Make personal contact with each child and make sure they don't blame themselves for their father's death.

• Help your children find others with similar experiences and reach out to them.

• Let go, when necessary. It was a challenge to not become overprotective, especially since the accident that took my husband also took two sons. But I also realized my children need to be exposed to "normal" family life. At times, it was best for them to be with other families to learn the give and take of normal home life, especially with a strong father figure.

• It helps to have people take an interest in your children. I had some friends who came for the weekend every so often. They planned activities or took us to the mountains nearby. They helped to get our minds on something else…to air our brains and not just think of the loss we suffered.

• Take nature walks and have little picnics in the woods or back fields. Work together, sing together, play together. You will treasure every bit of time you spend together. You will never regret the effort you took to give your children a happy childhood.

• Assemble three meals a day, even when the one who you cooked for is not there to enjoy your efforts. Your family deserves their mother's attention too.

• Forgive the misunderstandings, the ignorance, the criticism, the callous indifference, and the gossip. I need to remember that there may be those that hurt with us who simply do not know how to express the comfort they would like to. I understand—because I was there too at one time.

• If taking the lead in family worship seems too big to you, perhaps you could all take part and each one read the text verse by verse. Do not ask your older teenagers to lead; after all, you are the parent.

• To the younger widows: take courage! It hurt when my children claimed I did not love them when I disciplined them. I told them I do love them, or I would care less what they do. Now that they are older, it is a blessing to see each child confess and be baptized in the church. 🌺

God's Children

A WIDOW

I have a Peter in my family—impulsive, extreme, and very busy. My Peter will jump from the garage roof without thinking of the possible consequences, just as Peter leaped from his boat without seeing the waves. When watering, my Peter will be wet; not only his feet, but also his hands and his head. My Peter tells stories without considering the accuracy, not really knowing what he is saying. When life turns upsidedown, my Peter will go a-fishing for something, anything, to keep his mind busy. Did Jesus need to beseech His heavenly Father for patience with His Peter? Jesus loved His Peter, and He loves mine too! Oh, how I love my Peter, and I pray that when he is filled with the Spirit, he will feed the lambs and sheep.

I also have a Thomas—careful, suspicious, distrustful. "Are doctors only trying to get more money from us? Is someone covering up the truth? Does my friend really mean what he said? Am I doing what I ought to be doing?" Oh, how I love my Thomas, and I pray that he will learn to love and trust his Maker and Master with an unswerving loyalty.

I have a John—loyal, stable, humble. Personal relationships are important to him. He considers his words and does not use them very freely. My John stays in the background and is never in the center of the party. He is quiet, reserved, and gentle. I love my John, and I pray that he will be faithful in whatever calling God gives to him.

I also have an Esther in my family. She is alert to the moods and struggles of others and does not like to see them sad. She tries to replace their sackcloth with clothing. She wants to do what is right, but often needs the encouragement to do it, especially if it appears to carry the risk of not being accepted. I love my Esther, and I pray that she will be determined to wholeheartedly follow her Lord's will.

Do you have a sacrificing Dorcas in your family? A meek, speech-impaired Moses? A stubborn, rebellious Jonah? A crippled Mephibosheth? Perhaps a pessimistic Naomi, or a strong, careless Samson. Remember, God has a plan and a purpose for each of His children, no matter of what personality or temperament. He can use each one to His honor and His glory, even the child that brings you to the end of yourself most often. He can use a zealous Saul, a busy Martha, a relaxed Mary, a sickly Gaius, a daring Joshua. God loves each of our children, more than we can possibly love them ourselves. He made them, He sent His Son to redeem them, and He wants them returned to Him when He calls for them.

I Saw a Daddy

LMH *with apologies to Dorothy Hsu*

I thought I was healing. I had survived a snowstorm, church services, weddings, and family gatherings, without going to pieces. I had made it through the stomach virus, fevers, toothaches, and bicycle wrecks, and still retained my sanity. I had adjusted to calling the repairman, long-distance driving, and even to sleeping alone, so I thought I was healing. But it all came back in a sudden onslaught of emotion!

I saw a daddy…

Throwing snowballs and building a snowman with his children, just like my children's daddy used to do.

I saw a daddy…

Sharing songbooks with his son in church, just like my boy's daddy used to do.

I saw a daddy…

Gently rocking his sick baby daughter, just like my little girl's daddy used to do. And I knew that never in a lifetime will I adjust to seeing a daddy with his children.

How did you go about finding and accepting a father figure for your children? How does this work out for you?

Widows answer:

• Early on in my journey as a widow, I was told that although most children only have one daddy, my children will have many acting fathers. Naturally, I rebelled at the very idea! I wanted my children to be like everyone else and have *one* daddy…their very own daddy.

But as time passed, I came to realize that acting fathers were certainly better than no father! Today I rejoice that my children do have many fathers who care about them in a fatherly way.

When my husband's brother comes, he walks around the farm with my boys and tells them stories of when their daddy was a little boy. He tells them interesting details about the farming methods their daddy used. He asks questions and listens to their stories with a kind, fatherly interest.

My parents, siblings, and in-laws come to do repair jobs and they take time to show the boys how to use the tools. They give them hands-on experience to teach them how to be the fix-it men someday.

Often after church services, I notice other boys' daddies reach down and shake hands with my boys, then linger to chat with them.

May God bless all the fathers who take time for the fatherless.

LMH

• My children had no father figure. They were older and yet not too old to take some counsel. I wished I would have encouraged them to ask and accept counsel from older ones. I am not sure how they would have taken advice. I failed.

• My son has a father figure after four years! After trying and exhausting local willing possibilities, we asked my cousin to reach out to our ten-year-old son. He loves them. He goes several days and overnight in the summer. They have committed to long term. God bless them.

• I had a family who took charge in helping to raise my boys…it worked out very well…they learned to do farm work and many fix-it jobs that go with a farm. It took a load off my shoulders. Now my boys are upper teenagers and it seems the closeness isn't there anymore with that family. Was that family too demanding? Maybe the father didn't know how to handle their feelings? It has been a problem.

• It is thankworthy to God who daily supplies for the widow's children, the fatherless. It seems they have many dads and mostly respect their uncles on both sides of the family.

• My upper-teen daughters found it hard to accept me doing things that used to be Dad's role, such as giving direction to prayer when we have dinner guests. For that, we reached an agreement to have a married son or son-in-law do it. They also thought it was Dad's place to give direction on their social life, dress, etc. It was hard for them to take it from me. Maybe it was failure on my part to know how to do it. Maybe if he were here, they would have struggled with his decision, too.

• A word of encouragement to those with boys. You know, we cannot fill the role or responsibility of a daddy for our children and especially our boys. God does not expect us to fill that for the boys as they grow to manhood. There are faithful men that can fill that for us. Thank the Lord for providing in ways we cannot.

• What I found that really helps my boys is helping a father figure with work. It makes them feel worthwhile. I encourage mothers to have a father figure for your children, especially for boys. It can be a challenge keeping them busy with men's work which they enjoy most.

• My two teenage boys each have a mentor of the church who meet with them occasionally and they are accountable to them. It seems to work out well.

• Your children long to have a dad…to be like their friends, to show Dad how far they can hit the baseball, anything they can do with Dad. Remember your children will need a male figure in their lives….grandpas, uncles, or even a friend you trust. Beware; they may call them Daddy just for the idea of feeling they have a dad. Don't feel hurt. It is their way of having security. My daughter did this, and as we widows know, no one likes to hurt our feelings. The family tried so hard not to let me hear, but one time it slipped out. My friend was horrified; she didn't know how I would react. Now we freely let her call him Dad.

• Our oldest son helps with produce at his uncle's place once a week and helps a couple evenings a week with barn chores at our neighbors. Our next son will also, once he is a little older. They all enjoy spending time with uncles and grandfathers.

• I encourage couples to visit widows. Just a visit with a man along does wonders and shows the children he actually cares. Read a book, play a game, or just chat…never stop being involved in the children's lives; they need that man figure. After all, they *had* a dad.

• I often wished a man would come and talk to the children about death or spiritual matters; have short devotions and prayers with us. After all, we are not used to this difficult role…besides helping the children with their heartache. Please stop and take time for them. ❧

Death is the opening of a more subtle life. In the flower, it sets free the perfume; in the chrysalis, the butterfly; in man, the soul.

Adam

I walked a mile with sorrow and ne'er a word said she.
But oh, the things I learned from her, when sorrow walked with me.
Robert Browning

Seven Orphans

As one whom his mother comforteth, so will I comfort you... Isaiah 66:13

Seven Orphans

SUELLEN J STRITE

In April of 1918, my Great-Grandpap Ebersoles (Chris and Minnie) moved to a picturesque farm overlooking the Antietam Creek near Leitersburg, Maryland. They and their seven children worked hard to make this rented property a decent place to live. The house was badly infested with bedbugs, so they set the legs of their beds in cups of kerosene to try to keep the bugs out of their beds.

With the 110 acres being farmed with horses, and his oldest son only twelve years old, Father Chris needed a hired man. A young conscientious objector, David Ranck, from Lancaster County, PA, filled this need until he became sick with the flu (Spanish infuenza) and went to bed to recover.

This was 1918, remember, and this was no ordinary flu. Most people began to show signs of recovery in three days; and if not, they usually died. In this case the hired man lived, but Father Chris became ill. Even so, he dipped hot apple butter on a cool fall day. From the steam and the stress, he developed pneumonia, took chills with high fever, became delirious, and died—all in less than a week's time.

The eleven-year-old boy, Clarence, was sent to get his Grandpap Ebersole to help care for Chris during his last days. Their doctor was sick and all the other doctors were extremely busy with flu epidemic patients. When one finally had time to see Chris, it was too late.

As the children stood around their father's bed watching his life ebb away, their mother lay in the bedroom across the hall, seriously ill. When she was told that her husband had died, she said, "What will I do with seven fatherless children?" In less than twenty-four hours, she didn't need to wonder, for she was gone, too. She was of sound mind until her death at 6:00 PM, October 25, 1918. Her husband had passed away the evening before at 8:00 PM.

Undertakers were so busy that none could come until the morning of the funeral. The bodies were washed and laid in the bedroom until he came with the coffins. The bodies were then put in the coffins during the funeral service. Because the flu was so contagious, services at church were not allowed. There was a funeral service held in the barn. The minister used the text 1 Samuel 20:3… *Truly there is but a step between me and death.* The coffins were placed in the front yard where those who came could view as they left. Then the coffins were carried by a horse-drawn hearse to the Miller's Mennonite Church cemetery where they were buried in a double grave.

Irene (14), being the oldest, "mothered" her siblings around the grave. Baby Harold had his second birthday a month before the deaths. He was placed in a foster home before the funeral. He was very afraid of everyone. He did not want anyone to care for him except Irene; he did not cry for his parents, but for Irene. His new foster mother stood outside the graveyard fence with him, so he would not cry for his sister. Irene had been given the heartrending responsibility of packing little Harold's belongings and carrying them to his foster parents' car. He clung tightly to her before they parted, and she could hear him crying as they drove out the lane. Later, Irene dreamed at night that her parents came back and asked if they were going to get Harold back.

After the funeral, the children's Uncle Denton Martin took them back to their house. He had pressing duties and needed to leave. The grandparents were planning to stay for the night and had not yet arrived, since they had left the graveyard and gone home to gather more clothes and supplies. So, the six bereaved children were left alone in the parent-less house. Uncle Denton asked Irene if she was afraid to stay alone and she said, "No," but she later admitted to having had an awful feeling at being left alone in that house.

The grandparents stayed with the children a few weeks as plans were made for the sale, the fall work finished, and homes found for the children. In those days, children were often put out into other homes to help meet expenses, since making a living was not easy. So even if Mother Minnie had lived, she likely would not have been able to keep the children together.

Grandmother Ebersole thought the jelly would not bring much on the sale, so she decided the family may as well use it. After dark one evening, she asked Irene to go upstairs and get a jar of this jelly from the cupboard where it was stored. This was in the room where her mother had died and where her parents' bodies had both been laid to wait for the undertaker. Irene was never a person to talk back, but this time she said, "I can't." Grandmother offered that Irene's brothers could go along upstairs with her. She still insisted that she could not do it. Grandfather came to the rescue and told the boys to fetch the jelly. Eighty years later, Irene said, "I don't think I could have gone for that jelly if they would have whipped me."

Irene at fourteen was considered old enough to work for her board. She helped here and there, moving often, wherever the next job opportunity was. Pearl was seven when orphaned and she had a very hard life. Her age was against her, as she could not work enough to pay for her board, and she was shifted around into several less-than-ideal homes. Little four-year-old Leonard was moved often too. Naomi, my grandmother, was nine when her parents died and she had the blessing of being placed in a pleasant home. Neither did she have the trauma of moving every year or so. In fact, she was the only one of the seven orphans who ended up in a stable home.

Four years after her parents' death, Irene penned these poignant words:

"Dearest Father and Mother, Thou hast left us lonely here. Thy loss we deeply feel. But tis God who has begrieved us. He can all our sorrows heal.

Dearest Father and Mother, How thy dear face we miss, and thy loving hand who cared for us, and helped us in time of sickness, who smoothed our aches and pains, who helped in time of trouble and distress. And thy chairs are empty and thy place is vacant. Thy sweet and loving smile we do not see or do not hear thy sweet and welcome voice. Thou art sweetly resting in your heavenly home, where some sweet day we shall see each other face to face and we will never part anymore. Oh, that happy day will soon be here. Oh, how I long to come to thee, dear Father and Mother. But tis God who has parted us here on earth and He will help us through this homeless life. We put care and keeping in His hands.

Dear Parents, As oft as I think of thee in that heavenly mansion above and of Jesus on His great white throne—oh, how I long to be there too. Life is lonesome here on earth without thee. When thy grave I look upon, and think of thee neath the cold, cold clay—it makes my sad heart ache till it nearly breaks. As oft as I think of the kind words you used to speak to us and how you told us to do what was right, and love Jesus, and some sweet day could come to Him and sing with Him up there at that great white throne. The kind words keep ringing in my ears.

Oh Father and Mother, tongue cannot express how we miss thee and how much we loved thee and you cared for your seven children.

Dear Father and Mother, when the last time we looked on thy dear faces, how it hurt our hearts. And it seemed as though thy voice we must hear. But your soul had taken its flight from your bodies.

Written in the year of our Lord, 1922 by Irene Ebersole

I grew up knowing Irene and Pearl as the two aunts who came and helped us shell peas and peel peaches. These nice aunts told us stories while we worked and served us vanilla ice cream when we visited them. Irene helped out in many homes and nursed sad children in her adulthood. Between her various day-jobs, Pearl taught Home Ec. at Paradise Mennonite School, and Sunday school at Miller's Church for years. Naomi was the only girl in the family who married, and I became her granddaughter. Her heart was soft as pudding toward any unfortunate child, teenager, or adult. I dearly loved my grandmother and was sad that she passed away when I was twelve years old.

I know they never really stopped grieving their parents' death until they too passed from this life; yet these three sisters seemed to be happy, well-adjusted adults. How did they do it? How did they survive such a pathetic childhood? How did they manage to bless so many other people when they carried a weight of sorrow on their own hearts? I believe it was only as they gave their life to Jesus and looked forward to heaven that they were able to live above their sorrow. God did not forget these children in their hours of sharpest grief, and at the end of their life when death was swallowed up in victory, He had a mansion prepared for them. When these faithful sisters passed on, they never had to fear another move or another separation. They are with Jesus forever! Former things are passed away and God wiped all tears from their eyes.

No sorrow is so great that heaven cannot heal. That was true for the faithful among the seven orphans, and it is true for any widow's child today. Take heart!

Thou wilt keep him in perfect peace, whose mind is stayed on Thee, because he trusted in thee (Isa. 26:3).

Quiet tension is not trust. It is simply compressed anxiety.

The Gospel Thumb Tack

Too often we think we are trusting, when we are merely controlling our panic. True faith gives not only a calm exterior, but a quiet heart.

JC Macaulay

Question 21

Do you have any advice to give about helping children through grief?

Widows answer:

• "Grief is not a process of forgetting. It is a process of learning to cope while we remember. A child unaffected by the death of a loved one is a myth. A child may seem unaffected. They may go on playing as if the loss did not happen. They, like adults, are in a state of shock and denial. Death will not be resolved quickly, but will integrate slowly for the rest of their lives as they grow in maturity and understanding.

• In times of sorrow, we parents are wonderful mother hens. We want to gather our children and tuck them under our wings and shield them from the harsh realities of life and pain. In some ways it is easier to bear grief ourselves than to allow our children to experience it. They must face it, no matter what we say or do. Life with its heartaches and joys will happen to them. When we accept that truth, we can switch from overprotecting them to guiding them.

• Remember, the children are grieving too, and probably not with an older person's perspective. So, they may be hurting more, or in a different way than you are. God has reasons we may not understand, but accepting it as part of God's will goes a long way. But it is not something you do once and it is done. Often you need to stop and get your mind on the big picture...why we are here, and where we are going... Heaven will be worth it all!

• If possible, try to see your children's need of grieving. I was so overwhelmed with my husband's death that I did not realize how the children were hurting too. They never complained that I found out. It is just the thought in these later years that bothers me. One child had turned hyper who was a normally calm child. Thankfully it didn't last long. I tried to explain their father's death and that he won't be coming back as one of them thought. In later years I read a letter that one child

225

wrote saying she wishes someone had told her he won't come back again. I guess they had many unanswered questions, like adults do.

• My husband was sick a long time and I was with him almost all the time. Our youngest son was his hands and feet. The teenage children took over a lot of the farm/home responsibilities. It seems life for the children goes on, mostly. Their future is still ahead of them. In a way my husband's death has eased the strain and stress that went with all his ups and downs and the uncertainty of his life. With my husband sick for so long—no appetite; pills, teas, and tonics; dialysis supplies; runs to the doctor…not all was pleasant. I shared with the children that I don't miss some of those things…it is because it was a part of him that I "miss it." That gave them the right to not feel guilty if they were relieved to be free of some things and have a mother at home again.

We all knew my husband was dying. And the children knew of other families gathering around to watch their loved ones depart. They asked if they are required to do that; they didn't want to. God was so good. I got my heart's desire and was with my husband when he passed away… and most of the children got their wish and were not present at that time.

• We share memories of our dad/husband. But I find it hard to let my children see my deepest grief. My bedroom is my hottest battlefield. I don't know if this is good, or if I should weep more in front of them so they can feel free to weep also.

• Children need to be free to express their emotions, whether cheerful or sad. Young children especially can heal and accept quickly, and be ready to embrace their new normal of life long before we adults are.

• Those first couple years, there will likely be some strange behavior in your children. There might be occasional mad outbursts that leave you in tears of frustration and gets you on your knees. You feel so overwhelmed and insufficient with the responsibility of these behaviors. But looking back, this is a process. God is good and His promises are sure. God has called you to this position and you can do it.

• It is okay for your children to see you cry at times. One mother asked a doctor if this was emotionally damaging to her children. He assured her that it would not damage them as long as she was not crying all the time, and if there were happy times in between. This actually helps the child realize that it is okay to feel sad about Daddy's death.

• Through your own grief, don't forget children grieve too. They tend to grieve not in one year, but over many years.

Not only do we fail to look for answers to our prayers, but we are often surprised when the answers come.

How Death Affects a Child

THOUGHTS GLEANED BY DARLETTA MARTIN
from a seminar by Dr Kathleen Miller, Ellen Savoy, and Margaret Paul

The death of a parent is a severe loss to a child and it will have an impact on his life. The grieving mother realizes this. In fact, the realization that her child is suffering is part of her grief. Yet how can she be expected to analyze all the needs of her children at this time of her own loss? She needs some space to deal with her own grief. We continue to maintain a sense of compassion and wonder at how widows can survive these crises.

All children benefit from structure, clear expectations of what is going to happen, and regular and predictable responses from adult caretakers. Continuing with our responsibilities provides structure for children to recover. A realistic response is that we don't understand this completely and we wish it wouldn't have happened, but God is still in control.

Cases have been observed over the years and organized into lists to help us understand what we see. They can be used as general guidelines. Sometimes they are helpful. Other times we feel lost as we try to relate to them. It is important to keep in mind your own judgment about what you see. The idea that a child should come to a specific conclusion in such experiences must be viewed according to the child, not a theory.

Not everyone has the same reasoning or memory abilities. Still there is progression in each experience. If a child is exposed to repeated trauma, it is hard for him to find his way back into the world. Just as they come to a settled state, the problem opens again, making the child feel that resolution itself is suspect.

We need to be open to how a child reacts to loss. It can be very different for different children. When we talk about loss, we can make general statements, but when helping a child, we need information about that particular child so we can focus on taking the right steps for him.

A child who suffers loss early in infancy will show the impact in a very different way than a child who is at age eight. The younger the child, the faster he should recover. A child *younger than age two* who loses a parent will remember it differently than it really was. This is not pathological, just a part of the phase.

From *ages three to five*, children often see death as a reversible separation, a temporary state that is like sleep. For many months after the death, young children may ask, "When is Daddy coming home?" It is important to remember that intense experiences live in our minds. We adults can sometimes not get the thought out of our mind about someone we lost. Some people need to forget some parts. Does Johnny need to relive what happened, talk about it, cry, and discuss whether he feels responsible in some way? Bringing the memory back does not always get the child unstuck. If a child had a traumatic past, it may be best if he does not remember how bad it was before, but can focus on the present benefits.

Children *three or older* will have bits of memory that are not complete, because memory is not fully developed until after the age of eight. Young children do not have a sense of time the way an adult does. Their way of coping comes in different pieces. We may have a concept of the loss involved, but a child may have a very different sense of it. Try to hear or see what the child's experience of the loss might be.

Between the ages of five and nine, a child may accept the death of a person but not necessarily the fact that everyone will die, including loved ones and the child himself. The child frequently views death, not as due to natural causes, but as a result of strife, defiance of authority, retaliation, or punishment. Concerns about death often involve personal security.

The child wonders in a concrete way, "Who will drive us to church now that Daddy is gone?"

What can you do about a child who feels responsible for the death of a parent? Many children at this age feel responsible for everything that happens to them. It only makes sense to him that he is at fault. It is a terrible burden to feel responsible for death, damage, or sickness, but children just naturally do. It is important to not try to talk him out of it. We cannot use reason to attack an idea that develops out of something unreasonable. We can acknowledge the child's feelings and reassure him. Share your perspective with the child as he shares his. But finally, we need to help him come to rest in the fact that there are some things we just can't explain, and only God understands.

By *age nine or ten,* most children begin to comprehend death as an inevitable experience for everyone, including themselves.

The *adolescent* who faces the loss of a parent may feel awkward, fear rejection from his peers, and even experience embarrassment over the death. Adolescence is normally a time of inner turmoil, but with the addition of a parental death, young coping mechanisms are often strained to their limits. An adolescent may respond in any number of ways ranging from withdrawal to rebellious and anti-social behavior. The surviving parent, often immersed in his or her own grief, may be irritable, distant, inaccessible, or deeply depressed. Thus, the adolescent may feel unsupported or abandoned. Some adolescents express the feeling that at least temporarily they have lost both parents.

> Ah, when to the heart of man
> Was it ever less than treason
> To go with the drift of things,
> To yield with a grace to reason,
> And bow and accept the end
> Of a love or a season?
>
> Robert Frost

Helping Children Through Grief

JONATHAN KROPF

Children do grieve. They need your help as adults to cope with major loss. Like adults, they display a variety of reactions. They have many of the same needs, and experience many of the same symptoms and issues.

There is the double task of dealing with our own grief and at the same time trying to be there for the children. These tasks are extremely important, but they are emotionally draining as well. Some of us have been there and know what it is like.

There are several things we need to keep in mind as we help children through grief:

1. Children are immature in their thinking abilities. It is difficult for them to grasp the fact that death is permanent. Because of their intellectual immaturity and lack of experience, they may not know how to describe their feelings, thoughts, or memories. This fact is very important in resolving grief. It should not surprise us because we remember how difficult it is/was for us to identify our thoughts and feelings.

2. Children tend to take things literally. It is crucial how we communicate with our children. We should be careful how we talk about death to them or in front of them. If we say we "lost" someone through death, they may expect they can be found again. When we say it is mostly "old" people that die, the child may become very concerned, because even if you are

only 40, they may think that is old, and therefore you might die at any minute. If we say the person is "asleep" they may think they will wake up again. This is all very confusing to a child. We need to speak truth that is appropriate for their age.

3. Because a child is a child, they have little control over their lives. They are very dependent on their caregiver. They do not have access to resources like adults do. We may become overwhelmed with our grief and decide to go visit a friend. Children can't do that. They are very limited in their resources, and even if the resources were there, they cannot go out and look for them as you and I would do. A child needs to be provided with avenues that allow them to cope effectively with grief.

4. Children may not understand that the pain will eventually go away. As adults, we sometimes wonder if the pain will ever go away, yet in the back of our mind, we know that someday it will get better. This too shall pass. But a child may not have the background to know that. They don't have the reassurance that they will survive. This can leave the child without the strength to take future risks of loving other people.

5. Children do not have the capacity to tolerate intense pain like an adult. In order for a child to not feel overwhelmed, they may handle grief intermittently. This can go on for years. They will alternately avoid or approach their feelings so they won't feel overwhelmed. They have a built-in survival mechanism that adults often misinterpret. When the child plays happily, we may think that death had no impact on them. This may not be true at all. A child simply may not be able to grieve intensely for too long a period of time.

6. Children need to feel secure before they can let go of their feelings. The child's need for security and safety actually intensifies when a parent dies. We need to continually assure them of our love. Give them lots of hugs. There has to be a sense of emotional and physical security before a child will open up. Consequently, many children do not resolve their loss, but will wait for more favorable circumstances to arise where they feel secure enough to express their feelings, freely acknowledge their pain, and mourn the loss of their loved one.

7. Play is an important expression in the life of a child. It can actually be a way for the child to work through their problems. So when they play funeral, it may be they are actually trying to master their loss, as well as

take a break from their grief. It does not mean that they were not affected by the death. It is just a way for them to deal with it, and cope with what has happened.

8. Children should not be overprotected from the reality of loss. They need to be able to express their feelings. Simply not talking about the death around your children is a mistake. They need to be included. There can be feelings of insecurity and abandonment when they see the adults in their life sharing in an experience that they cannot share. The fantasies of children are often worse than reality; therefore, they need help to understand what is going on in your own grief process, lest they draw incorrect conclusions that will hinder them later on. Remember they feel the loss as keenly as you do.

9. Children should not be burdened with the responsibilities of the parent who died. Small children should not be told that they are now the "little man" or the "little woman" of the household. This can feel overwhelming, and they simply are not capable of being something they cannot be.

10. Our children have real fears and real faith. Listen to them. Sometimes their simple faith can put us to shame. They also have real hurts and real hopes. With a little guidance these hurts, hopes, fears, and faith can be a means for them to learn to trust in the God who will never leave them nor forsake them. Remember, children are not looking for solutions as much as they are looking for models. Model your faith and they will follow.

You and your children are building a castle out of sand on the ocean beach. You are nearly finished with the castle and you stand back to admire it. Just then a huge wave comes along and levels it. There's not much left but a few humps and bumps. The wave was unexpected. The loss was great.

Death is that wave that washed over our children. Their future was being built, when suddenly the death wave flattened what they thought was their future, leaving only a few humps and bumps of memories. By God's grace we can help our children rebuild their lives. He has promised to supply all our need according to His riches in glory. And that is an exhaustless supply. May we recognize God's hand in our lives and build around His plan for us. ❧

When I Tried to Take God's Place

PHEBE J MARTIN

It was all over…The subtle symptoms, the shocking diagnosis, the surgery, the few short weeks of compromised living, and then death. Now my mother was a widow. The first time we had met with the hospice nurse during my father's illness, Mother sobbed, "But I don't want to be a widow." Who does?

My father was a strong leader and my mother depended on him for so much. Now he was gone and who would she lean on? I felt responsible. Some of my siblings had health issues, some lived far away, some had small children to care for. I felt responsible.

I pitied my mother. Her grief was so intense. I wanted to bear it for her. I wanted her to be happy. I wanted to take away her pain. I felt responsible.

One day each week I went to her house. I helped her with the heavy house cleaning; Dad had done that before. I helped her decide not to dispose of his things in the first two weeks; she later thanked me. She needed a new sofa; I took her shopping and helped her choose one. Her worn sofa pillows bothered her; I made new ones.

One evening a week, my family went with me to visit her. We cleaned her garden, mowed her lawn, and fixed her stove. We helped her clean out the garage and dispose of Dad's tools. I gave her the advice and courage she needed to write a will. It was canning season, so I ordered her fruit and helped her can it. Some of the rest of the family helped too, but I felt responsible.

I worried about her when she needed to drive through the dark or the rain; these were all new experiences for her. I talked to her on the phone and helped her work through her feelings when she was tempted to envy those who still had their companions, or when she was tempted to give into self-pity. I helped her to accept her new place in church life, since Dad had been a minister. As I listened, she leaned. And the more I listened, the harder she leaned. I pitied her and I felt so responsible.

I helped her decide to make the out-of-state trip. I was at her house when she returned because I could not stand the thought of her returning to an empty house. I painted her living room walls after helping her choose the color. I listened to her loneliness and memories. She cried and I cried. The more I did for her, the more she expected me to do.

Thanksgiving and Christmas with special meetings and family gatherings were hard days. I stayed close to her and listened as her grief poured out. I somehow wanted to make things better for my mother. I wanted her to be happy. I helped her to accept the sympathies of others and also to accept the fact that others moved on in life.

One day as I drove home from my mother's place, I became aware of a tingling feeling. It seemed as if the nerve endings in my arms and legs were on fire. It soon passed and I forgot about it… Until it happened again and again… What was wrong? But I was too busy "carrying" my mother to think about it for very long.

I found myself struggling with anger. I had never had a temper that flared. My temptation was to be irritable and grouchy. But now over the smallest and strangest things, I felt this flare of anger. What was happening?

And then my daughter got sick. At first, we were not too concerned—a cold, a sore throat. But over the next two weeks she got sicker and sicker. Her throat became so swollen she could only swallow clear liquids. Strep tests were negative although the doctor made all kinds of dire predictions. It was almost a relief when the diagnosis was mono. It was curable!

But she needed rest. She needed my care and someone needed to fill in with her chores. How would I care for my daughter and my mother at the same time? My daughter was my first responsibility, so I stayed home. I distanced myself a bit from my mother's needs. And as my daughter began to recuperate, I relaxed…and found it a blessed feeling! I still talked to my mother by phone, but there was a difference. Instead of talking only about herself, she asked about me and my daughter. She began to make a few decisions on her own; do a few more things by herself. And the rest of the family helped her. They had been helping all along.

Many weeks later, when my daughter had recovered, we once again visited my mother. But what a blessed difference. I was no longer "carrying" her. How foolish I had been to think that I could! Only God could do that for her. He was well able and willing.

Now I was back to being a daughter…a helpful daughter, a listening daughter…but just a daughter. One day I realized that my nerves no longer tingled and my temper no longer flared. Why? Because I was no longer trying to be God. It was so relaxing to let God carry my mother.

Both the grieving persons and their friends need to understand that it takes time to get through deep grief. There is no good way of rushing the process. Those not closely related to the departed one will soon readjust to life. It is hard then for them to watch one who has been deeply affected by the death struggle on for months and months. Friends must be patient and understanding. Telling grieving ones to get over it will be counter-productive. Carl L Eby Jr

Gifts

AMY SCHLABACH

There is one day in my life that will be etched on my heart as long as I live. It started out as a normal Saturday in July. The sky was a clear blue, and birds were singing in the woods around our house. All was good.

Until the news came. An accident. My dad. *I'm sorry, so sorry. He didn't survive.*

I sank down onto the back steps where my husband had gently brought the words he could barely speak. I stared at the harsh, unyielding concrete. Long moments passed. I felt detached. They must be mistaken. My dad? Not my dad. He was only fifty-nine. Healthy. Whole.

When I finally lifted my gaze, the world took on an artificial cast. The sky looked plastic. No longer singing, the birds' calls were jarring, cruel.

Stop! I wanted to yell. Why is the sun still in the sky? Why haven't the clouds covered everything? How dare people drive past on the highway, jolly and uncaring? Why is life still strolling along?

I moved through the next days in a fog. The community rallied around us and carried our family in prayer. I was grateful. How, I wondered, did people survive a grief like this without a supportive church family? Without friends? Without God?

The numbness wore off, and the pain pierced deep. My tears dried up, and I went through the necessary motions with scratchy eyes that grated in their sockets.

Words started to penetrate into my heart. My dad was a quiet, unassuming man. Very talented, but never one to promote himself. But now everyone had a story.

His co-workers came in droves to tell us how he would fix them up whenever they got hurt at work. "He could bandage us up better than anyone else," they said. "He kept us out of the emergency room all the time."

"He could fix anything, absolutely anything," his boss assured us.

Among the hundreds that attended the calling hours were business associates that we didn't know, except that Dad had mentioned them only in passing. They shared how he had helped them, by listening quietly and offering solutions to problems ranging from marketing to marriage.

People from church came with tales of behind-the-scenes help they had received. Extended family had stories of casual counseling and advice. People came and came and came. Even the UPS driver was his friend.

Finally, I couldn't take it anymore. "He was *my* dad!" I cried to my husband. "Why is everyone trying to tell me who he was? What he did?"

"They are only trying to honor his memory," he assured me. "They don't mean to hurt you."

But it hurt. It felt like everyone was trying to seize a piece of Dad's memory, and I wanted to cling to it for myself. It didn't make sense to me, and I couldn't put it into words. I tried to smile at each new storyteller, and nod my head and murmur appreciation. But my heart rebelled.

My husband's words kept ringing in my mind, and suddenly I felt ashamed. Dad's friends, neighbors, and co-workers were grieving, too. Not in the same way as I was, perhaps, or my mother, but still it was grief. The words they brought were gifts, laid at God's feet. Why did I want to fling them away?

He was my dad, yes, but more importantly, he was God's person.

The Memory Book

AMY SCHLABACH

My father was unique. He was quiet, usually letting others do the talking. When he did speak up, others listened. He had a sense of humor that simmered just below the surface. Our family had lots of private jokes, things that left other people scratching their heads.

After my dad died in an accident at work, our family felt rudderless, at loose ends. Though a laid-back person, he had lived his faith and steered our family toward God. In an effort to hold on to all the memories, all the funny, all the quirks, we put together a memory book. The finished product was a thick, chunky tome of photos, journaling, and jottings about Dad. It was a labor of love. Many were the tears that dotted its pages.

"Remember when Dad did this?" we'd ask each other, tracing a drawing one of the grandchildren made. Or, "Remember how Dad always said that little rhyme from his school days? How we clapped our hands over our ears?" "Remember how finicky he was with his tools?" we'd say, wandering out to his shop, memory book in hand, to run our hands over the clean surfaces that would never again see the dust of one of Dad's projects. "Who else had a workshop so well kept?" "Yes, and remember…" we'd say, tears streaming down our cheeks, each memory another jagged wound to our hurting hearts.

Finally, we closed the book, and set it on a shelf. For later. It hurt too much now.

Every now and then we'd get the book off the shelf and turn the pages. Read what we wrote in the depth of our mourning. Wipe a few tears. Give the book a loving pat and set it back.

Then one day, we got the book down to show one of the grandchildren a picture of Dad's Golden Retriever. The book fell open to an especially funny trait of his, and we passed it around for all to see. Suddenly, I held my breath. Everyone was laughing. Uproariously. Like we used to when Dad was here. We laughed until our sides ached, until tears flowed. Tears of healing, tears of joy.

Our grief had come full circle—from stabbing, raw, angry pain, to a remembering, healing love.

Question 22

Do you have any encouragement for other fatherless children? Or, do you have some insights that would benefit another widow?

Widows' children answer:

• Since I don't remember Daddy, all I knew was life without a father, therefore, I had no memories of situations that I still wished I had. Because I didn't lose my father while growing up it wasn't like friends showered me with gifts and thoughtful deeds after his death. I never heard mother bemoan her lot as a widow. She did not have the attitude that folks should be doing this and that for her and us. In fact, I thought she wished people wouldn't feel like they had to help her. I have always struggled with feeling inferior, unsure of myself, anxious and fearful, also thinking negatively. I really don't know if that has anything to do with being a widow's child or not. Keep your family all together with you if possible. Years ago, a widow's children sometimes were put out in other homes. I am grateful that it wasn't that way when Mother became a widow. I am thankful that Mother was able to be at home while still providing a living. If that is not possible in every situation, it is nice if Mother can be at home when the children leave for school and when they come home.   *Daughter: two years old when father died*

• A hard thing for me, as the oldest son, was taking over some of the farm responsibility without Dad. Neither was it easy to do things for the first time myself, which Dad had always done. Before Dad's death, I never really seriously thought something like that would happen to us, or never thought it would be that real. People just came by and showed their sympathy by helping for a few hours or showed their interest in what I was doing and encouraging me. Never put widows' children down by saying, "You are not doing that like your dad did." Don't ignore them. Don't tell them to stop grieving and get to work. I thought my mother related well and accepted it well. It helped me heal better when she accepted God's will. Let other people chip in and help with the work and don't feel obligated to be responsible, especially the first weeks or months. To the children: if you feel a need to talk to someone, don't hesitate! Open yourself up to someone you feel confident in, and you won't regret it.

Son: fourteen years old when father died

• I felt very much alone as my friends talked about their father and the things they were doing together. I needed to sit with my mother in church if my grandfather was not with us. To find somebody to sit with when I was older was a challenge. I don't remember having misconceptions about my father's passing, as my grandmother and mother helped me understand the best I could as a child. We enjoyed company who had children to play with. My grandfather meant so much to me. He cared about my loss which was his loss as well. He died when I was 12. God provided several brethren who taught me good things over my childhood and youth. Never tell a widow's child: "You don't know what a sound smacking is like." "You can do as you please." "You don't need to work hard like we do." Mother related very well to her widowhood. She would cry with us when we would talk about Papa's death. Other times, she braced herself to make it easier for us. She expressed much appreciation for our caring brotherhood. She taught us to respect people no matter what they said, whether meaningful or not. Advice for the widows: Read, sing, and pray together. Have living room conversations about the passing of Father. Visit other families who lost their father. Reach out to others. Grandpap told us to think of those who had greater problems. Be thankful for what God is doing. Teach love and forgiveness.

Son: four years old when father died

• I miss my father's leadership and advice. I appreciate when people come by or offer to help us. It is especially meaningful when a busy father takes time to come and give us a lift with chores. I also found all the cards, letters, and notes encouraging. It means a lot if people accept us just as we are. I thought my mother accepted it as God's will and it helps me accept our lot in life. It is encouraging to do something for someone else if I myself am grieving.

Daughter: twelve years old when father died

242

• I cannot remember my father, but Grandmother smothered me with photos. Was this helpful? At different ages I felt differently about the helpfulness of it. I cherish a few special ones. I heard my father's chuckle on a family music recording between songs. Jesus is the dearest to all saints. God did not give mankind a photo to remember Him by, nor a recording of His special Sermon on the Mount (Matt. 5-7). God could have, but chose not to. Let's be moderate.

It was hard for me to do without siblings. I was often bored because I was an only child. It was hard to learn that God only sends babies to complete families. It was very difficult to be stared at as an unusual object, like some zoo animal! Three things I could not bear: #1 Being pitied, #2. Being pitied, #3 Being pitied!

The Christian widow's child has much more opportunity to learn about death and to know the truth and the facts, as their family experiences it closely. As Christian friends associate/fellowship/support the widow, the widow's child will gain proper conceptions of death if the people they listen to have a biblical concept of death.

Once a year, a "rich cousin" gave gifts. This was a delight, but helpful?? I don't know. Two uncles and wives acted interested in our family. Two grandfathers and grandmothers were always there for us. Almost everyone included us in their lives and we had a *big* family. A caring family! Some special memories: Receiving *nice* handed-down dresses, toys, supplies; other people's surplus was so interesting and delightful. A mother who took time for children. We had a wide variety of friends.

I never knew what all a father's presence added to a home. I never really "lost" a father since my adjustment time was all before my memory. Maybe I was treated more special since my mother lost her husband. Did she dote on me? Was I spoiled? Maybe Mother did not try to convince me how difficult her life was, and so she didn't focus on my difficulties either. Once I got to sit with a girl cousin in church (as a fourth grader) on the *men's* side, with her father! This is still a special memory! She said, "Let's sit with Papa. He lets us get by with more than Mama." Oh! I was learning things! I had no option to get by with something when Mother said, "No"! I was surprised the first time I heard another widow refer to how unruly I was as a child soon after my father's death, that I nearly caused my mother to despair in her parenting...but maybe it helped to hear that in the long run...likely it was good to learn and face the facts and be humbled.

Never say, "You poor thing!" Never say, "You don't have a father." "Oh yes, I do!" I wanted to shout back, "But he is in heaven! I am not an illegitimate child of an unmarried female." (This answer was all kept inside.) Don't tell a widow's child, "You have it worse than other people. It will be hard for you to grow up and be true, without two parents working together on you."

My mother believed God allowed this. "Now let's talk about something else," she would say. "Let's sing, let's pray. Let's find someone to encourage. Let's act interested in other people. Can we help others in difficult experiences? We can live one day at a time. Our circumstances are not worse than most people's. People care about us. People mean to be helpful. People want to be friends. God cares. God is faithful. God is good. I have been blessed. I won't benefit myself or others by pitying myself."

My advice to other widows: Don't focus on the differences. Notice how others have similar or worse struggles. Notice God's faithfulness to other struggling saints. Believe in God's promises. Work on today. Look up into Jesus' face. Nestle in His loving hand. Allow yourself to feel it all...the pain and the promises. Forget how "different" you feel. Don't expect that someone will always want to do something for you. (Most wives learn to patiently wait for the back storm door to be fixed.) People let me know that they thought my mother's choice to "talk about something else" was not healthy. Oh yes, she told me stories about my father, by times, but not on a frequent basis. That is what worked for her and I became comfortable with that...So why criticize? Really, how many stories come from two years of married life? I wonder if other people hate to be pitied. Don't we all want to be accepted with the great blessings God has given us? Doesn't God want us to circle arms of love around all nationalities, handicaps, or unwished-for circumstances? People have needs because they are people. I wished my father would have lived, but far greater in my mind, I wished for a sibling. My mother went regularly to homes with children (cousins, etc.) to try to give me playmates. Widowhood is

244

temporary, short-term…it ends with time.

Daughter: 1¾ year old when father died

• I felt the stigma of being different, and truly felt the vacancy my father left. Though others were caring and very helpful, I felt we were a sorry case in need of help and sympathy. I pitied those that died, even though I was taught they were in heaven. I guess my finite mind couldn't grasp that heaven would be far better. People invited us for Sunday dinners, sent mail and visited, took us along on little day trips. Never remind a widows' children that they have no father. Never make fun of them. My mother did shed tears at times, but she tried to be brave for us children's sake. Because my brother and I were 17 and 18, we discussed issues and decisions together with Mother. Be cheerful! Visit and enjoy other people! Share in their life's experiences.

Daughter: eighteen years old when father died

• Growing up without a father, I would see how other little children would interact with their father as they grew older…that was hard. Never mock or look down on the widow's child, like you think they are not as good. We cannot help that our father died and that does not make us less worthy of friends. I don't remember of ever hearing my mother complain about being a widow, but she was one who lived with how her circumstances were and didn't let them keep her from going on in life. God is able to provide for us no matter if we are a widow, a widow's child, or anyone else.

Daughter: five years old when father died

• It was hard to watch my brothers have no father figure to look up to who was an upbuilding church member, and no grandfather that cared about their soul's well-being. The ones that they looked up to were on the rocks spiritually themselves. It was helpful to hear someone say, "I don't know why he said that. I am sorry that he had the nerve to say that. We won't sell your mother out unless she says so." Never say, "Well, since the boys are lazy and won't do anything, let's sell out." Or… "His daddy died, so he will never amount to anything now." It did not hit home to my mother until nine months later. It seems the stresses of rebellious grieving teenagers almost did her in. The ministry did not understand that she was sincere when she asked for help, so my siblings had support against her instead of help to respect her. Widows and her children need a good relationship with the church to help carry them through the trials of grief. I hope I do not sound bitter, but truth is stranger than fiction. In real life, experience teaches lessons we never forget.

Anonymous fatherless son

• Having people ask me who my dad is was hard. I did not want pity when they knew who I was or have them feeling sorry for me even when I was only ten. Those people that included us children were special… they treated us in a way that made us feel we were normal. I knew our home life was different than that of my friends, but I didn't want to be in the limelight. Never say, "You are fortunate not to have a strict father." "You probably do more things you want to without a dad." Children can be cruel. But I was reminded they had no idea what we were missing as young teens. I do not remember adults saying things that hurt. My mother had times where she could have blown up. She never said much to us children. If we did find things out, her sense of humor helped us all. When some people tried to take advantage of Mom's situation she was not easily blown over. It was a good example to us children to stick to the right way. Advice to widows: Keep communication lines open with your children. I came home from a five-day-a-week job, from my sixteenth birthday until I got married at twenty-one years. I always felt loved in spite of having to do a lot of work. My mom kept on farming with us children's help even if I was the oldest. We had good times working in our produce patch together. Never expect more from widows' children, and if they make mistakes don't assume it is because they are a widow's child. Sometimes it seemed we were being watched. I did have a heart for the bishop's children at least.

Daughter: ten years old when father died

• My mother needed to work away from home. My friends had baby brothers and sisters born into their home; we didn't. Summer days were long and lonely at times. Mama and Grandmother spoke of death as a gateway to heaven. They talked about heaven a lot and said that our loved ones are resting in God's care. They often asked in their audible prayers that we children would be good children and grow up to be faithful Christians and that not one would miss heaven. Sometimes we were invited to go along with a family on their summer trip for a day. I liked when people shared a memory of my father with me. He was a real person! Never say, "I pity you." Children don't like to be different. Mama was a positive thinking person and related to her experiences with a strong faith in God. She accepted her widowhood as God's direct plan for her life. This attitude made our home a happy, secure, stable home in spite of the difficulties. (I should mention that acceptance is not a once-and-done experience. She labored to keep that attitude.) It is helpful when mothers can be at home with their children, but it is not always possible. When Mother needs to be Father also, the children do well to obey and respect her and not resent her instruction and discipline. Keep up the family worship and pray audibly for your children. Teach them how to pray and talk about God's love and goodness freely. Keep a cheerful attitude.

Daughter: three years old when father died

• Once I was old enough to go to my friends' houses for a meal, I would notice they had their dad at the head of the table instead of their mom. I was sure my dad would come back to us just as Jesus arose and came back to His disciples. When couples came to visit my mom, we really appreciated if the men fixed up our broken bikes, etc. Never for any cause should people say that the reason we turned out the way we did is because we have no dad. After all, what's their excuse for the way they turned out? Mom kept quiet through her grief, which in turn taught us to keep our problems to ourselves. Keep your children as other children and not singled out as some strange specimens. As for the widows, keep in mind that they might not want to remarry.

Daughter: seven years old when father died

• We children had to hitch up the horse on Sunday mornings. Sometimes it was hard to make ends meet, but God always provided.

God has been very, very good to us. On my wedding day there was an empty spot; and I am sure Dad would have enjoyed seeing my first baby… My mom took one day at a time. I am sure there were times she felt very overwhelmed with all the responsibilities that go with raising a family. Since I am married and have a child, I often look back and am amazed by the awesome way she handled things and trusted in the Lord through difficult times. Heaven will surely be worth it all. Heaven looks a whole lot sweeter with one of your loved ones gone on before. One thing I can hardly imagine, though, is how awesome and beautiful it would be to actually have your home in heaven. I wish and pray for all the widows and their children for strength for each new day. God will never forsake us. He is always right here; all we need to do is say, "Lord, help me!"

Daughter: ten years old when father died

• I wished Dad could have been here on our wedding day. I always thought Mom was a very positive person. She of course had her difficult times too, going through her widowhood, but she was always helping other people first, before herself. She used to tell us, "God has beautiful promises for the widows." She was outgoing and made a lot of widow friends. I would encourage widows' children to be obedient and help their mom the best they can.

Anonymous fatherless child

• My father became ill soon after I was out of school. I felt that I missed the opportunity to work with him on the farm and learn many of the skills needed such as welding and the basics of crop care. Many people helped with the farm work during my father's illness and death. People should avoid pushing their help and advice onto those grieving. People relate to grief differently. Some find healing through keeping on with normal responsibilities as much as possible. Those wishing to be helpful should be available but not intrude where they are not wanted. Appreciate others' attempts to extend comfort and help. Overlook the words that seem ill suited to the need. Remember that others want to help because they care. Be alert to the danger of allowing self-pity to control your responses to life and your friends.

Son: seventeen years old when father died

• Seeing my mother need to live alone was hard. My mother related to her widowhood as she did to everything else in life…with calm acceptance. That provided tremendous stability for the family. I was almost an adult when Papa died, and I moved away from home to teach school less than a year later, but I certainly have no memories of life going to pieces in any way.

Daughter: almost twenty years old when father died

• At my age, the hardest part was seeing Mother go through the pain and grief of parting with the one dearest to her. We all have failures, but the death of a loved one is *not* the time to bring up a failure of theirs in the past that has been taken care of. It hurts and is hard to be appreciated. Mother accepted her lot and found fulfillment in reaching out to others. She drew closer yet to God. That was a faithful example of where we need to turn with our heartaches and troubles. Talk about your loved one and share memories; they help to heal. Listen when widows need someone to talk to…they no longer have the one they shared everything with.

Daughter: twenty-seven years old when father died

• I didn't like when all the other schoolchildren made Father's Day gifts or when my friends griped about something they didn't like that their dad did. Now that I am older, I realize how awkward it is to invite company; you have to always invite at least two families so it's not just one man. Now I realize why when people came to visit it was usually two families. It is hard to be mocked, looked down on, or pushed back because, "You don't have a dad." I grew up being used to people giving us things, but now since I am older, I don't like when they make a big spaghetti supper to "benefit the widows" because I don't think we need it and I don't like the big show that they make out of it. I am glad I was as young as I was. I just sort of grew up with "that's just the way our family is" but I think I must have sort of an unconscious longing there for a daddy, because I imagined picking out a daddy from all the men at church, or an uncle that looked the most like Daddy at a family gathering. I never clung to one certain one though; it was always changing. Now that I am older, I don't think I do it as much because I worry that it is sinful. As a child,

I enjoyed all the gifts people gave us, and things they did for us but I know now that Mom didn't want us to grow up with the attitude that people owe it to us, because we don't have a dad. I know Mom didn't tell us when we were little, how much money people gave us. Sometimes I think it would be nice to have a dad when I don't feel like helping feed calves after a day of school teaching or when we have to skip youth activities that are afternoon and evening combined, because we need to help Mom with chores. But I suppose it is good for me to have to do things I don't feel like doing. I often worry about Mom doing skid-loader work by herself while I am at school. I don't think I could stand it if something happened to Mom. I wonder if girls with no dad have a harder time giving up their brothers when they get married, or if I was just too sensitive to our family being pulled apart. I have developed a firm resolve to never get married. After a brother was killed in 2007 and another brother with a baby was killed in 2014, I realize the serious pain you go through. I did not feel that much pain when Daddy died because I was too young. If losing my brothers was that bad, I don't know what Mom must have gone through when Daddy died. I am happy being single and intend to keep it that way.

Daughter: six years old when father died

• Mother did not seem to realize her children were also grieving to a degree. I am sure it was not like a companion, but he was our father. Children should look out for their widowed mother, but the mother needs to respect family mealtime and bedtime of her married children. Especially when the husband is gone all day. If only one of your children come to visit, the son-in-law should not be stuck in a room alone. If grandchildren are going to learn to know their grandparents, how will they if the men and boys are never allowed to sit with their grandmother? It can make the in-laws feel rejected.

Anonymous fatherless daughter

• Only until I saw my mom come to grips with the reality of loss and make it a healthy part of her life, could I know how to do the same. Children learn how to cope with challenges by observing the behavior of others, so the responsibility rests on our shoulders. Allow your children to cry, and cry with them. Encourage your children to talk, recall good times, and humorous incidents. Good memories are precious gifts to a child who feels alone. Be a good listener. Write to them and call when you are away.

Anonymous fatherless son

• The most difficult thing for me was my wedding day. My father was our bishop, and I always expected he would perform my marriage. The most helpful were those who came to visit soon after Dad's death, and would sometimes have evening prayer with us, which we greatly appreciated. My only advice here is to practice the Golden Rule. If you are speaking to the widow's child, speak in love. If you are the widow's child and being spoken to, listen in love. Sometimes our words do not come out like we mean them to. I consider my mother a strong person. No, maybe I should say a person with a settled trust in our Almighty God. I never heard Mom complain about bearing the load, and enduring the pain and grief after Dad died. I am sure her attitude helped me turn to my heavenly Father for strength and submission to accept the loss of my earthly father. With God's help, be open. Share memories good and bad, even if they make you cry. And remember, heaven will surely be worth it all. To think, God Himself will wipe away all our tears (Rev. 21:4).

Child: sixteen years old when father died

IN LOVING MEMORY OF VIRGIL LAMAR HOSTETTER

Our Daddy Was a Christian Man

DARLETTA MARTIN

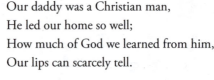

Our daddy was a Christian man,
He led our home so well;
How much of God we learned from him,
Our lips can scarcely tell.

He loved our mother very much.
And filled her life with cheer;
He did such special things for her,
She often called him dear.

He sang our favorite songs with us,
He prayed about our fears,
He listened to our joys and pains,
And kissed away our tears.

He played with us and made us toys,
He filled our box with sand,
We loved to ride along with him,
And help him farm the land.

He memorized God's Word with us,
He helped explain our math;
His many little deeds of love,
So often smoothed our path.

Our daddy was a Christian man,
Who taught us Jesus' way;
We'll follow in his steps to heaven,
And meet him there someday.

Dear Young Children,

As you know, your mother is a widow. That means your father is no longer living. Perhaps you remember your father. But maybe you don't. Maybe you were very young when your father died. Either way, you are a widow's child.

The Bible talks about the widow's children and says God will care for them and be their Father. One fatherless girl felt very sad at nighttime and could not fall asleep. So each night her mother helped her find a verse that mentions the fatherless. Here is part of the list they made:

*Leave thy **fatherless** children, I will preserve them alive: and let the widows trust in Me* (Jeremiah 49:11).

*Thou art the helper of the **fatherless*** (Psalm 10:14).

*For in thee the **fatherless** findeth mercy*. (Hosea 14:3).

*A father of the **fatherless** and a judge of the widows, is God in his holy habitation* (Psalm 68:5).

As the girl read these verses, and others similar to it, she realized that God does see and remember the fatherless children. That was comforting to her and she was able to sleep better.

There are also stories in the Bible about times God provided for widows' families. You can ask your mother to help you look them up and read about them.

Maybe you want to hear more stories about other children like you, whose father died. Do you feel like you are the only family who does not have a father? Do you think life is not fair? Do you feel alone sometimes?

If so, then you will want to read these stories about widows' children. These stories were put in this book just for you.

Sincerely,

"Aunt Tulip"

Jaylon's Daddy Goes to Be With Jesus

SUELLEN J STRITE

Jaylon was a little boy, six years old. He had two brothers and three sisters, and they all liked Daddy a lot.

Daddy was tall. When Jaylon stood up on Daddy's shoulders, he could reach the ceiling! Sometimes Daddy got down on his hands and knees on the floor. Jaylon, Kevin, and Lyndon would climb onto Daddy's back. Then Daddy gave them a fun ride across the floor. The boys all squealed and laughed.

The boys had other fun rides with Daddy. He took them along in the truck to take bull calves to the auction. He took them on rides in the cab tractor to mow hay. One time when they were mowing hay, Daddy saw an unusual animal. Daddy stopped the tractor and helped the boys down. Daddy and Jaylon and Kevin and Lyndon all crept up on the animal very quietly, so that they could get a good look at it. They were afraid it would run away. But it didn't! It lay very still.

"It is a dead animal!" Jaylon said.

But Daddy shook his head. "I don't think so. I think it's an opossum! If we are quiet maybe I can catch it."

Daddy almost grabbed it, but just like that it slipped away. The boys were disappointed.

"I wanted a pet possum!" Jaylon said as they all climbed back into the tractor.

Daddy told Jaylon that a possum would not make a very good pet anyway.

"Then why were you trying to catch it?" Jaylon asked.

Daddy smiled. "I thought we could take it to the house for Mother and the girls to see. Then we would have let it go again. Possums do not like to be penned up and petted. Besides, don't you think you already have enough pets?"

Enough pets? Jaylon counted them on his fingers. They had six baby kittens and two baby lambs. The baby lambs drank milk out of bottles. It was lots of fun to feed them. Jaylon decided they really did not need an opossum after all.

After supper that evening, Daddy played ball with the boys. After Monica and Gwenda helped Mother with the dishes, they came outside too. Daddy helped the girls practice batting the ball.

Then Jaylon said, "Hey, Daddy, can you bat a ball for us?"

They all liked to watch Daddy bat balls. He could bat them far, far away.

So Daddy got the bat and smacked the ball. Whew! Up, up, up, it sailed. Across the tree…and on out across the barn roof! It never had gone that far before.

"Look, Daddy!" Jaylon hollered. "The ball went the whole way across the barn roof!" They all laughed and laughed. It was so much fun when Daddy played.

After dark, they all trooped inside for devotions. Mother held Baby Andrea. Daddy held Jaylon, Kevin, and Lyndon all three. They were sort of squished, but they all wanted to sit on Daddy's lap. Daddy was teaching the boys the 23rd Psalm. It starts out, "The Lord is my shepherd." Daddy had helped Monica and Gwenda learn it when they were younger. Now the boys were learning it.

After devotions, Jaylon told Mother and the girls about the opossum they had seen in the hay field. Daddy got the encyclopedia and found a picture of an opossum. The opossum was hanging upside down in a tree. "How would you like for me to carry you boys up to bed that way?" Daddy asked.

"Yes, yes, I want you to, Daddy!" Kevin yelled.

Jaylon wasn't so sure. Usually Daddy carried him up to bed on his shoulders. What would it be like to be carried like a possum? Jaylon decided to wait and see what it was like for Kevin.

Daddy picked Kevin up by his feet and slung him over his back. Kevin hung upside down on Daddy's back. He laughed the whole way up to his bed. Next Daddy carried Lyndon up like a possum. Jaylon decided it looked like fun. Daddy carried him up next. It *was* fun. He could hardly get done laughing when Daddy plopped him into bed. "Do it again," the three boys begged.

But Daddy said, "Not tonight. It's time for my little Farmer-Boys to get some sleep."

Daddy often called them Farmer-Boys, because they rode along with him in the tractor and helped him feed the calves. It was fun to help Daddy farm. They all liked Daddy a lot.

Then one day, something very, very sad happened. Daddy was in a farm accident. He was hurt so badly that he died.

When Mother first told Jaylon that Daddy died, he did not really believe her. Jaylon remembered when Grandpa died. But Grandpa had been sick for a long time. And besides, Grandpa was much older than Daddy.

Daddy was not very old yet. And he was not sick at all. Jaylon thought it could not be true that Daddy had died.

Pretty soon Grandmother came. "Daddy didn't really die, did he?" Jaylon asked Grandmother.

Grandmother pulled him up onto her lap. "Yes, Jaylon. Daddy got hurt really bad. He was hurt so bad that he died. Now he is with Jesus."

Grandmother's eyes looked funny, like she was crying. But grandmothers don't cry, do they?

Jaylon did not cry, but he was very unhappy and afraid. Why did Daddy die? Who would give him tractor rides now? Who would play ball with him? Who would carry him up to bed at night?

That day was all mixed up. Lots of people came. Some people brought food. Almost everyone was crying. The people all talked to Mother. Jaylon did not have a chance to talk to Mother. He was glad that Grandpap and

Grandmother and Aunt Evaleen stayed all day. Grandmother read stories to Jaylon and Kevin and Lyndon. Aunt Evaleen gave them swing rides.

That night, all the people left, except Aunt Evaleen. Jaylon was glad that Aunt Evaleen stayed to sleep at their house. But he was still sad. Mother held Jaylon. She looked tired and very, very sad. He had never seen Mother cry before. But today she was crying almost all day. Jaylon knew that Mother had liked Daddy too. Daddy often did nice things for Mother. He helped her in the garden. Sometimes he gave her pretty cards that made her smile.

Now Daddy was not here to make Mother smile. Mother held Jaylon and told him that Daddy is with Jesus. "Daddy is very happy with Jesus," Mother said. "We are sad because we wish Daddy could be with us, but if we love Jesus, someday we will go to heaven, too."

It was hard to go to sleep that night. Jaylon tried to remember that Daddy was happy. But Jaylon was so sad. Finally, he just cried and cried. Aunt Evaleen sat on the edge of Jaylon's bed and patted him. Eventually, he went to sleep.

Two days later, Mother told Jaylon that today would be Daddy's funeral. Jaylon remembered Grandpa's funeral. It had been a church service. Then they had buried Grandpa.

Jaylon did not want to go to a funeral for Daddy. He wanted Daddy to be here with him. But he went along with Mother and Aunt Evaleen to the funeral. It was a very sad day. Everyone in church was crying. After the church service, everyone went out to the graveyard. There they buried Daddy. Jaylon thought this was awful. He did not want to watch, so he looked the other way.

That evening, Mother explained to Jaylon that the men had not really buried Daddy. "That was only Daddy's body that they buried," she said. "Daddy is really in heaven with Jesus."

"But how can Daddy be in heaven while his body is being buried?" Jaylon asked.

"It is very hard to understand," Mother said. "But when Daddy died, he did not need his body anymore. God will give him a new body in heaven. Daddy got hurt the other day. But now he is with Jesus and he is not hurting anymore. We are sad because we miss Daddy, but we want to remember that Daddy will never be sad again. He will always be happy in heaven with Jesus."

"But how will Daddy get up to heaven?" Jaylon asked. Heaven seemed so far away. How could Daddy be hurt and get up to heaven?

Mother smiled a little. "Do you remember the Bible story about Lazarus?"

Jaylon nodded.

"Well," Mother said, "the Bible says that when Lazarus died, the angels carried him to Abraham's bosom. I like to think the angels carried Daddy to be with Jesus, don't you?"

Jaylon nodded again. If the angels had carried Daddy to be with Jesus, Jaylon wished he could have seen them. He wished he could ask Daddy what it felt like. He wished Daddy could be here right now! He did not want to go to bed another night without Daddy! Jaylon began to cry.

Then Mother started crying. And Monica and Gwenda, and Kevin and Lyndon. Baby Andrea saw everyone else crying, so she started to cry too! Jaylon had never seen Mother crying before Daddy died. Now Mother seemed to be crying all the time.

Soon, though, Mother wiped her eyes and blew her nose. "Come children, let's pray and ask God to help us not to be so sad."

After they prayed, Mother said, "Now let's try to say the 23rd Psalm. If Daddy was here, he would want you to finish memorizing it. Let's all say it together, this time."

The Lord is my shepherd; I shall not want. He maketh me to lie down in green pastures; he leadeth me beside the still waters. He restoreth my soul: he leadeth me in the paths of righteousness for his name's sake. Yea, though I walk through the valley of the shadow of death, I will fear no evil: for thou art with me; thy rod and thy staff they comfort me. Thou preparest a table before me in the presence of mine enemies: thou anointest my head with oil; my cup runneth over. Surely goodness and mercy shall follow me all the days of my life: and I will dwell in the house of the Lord forever.

The next several days and weeks were very different for Jaylon. He did not like going to bed without Daddy. He did not like that he could not take rides with Daddy anymore. He did not like that Daddy was not here to play ball anymore. He did not like going to church on Sunday without

Daddy. Jaylon was very sad.

But there were people who tried to help Jaylon and his family to have some happy times. Aunt Evaleen came and slept at their house every night. She helped Jaylon and his brothers get ready for bed each evening. Even though Daddy couldn't be here to carry him to bed like a possum anymore, it was special to have Aunt Evaleen tuck him into bed.

Grandpap and Grandmother came to Jaylon's house almost every day. Grandpap read Jaylon and Kevin and Lyndon stories. Grandmother helped Monica and Gwenda with the dishes and laundry.

Jaylon's uncles came and did Daddy's field work for Mother. The uncles took Jaylon and Kevin and Lyndon on tractor rides. That was fun.

Some other friends took Jaylon's whole family for a picnic. Then they took a walk on a trail. One of the men carried Jaylon on his shoulders. Jaylon liked that. It almost felt like Daddy was carrying him.

On Sunday at church, some of the other boys' fathers shook Jaylon's hand and talked to him. Since Jaylon's daddy was in heaven, he liked when other daddies talked to him.

At first, when Daddy had died, Jaylon thought he would never have any fun again. He thought he would never feel like smiling or being happy again.

But Jaylon learned that the Lord was taking care of him and his family. They would always miss Daddy. They would never forget all the fun they had with Daddy. But God was taking care of them. Other people were very kind and helpful.

Jaylon found out that he could be happy even though Daddy was in heaven. And he wanted to always love Jesus like Daddy did. Then someday he could go to heaven, too. Then he would be happy for always!

God Cares for Little Girls

KAREN LOUISE MARTIN

"Beep! Beep! Beep!" The persistent alarm clock pierced through Karen's deep sleep.

Thump! Karen's feet hit the carpeted floor. Why was Mom and Dad's alarm clock beeping? In a moment she was in the next room and switched it off. She padded barefooted back to the bedroom she shared with her sisters. By then Laura, Kaitlyn, and Janea were rubbing their sleepy eyes.

At that time their family consisted of four girls and a baby boy. Mom and Dad were in their mid-thirties. Karen and Laura were eleven and nine. They were Mom's big helpers. Kaitlyn, a small stocky girl with lots of spunk, had her seventh birthday just the day before. These three girls were blond-haired with blue or green eyes. Four-year-old Janea was a kind of her own. With dark hair and brown eyes, she favored her father. At five months old, Daryl was a baby doll: blond and blue-eyed with a round face and chubby cheeks. He was everyone's joy.

Being bothered about where Mom was, the four girls didn't think to dress for the day. Coming behind the others, Karen thought of taking a dress downstairs with her. "Hmm, which one should I wear?" Today was the big day. After school, the family had plans to travel to the state of Virginia. Everything was laid out or packed and ready to go. She grabbed an ordinary school dress and padded down behind her sisters.

The girls stopped abruptly at the living room doorway. What was Grandma Ada here for? The girls loved Grandma Ada. She was not related to them, but she was widowed and lived alone in the house next door, so they counted her part of their family. But…Grandma Ada wasn't Mom!

"Where's Mom?" the girls asked.

"Come here, girls. I have something to tell you." Grandma Ada had baby Daryl in her arms as she sat in the recliner. Four pairs of confused and worried eyes gazed upon her. "Mom is in the hospital because your dad was in an accident. He was going to an ambulance call and they hit an ice patch."

"Was he in the ambulance?" Laura interrupted.

"No, he was still in the van heading toward the ambulance building," replied Grandma Ada.

"Is the driver in the hospital, too?" Karen wondered.

"I don't know."

"Will he be better soon?" Kaitlyn asked in childlike faith.

Grandma Ada swallowed, trying to control herself. "I will let Mom tell you when she gets home. She should be here soon."

Grandma Ada's heart was breaking apart. Tears wanted to overtake her. These dear children were still innocent to the fact that their daddy had left this earth, never to see them again. She couldn't bring herself to break this terrible news. Unknown to the children, much had happened while they slept peacefully. Early in the morning Mom was contacted by phone and told to come to the hospital. She was told her husband was in an accident and further details would be told in person. In panic, Mom called Grandma Ada and asked her to come and stay with the children. Ada advised Mom to take someone with her. "You don't know what it'll be. You might want someone with you." So, two phone calls later, she had a neighbor friend to give her a ride and her brother-in-law to go with her.

After Mom left, Grandma Ada busied herself folding laundry that had been left unattended the night before. Her mind was spinning with the possibilities of what could be in store for this young family. The memories of losing her own husband six years earlier was still fresh in her mind. "Surely not, Lord," was her prayer.

As she busied herself in the quiet kitchen, she was startled to hear a knock on the door. Who could that be? Her heart jumped when she saw the people dressed in uniforms. This was not a good sign. In her heart she knew this could mean only one thing.

"Good morning," she greeted them.

"Good morning. Are you Mrs. Nolt?" they asked.

"No, I'm the neighbor lady. Mrs. Nolt was called to the hospital."

"Oh!" they said looking bewildered. Why had the hospital called out? Grandma Ada could wait no longer, "Is it over for Mr. Nolt?"

"Yes, it is. He was instantly killed when the van hit an ice patch, flipped on its side, and hit a tree."

All was silent as tears flowed down Grandma Ada's face. Her worst fear was reality. How would this precious young family live without their daddy and husband? Mr. Nolt had also been a great help to Ada since her own husband had passed away. Each day she had seen him arrive home to his family. It was hard to grasp that she would no longer see this man. And these dear children! This young baby boy in her arms would grow up without remembering his daddy. Surely this was all a mistake!

The officers moved into the house. They realized they could not leave with Ada in this state. They would have to tell the children.

As Grandma Ada sensed that they felt obligated to stay, she gathered her emotions together. "The children are still in bed. I will keep myself in control. You are welcome to move on."

After they were assured she was okay, they expressed their sympathy and left.

Tears flowed again as the door closed behind them. Overwhelming sorrow overtook her. "God, why would You allow this to happen? This is too much for a young mother with a long future before her. Why, God? Please be with Mrs. Nolt as she receives this dreadful news."

It was with this great sorrow that Grandma greeted the dear children that snowy morning. She couldn't find the strength to tell them the whole story, but she tried to answer their questions the best she could.

"Will we go to school? Will Daddy be well enough to go to Virginia?"

"No, probably not." She arose from her chair. "Let's make breakfast for everyone."

Breakfast was over and Mom was still not home. Karen was in the bathroom brushing her teeth vigorously. Many thoughts passed through her mind. Suddenly a small voice in her heart whispered, "Suppose Daddy would die?" Her heart froze; the voice was so real! "But no, surely not. God would not take a daddy so young. He was only thirty-six years old." Ah, she felt better as she comforted herself.

"Suppose he would die?" whispered the small voice again. Again, she froze, and again she tried to shrug it off. But the voice was persistent, "Suppose Daddy would die?"

All in a moment's time, these thoughts raced through her mind. Then she heard the front door open. For a minute she froze and listened. All was quiet. Soft voices spoke that could not be understood from her place at the bathroom sink. She quickly finished as Laura came to the door. Her face was white. "Dad died."

"No, that's not true," Karen responded.

Right behind Laura were Mom and Karen's sisters.

"Mom, is it true?" Karen inquired.

"Yes, Karen, it is," Mom replied. A bombshell fell on these young, tender hearts. How could Dad be gone?

As they reentered the kitchen, Grandma Ada saw a sight she would never forget. The look of shock and dread was written all over their sweet little faces. She wanted to gather them in her arms and smooth the hurt away, but it is only God who can heal a broken heart.

In the kitchen stood the sad little party. Uncle Nevin and the neighbor lady were still there. She had worked with Mr. Nolt through the ambulance and was a family friend. She also felt the pain of loss. No words were said as silent tears of sorrow flooded each heart. "What is to be done next?" was the question.

From there, many heart-wrenching phone calls were made. Again and again the piercing words were said, "Mr. Nolt was killed in an accident."

Aunt Sarah came as soon as she could so Grandma Ada could go home. Together Mom and Aunt Sarah grieved as they tried to grasp the life-changing news.

In the afternoon friends, neighbors, and family gathered in what they always thought was a large kitchen and living room. It was full of people!

Like mice, the four girls sat on the couch hidden behind many black-attired women. Many looks of sympathy were sent their way. Karen thought, "Just go away! This isn't happening! Daddy will come home soon."

Some of the ladies were brave enough to give them hugs. As one dear neighbor lady gave Karen a hug, Karen's first tears filled her eyes. Her heart had been touched, but her mind still screamed, "Go away! Leave me alone. I will not cry!"

A few days later were the viewing and funeral. With numb minds and bleeding hearts they made it through. It was only by God's love and grace that Mom kept from falling apart. During the viewing the girls did not sit in the family line. They rebelled to all the crying and sympathy. Karen's thoughts were, "This is all a dream. Let's get this over with so life can be normal again." She could not grasp that it would never be the same again. She felt no connection to the man in the coffin. It seemed her daddy was alive somewhere. Somehow he would come back, wouldn't he?

I am Karen in this story. Eleven long, yet short, years have passed since that fateful morning when I found out that sometimes God does take little girls' daddies. But in those years, I have found out something else as well. *If a daddy dies, we don't want him to stay dead forever, so we want God to take him. And when God takes a little girl's daddy, He will care for her and comfort her and never leave her.* We still miss Daddy. At times we gather for prayer at the dinner table and I get the feeling that someone is missing. Without Dad, our family is not complete. Yet God has helped us, and we have found healing. It is only through His help that we did not become a bitter, unhappy family.

If you struggle with bitterness and feel like life is not fair, remember God has a special plan for you. He is preparing you for His heavenly splendor. Even if your earthly father died, God will be your Father, and He will never be taken away!

When God Was My Father

"ROSE'S FRIEND"

I will never forget the day my father died. I was just a little girl then, only eight years old. But the memories still linger. How well I remember my grandfather's strong hand on my shoulder as he said with tears in his eyes, "Rose, dear, your father has gone to heaven to be with Jesus. He doesn't hurt anymore and he is happy." But then Grandpa could not talk anymore. Grandpa always seemed so strong and well...so grown up. But he was crying, and so was Grandma.

I turned to look at Mother sitting on the chair in the corner of the living room. She smiled a sad smile at me and held her arms out toward me. I sat with her on the recliner a long time that morning and watched as people came and went. It was confusing and strange.

At Father's funeral, our minister, Brother James, read a verse that said God will be like a Father to us now. That was hard to understand, too. How could God be my Father? How could God, whom I could not see be my Father? I felt mixed up.

It made us sad that our father died, but Mother and the rest of us tried to go on as best as we could. There were days I did not think about it so much, but there were other days that I missed Father very badly. Sometimes I would see a shiny tear on Mother's face, but usually she was wearing a smile. When I felt really sad, Mother would comfort me. She would tell me how happy Father was in heaven and how she wanted us all to grow up to be good men and women so we could be with Father someday. Sometimes she would remind us of that same verse that Brother James had read at Father's funeral. The one about God being a Father to us.

But how can it be, I wondered. How can God take care of Mother and us children like our father had?

A few months after Father died, I suddenly remembered that it would soon be Mother's birthday. Father always did something nice for Mother's birthday. Nothing really special, but he helped us sing to her and we did other little things that made Mother smile. It was a happy day, but now…Father was gone. How could Mother's birthday ever be the same?

Sure enough, the day of Mother's birthday arrived. I wanted so badly to do something special for Mother. But what could a little eight-year-old girl do? I made her a card, and I even helped my little sisters, Jewel and Joy, make cards for Mother. That was nice, but it did not seem like enough. Then I thought of a plan. Maybe I could make something special for Mother for lunch. Without a lot more thinking or planning, I took a paper and pencil to Mother.

"Mother, can you write on this paper what you would like for lunch, because it's your birthday?" I said eagerly.

Mother's eyes looked a little sad. "Oh, Rose, how could you get lunch for me?" But then she smiled and said, "All right, I'll think of something."

Mother thought for just a moment. Then she wrote something on the paper. It did not take long at all. I could hardly wait to see what she wrote. Mother slowly folded the paper and handed it to me. "Rose, you are a dear daughter," she said, as she smiled one of her special smiles to me.

I quickly unfolded the paper. In her neat handwriting, Mother had written one word: subs. For a moment my heart jumped. That sounded delicious! What a good idea! But just as quickly I felt very, very sad. How could I possibly get subs for our lunch? There was just no way that could happen. Why had I ever asked Mother what she wanted? Oh, how I missed Father! If he were still here, I could just run the paper out to the barn and show him. He would help me out. I knew he would.

But Father was gone. And I suddenly missed him very much. Here it was, Mother's birthday, and I could not even do anything for her.

But Mother understood. "It's all right, Rose," she said softly.

I sadly went back to my play, but my heart was heavy. Why did God let Father die? God said he would be a Father to us, but I just could not see how it worked. I needed Father.

Suddenly I heard Mother talking in the kitchen. "Sure, come in." I ran to see who had come to see us.

It was Sister Sarah, one of the women from church. And oh, look, she had a box in her arms. Mother held the door open for her and Sister Sarah set her box carefully on the table.

"I remembered just this morning that it was your birthday, and I wanted to bring you a meal," Sister Sarah was saying. "But I hardly had time to make a big meal for you. I hope you like subs," she said, almost apologizing.

Mother's mouth and my mouth dropped open at the same time. Subs? It was almost too good to be true. But look! Sister Sarah took out of her box a package of rolls. The long kind that you make subs with. And then meat, two kinds. Then cheese, tomatoes, lettuce, and onions. And even a little container of mayonnaise.

I was too surprised to speak. How could this have happened? How did she know? I was still surprised when I heard Sister Sarah say, "Well, I better be on my way. God bless your day." The door clicked softly shut behind her.

Mother just stood in the kitchen and looked at the food on the table. I looked at Mother and then at the food. And then at Mother again. Did I see right? Mother had a little tear in her eye, didn't she? Why yes, there it went down her cheek. But she was smiling at me, so I knew she was all right.

"Rose," Mother began. "Do you remember that verse that Brother James read at Father's funeral about God being a Father to you? Do you remember how he said God would take care of you children and me just like a father would? Rose, God is wonderful. Just look at how He provided for us today. Right here, Rose. You wanted to make subs for lunch, and you were sad because you did not know how to do it. But just look. God reminded Sister Sarah that it was my birthday. Then He helped her think of all we needed for subs. Isn't that amazing!"

My head spun as I tried to comprehend it all. God was my Father. He really was. He did for us what Father would have done if he were here. He answered my prayers before I even prayed them. And that meant God heard me ask Mother what she wanted for lunch. That meant God was here, right here in the living room with Mother and me.

Oh, I was still overwhelmed with surprise and joy when I heard Mother say, "Why, look at that, it is almost lunchtime. Shall we set the table, Rose?" And in a daze, I reached for the plates.

"Thank you, God, for being my Father," my heart sang. I looked at Mother. Her happy face made me take a little skip as I went back for the cups. God is so good.

Gifted Twice

DAVID HEGE

"Mother, Evan has a birthday coming up next week. Shall we ask him what he wants for a birthday gift or is that too risky?" Daddy looked at me with a grin. "What do eleven-year-old boys need, Evan?" he asked. "A new doll baby? Tea party set? Coloring book? You'll have to tell me. I never had an eleven-year-old son before."

I had my answer ready. "I want a puppy." I knew Daddy didn't like dogs, so I talked fast. "Uncle Peter's dog had six puppies and Aaron told me he would sell one to me for twenty dollars. A puppy would be useful, Daddy. Really useful. We could train him to do lots of things."

Daddy looked surprised. "You did think of something. But who is going to feed it? Who is going to train it? Have you thought about that? Who is going to keep it off the road?"

"Daddy!" I laughed. "I'll take care of it. Me and Douglas will."

"Hm-m-m." That was all Daddy said. I asked him later if he had talked to Uncle Peter yet, but he only said birthday gifts were supposed to be a surprise. "You know a dog can be a nuisance," he reminded me. I didn't know what he was thinking. He wouldn't say.

On the morning of my birthday, I was disappointed to merely find a shoe box beside my plate. It wasn't heavy. I tried to act excited as I cut the tape. Inside the box, there was a crisp, twenty-dollar bill and a note

269

that read, "Happy Birthday, Evan! You and I are going to go talk to Uncle Peter this morning. From Daddy."

I jumped up. "Right now, Daddy?" I asked.

Daddy smiled broadly. "May I eat my oatmeal first? I'm hungry. We'll go right after breakfast."

It was hard to choose just one puppy. All six were cute. I finally settled on a tan and white female. Douglas and I had her named by the time we got home. We called her Sandy. "Now, boys," Daddy reminded us, "if you want to train your dog to have good manners, you will need to do it while she is young. Mother is worried about her flower bed, so that will be one of the first things to work on. Teach Sandy that the flower bed is off limits."

"I will," I promised. "I want to teach her to do tricks, too." After supper that evening, Douglas and I hurried back outside to play with Sandy. Daddy came out and helped us build a house for Sandy out of straw bales. Daddy stayed out with us until bedtime. He laughed when he heard me telling Sandy to sit, for the fiftieth time that evening. "Evan," he said, "puppies are like little boys. You can't teach them everything in one day. You'll have to keep working on her."

"I thought you didn't like dogs, Daddy," I said as we walked to the house. "And yet you spent all evening playing with Sandy!"

"I don't really like dogs," Daddy said smiling down at me. "But I love my boys. If they want a puppy, why should I say no? I think Sandy will be well taken care of. Maybe I will even decide to like her."

I will remember that evening for the rest of my life. The next morning, Daddy took three bull calves to the auction. Douglas and I were supposed to be helping Mother and my sister Jenny pull weeds in the garden. We heard a lot of sirens and then things were quiet. Daddy wasn't coming home. "I am going into the house to call him," Mother said finally. "I wonder if there was an accident and he is sitting in a traffic jam." She came out of the house a little later, looking worried. "He won't answer his phone," she said. "I hope he is all right."

He wasn't all right. A police came and talked to Mother. She was crying when she came back over to the garden. It was Daddy who had been in the accident. A semi-truck had crossed over into his lane of traffic and crashed right into his truck. Daddy had been killed instantly.

The rest of that day and the next few weeks are hazy in my memory. A lot of people came and went. Some of our cows were sold. Two of Uncle Peter's big boys came over every morning and evening to help us do our chores. If we needed more help, Uncle Peter came as well. Douglas and I spent hours playing with Sandy. Somehow, playing with Sandy made us feel closer to Daddy. I often wished we could show him how smart Sandy was.

Just for an example, we came home from church one Sunday and, like usual, Sandy tried to jump up on us. None of us liked her messing up our Sunday clothes, and Mother had told us several times that we should teach our puppy better manners.

"Sandy," I said sternly, "go sit on the porch." Since we had just started teaching her to obey that command, I wasn't sure if she would obey. But she did!

"That's quite a dog!" Mother actually smiled, something she rarely did those days.

"Yep. You should see what all she does. She is the best birthday gift Daddy ever gave to me. I wish he could see her now."

That made Mother look sad, and I almost wished I hadn't said it. But it was true. Suddenly, I thought of something else…Sandy was the *last* birthday gift Daddy would ever give to me. I had never thought of that before. (Two years later, I did get a birthday gift from Daddy again. I'll tell you about that after a while.)

None of us wanted to go back to school that fall, but of course we had to. At least I got to see my friends every day again. Jerry was one of my best friends. He was Isaac Diller's boy, and they lived on the farm just west of us. Mother gave me permission to invite him over one evening. We had a lot of fun with Sandy. "I wish I could have a dog," Jerry said wistfully. "Mother would let me have one, but Dad's too stingy. All he can think about is work, work, work, and besides, he probably wouldn't be nice to a dog anyway if we did have one. I can hardly stand the way he beats the cows sometimes." Jerry sighed. "Sometimes I feel like using the cow cane on him, just to show him what those cows must feel like."

I was shocked. I had always liked Isaac Diller. He had told us more than once to be sure to call him if we needed anything. "Just be glad you have a dad!" I spluttered. "So what about a dog?!"

Jerry shrugged. "Dads aren't everything," he scoffed. "In fact, if I don't get home soon, he'll probably call and tell me it is bedtime. He makes me go to bed early, so I can get up early to help with the milking. He reminds me of those slave drivers in that book Sister Elizabeth is reading to us at school right now." Jerry reluctantly got to his feet and brushed the straw off his trousers. "Want to run north to freedom with me?" he joked. "We could start tonight."

That conversation stayed in my mind. Isaac Diller was a husky man, and every time I saw him after that, I thought of those big burly slave drivers. But... Isaac was nice! Douglas and I sat with him at church sometimes, and he would talk to us just like we were men. When I got a little older, I found out that he was the one who owned our farm. After Daddy died, he told Mother that if she wanted to keep living on the farm, the rent would be a lot less. As far as treating animals nice, I don't know about that. But I do know he treated Sandy nice one day.

It happened on my thirteenth birthday. Sandy was just a little over two years old. "Is that Sandy?" I asked Douglas that morning as we came out of the house after breakfast. It almost sounded like a person was crying down in the hay field. We followed the sound, and found Sandy in the fence row beside the hay field. Her front leg was caught in an old, abandoned coyote trap. "Oh, no." I stooped down to look. Her leg was bloody, and obviously broken. Sandy's eyes were glazed with pain as she made another pathetic struggle to free her leg, whimpering all the while. "Hold still, Sandy." I laid my hand on her head. "Let me check it out." I looked at the heavy trap, but I couldn't figure out how it worked. I tried prying the jaws apart, but Sandy growled and snapped at me. Then she jerked back and forth again, trying to get loose.

Douglas was in tears. "I am going to have to get help," I told him desperately. "You stay here and try to keep her calm. I'll run to the house and call Uncle Peter."

Nobody answered the phone at Uncle Peter's. "What shall I do?" I wailed to Mother. "We have to get her out of that trap before she hurts herself worse."

272

"Try Isaac Diller," she suggested. "Maybe he would be able to come over."

Isaac? Jerry still talked about how mean he was to animals. But I had no other option. I quickly dialed his number. "Sure, Evan," he rumbled in his deep voice. "I'll be right over. In the south field, you say?"

Isaac whistled when he saw Sandy. "I don't know, boys." He lifted the sore leg gently. "This leg is chewed up bad. It would probably be an act of mercy to put her to sleep. She lost a lot of blood."

"No!" I choked. "Please, at least get her loose so we can see how bad it is."

Isaac bent down and examined the trap. Then he went to his truck and got a heavy pair of welding gloves and pliers. "Can you hold her, Evan?" he asked, pulling on the gloves. "I think I can squeeze the trap open with my pliers. She won't bite through these gloves, but she will need to hold still so I can work."

I looked Sandy in the eye. "Freeze," I commanded, squeezing her muzzle shut. Isaac's big muscles bulged as he pinched the pliers. He used his other hand and gradually worked the mangled leg out of the rusty trap. With her leg free, Sandy seemed to lose her fight. She just lay there panting and moaning.

Isaac ran careful fingers up Sandy's leg. "It's bad, boys." He looked up at us. "What do you think?"

"Could the vet fix it?" I asked, my voice wobbling.

Isaac studied Sandy a long minute. "We'll see what he says," he decided at last. "Run to the house and let your mother know where we are going. We'll drive Sandy over to Doc Dan's pet emergency room and see what he says."

The vet's assistant gave Sandy a shot to sedate her. Soon, Doc Dan himself came into the room. He pulled on a pair of latex gloves and spent a long time cleaning Sandy's leg. Finally, he looked up. "This your dog, Mr. Diller?" he asked Isaac. "She has a nasty break, but I am 95% confident that I can have her up and running around again. It's your call. She will not be a cheap dog by the time I am through with her."

Isaac looked at us like he hardly knew what to say. "The dog is not mine," he said finally. "She belongs to these two young men. What do you think the total bill will be? Can you give us an estimate?"

Doctor Dan seemed to notice us for the first time. Douglas still had tears in his eyes, and I hoped I didn't. "You boys look familiar." The vet studied our faces. "I think I should know you. Who is your dad? Do you want to call him and see what he says?"

Did I ever! "Our father was Loren Miller," I answered, willing my voice to stay steady. "You still come out to our place sometimes to check a cow for Uncle Peter. I don't know what Mother would say." I looked helplessly at Isaac.

"Ah, yes." The vet's eyes softened behind his thick glasses. "Loren Miller. You boys had a wonderful father. He was one of my favorite clients." He drummed his fingers on the table, then suddenly snapped to attention. "Okay, boys," he said briskly. "I need to get Sandy into surgery as soon as possible. We'll keep her in here today to make sure she wakes up feeling well. You come back in at 5:00 this evening, and she should be ready to take home. I'm warning you, though, she'll have to take it easy for the rest of the summer. See you, boys. Five o'clock." He turned to his assistant and started telling her what to do.

"But...but the bill," I stammered. "I need to ask Mother first."

"Your father already paid the bill," the vet answered. "Ask no questions for now. I need to get this dog into surgery. Come back at five, and I have a story to tell you about your father. Now scat! I want to work!"

"I am as puzzled as you are," Isaac said on the way home. "I'll be back over to your place late this afternoon to take you in to get Sandy. I guess we will have to wait until then to find out what the vet meant."

Sandy seemed glad to see us when we walked into the pet clinic, at 4:55. Her front leg had a heavy bandage on it. "She should be good as new in two or three months," Doc Dan told us. "Just make sure she doesn't find any more coyote traps!"

"Thanks a lot, Doc," Isaac said gratefully. "Do you have your bill ready for us? This dog means a lot to these boys. I understand their father gave her to Evan exactly two years ago today for his birthday. He died in the accident the next day."

"I see." Doc Dan looked at me. "Well, Evan, this is the second time your father gave you this dog for your birthday gift. If it hadn't been for him, this dog would most likely be buried by now."

"Douglas and I wanted to hear that story," I reminded him.

The vet nodded. "It must have been almost eight years ago," he began. "I was coming home from an emergency farm call about 1:30 in the morning. There was a foot of snow on the ground, but the roads were fairly good. Anyway, I must have dozed off while I was driving past your farm. I missed the corner, and my truck landed in the ditch beside the road. The one tire hit the concrete culvert head and blew out. I was sitting in a snowdrift about two feet deep, with a flat tire, five miles from home."

"Say, I almost think I remember that," I said. "Daddy took you the rest of the way home, didn't he?"

"He sure did," Doc Dan continued. "I hated to knock on his door at that time in the morning, but I didn't know what else to do. But that isn't all. The next afternoon, one of my friends brought me out to fix the tire and dig the truck out of the snow. I wasn't looking forward to the job. But we found that truck sitting in front of your dad's shop with a brand-new tire already mounted. That surprised me! Your dad wouldn't let me pay a cent for the tire nor for all his hard work. He told me he might be the one who needs help the next time."

"Today," the vet looked at us over the top of his glasses. "Today, I finally had a chance to repay your father. That makes my day. I get past your place sometimes, boys. I'll stop in every now and then to check up on Sandy. Take good care of her!"

"We will," Douglas and I both said at the same time. "And thank you, Doctor Dan," I added. "I often think of Daddy when I see Sandy. Now I'll think of you, too. If you ever run off the road in front of our house again, I will be glad to help you."

"Thanks, young man," he smiled at me. "It's good to know that."

Isaac helped us get Sandy nestled into a nest of straw. I couldn't understand why Jerry talked so ugly about his father. He was one of the nicest men I knew.

As soon as Isaac left, Mother and Jenny came out to the barn to see Sandy. Mother almost cried when we told her what Doc Dan had said about Daddy. "I remember that day." She looked out to the road. "Daddy had a lot of work to do, but he wanted to take care of that truck first. He never dreamed that his kindness to the vet would be returned to his boys someday. *A birthday gift from Daddy.* I like that, Evan."

"This reminds me of two years ago," Douglas said wistfully. "We had Sandy up here in the barn and Daddy came out and played with us all evening. Remember how he used to…" We ended up talking for nearly an hour.

"Well," Mother said as she slowly stood up and brushed the straw off her dress. "We should be going in for supper." We all went into the house and washed up.

Jenny started setting the table. "What's wrong?" I asked, when I heard her gasp.

"I set a place for Daddy!" she exclaimed. "I've done that before, but it has been awhile. It just seems like he will be here this evening."

I knew what she meant. "Just leave the place for him," I suggested. "We can pretend he is here." It was easy to pretend that evening.

The Way of the Transgressor

DAVID HEGE

"Good job, Sandy." I rested my hand briefly on the furry head as I chained the holding area gate. Nearly five years had passed since her encounter with the coyote trap. She still carried a slight limp, but it didn't seem to hinder her in any way. She was a superb cow dog.

A lot had happened in those five years. When I got out of school, Uncle Peter decided Douglas and I were capable of handling the farm with my older sister Jenny's help. Uncle Peter's boys, who had been helping us, both got married that year, so the timing was about right. On top of that, Uncle Peter had been ordained deacon in our church, making him a very busy man. He still came over every now and then to check up on things. He was also on call if we ran into a problem we couldn't handle.

Jenny was waiting for me to start milking. I went into the milking parlor and we soon had the cows flowing through smoothly. "You taking us to Clear View some evening?" she asked brightly, partway through milking. "You are remembering they are having evangelistic meetings there this week, aren't you? Douglas and I want to go."

I had already forgotten. "I don't know," I said. "Clear View is so far away. There really isn't any reason we need to go. It will just make another late night. As far as I'm concerned, we can skip it."

Jenny looked hurt. "Mother even said she would like to go one evening," she said. "I guess if she goes along, we can have Douglas drive for us since he has his permit now. I was hoping to go several nights though. What do I need to do to get you motivated? Want a sticker?" She flashed me a smile. "When you were a little boy, you would do almost anything for me if I promised you a sticker."

I had to give in to her. She is like that—irresistible. "Well, I'll try to work it in some evening," I promised. "Not this evening, though. Jerry Diller and I want to hike on the Appalachian Trail this evening."

"I am guessing you would get home earlier if you went to Clear View instead," Jenny said pointedly. "Really, Evan, it is none of my business, but I think you get with Jerry more often than what's good for you. I happen to know that Mother thinks so too. He isn't exactly what you would call a good influence. Did you tell Mother what you want to do this evening?"

I ignored her question. "What's wrong with Jerry? I can't stand the way he talks about his father, but other than that?"

"You answer that," Jenny challenged. "You know him better than I do."

I gave her the silent treatment.

"Look, Evan, I didn't mean to upset you," Jenny said in a carefully controlled voice. "But if you don't talk, I am going to. You know as well as I do that Jerry was excommunicated from our church fellowship. He is not a conscientious young man. None of us like the way he is rubbing off on you."

"I don't like that the church kicked him out, either," I shot back. "But Jerry says he doesn't even care. He was tired of being picked on all the time. I know the feeling. It took you and Mother a long time to get over it when I started wearing a belt. Uncle Peter didn't get over it yet. I am sick and tired of it."

"Why?" Jenny asked simply.

"What's wrong with wearing a belt?" I huffed. "The church allows it."

The look Jenny gave to me just about did me in. She didn't know it (Or did she? Never can tell with Jenny.), but I could hardly stand to have her so disappointed in me. She had filled an important place in my life since Daddy died. She knew me inside out. I couldn't tell you how she did it, but she had taken control of my life so completely that the question,

"What would Jenny think?" was almost more of a deterrent to me than, "What would God think?" That sounds almost sacrilegious when you put it on paper, but I don't know how else to say it.

Jenny was still looking at me. "Mother and I both decided it was time to quit nagging you about wearing a belt," she said quietly. "We could see that it just aggravated you, so we knew your conscience was working." (She ignored the shocked look on my face.) "Evan, the church does not forbid wearing belts. You are right." She looked thoughtful. "Maybe we need to be explaining ourselves a little better. I am sure you are aware of the fact that there are many in our church fellowship, including our ministers, who still appreciate the use of suspenders, considering them to be a part of the conservative, traditional dress we value."

"But the church does not require it," I insisted stubbornly.

"But your parents did," Jenny answered quietly. "It is the attitude of disrespect for parental conviction and teaching that bothers us. Am I making myself clear?" She looked at me imploringly. "I still remember how shocked you were the first time Jerry showed up here in a short-sleeved bold-striped shirt and light blue jeans. You knew his father would not approve. We feel the same way about you wearing a belt. Your father would not approve. I know he is not here, but we are still disappointed that you are not respecting his convictions."

"Huh," I scoffed. "I could name more than one person in our church who wears suspenders and doesn't act like a Christian."

"So could I," Jenny agreed. "But that is completely beside the point. Can you name a genuine Christian young man in our church fellowship who changed from wearing suspenders to wearing a belt against his parent's wishes who has no other indications of rebellion in his life? I can't."

I didn't answer. She wasn't being unreasonable.

"It is time for me to stop," she said. "But think about it. When a young man does not respect his parents' convictions in relation to dress, he loses a lot of respect from everyone whose respect is worth having. You did not impress anyone but yourself when you started wearing that belt. And, Evan," her eyes bored into me. "You can't fool your sister. *You didn't even impress yourself!*" She turned abruptly and started dipping cows as if her life depended on it.

I felt like exploding. But I couldn't. Not to Jenny. There was a Cold War between us until all the cows were milked. Douglas had no idea how glad I was to see him walk into the parlor to take Jenny's place. "Thanks for your help," I told her stiffly as she sprayed off her boots. I hoped she didn't take a double meaning out of that "Thanks." I was still seething.

Not Jenny. "You are very welcome," she chirped. "Mother and I will try to have supper on the table by the time you boys get in. I guess you want to leave as soon as possible for your hike."

The minute I walked in the door, I could tell that Jenny had told Mother about our conversation. She had that somber look on her face. "Supper is ready as soon as you get washed up, Evan," she said quietly.

"I won't be needing supper," I said into the towel. "Jerry is planning to stop at Arby's on the way."

"No." Mother's voice was firm. "My men don't eat in restaurants as long as their mother is able to serve them. Besides, you need to think about the company and the environment. You are a man, Evan—I can't stop you from going out with Jerry. But, please, stay out of Arby's."

I knew better than to argue with her. "Go change your clothes," she suggested. "I'll pack a supper for both you and Jerry to eat on the trail. That way you can get started sooner, and get home before too late."

I wasn't sure how Jerry would react to that, but he just shrugged his shoulders. "I know what it's like," he said. "My old man throws a fit like that sometimes, too. Sooner or later, they will need to come to grips with the fact that we are not little boys anymore. Never mind, Evan. We'll sneak into Arby's some other time. I did want you to see the new waitress there. She's a cute one."

I felt sick on the stomach. Was Jerry really that far out? Needless to say, I did not enjoy the evening.

The next morning, Douglas helped me milk. "I guess we will have to get Uncle Peter over to check 307," I told him. "It looks like she is down with milk fever. I already called him, and he said he will be over right after breakfast."

"I hate to bother him again," Douglas said. "You don't think we could get the calcium and dextrose into her ourselves?"

"I don't like to pester him with our troubles, either," I agreed. "But every time I try to IV a cow, I have trouble getting the needle into the vein. He is so slick at it, I figured I might as well call him."

I still decided to try it myself after breakfast. After sending Douglas out to mow hay, I put a halter on 307 and pressed my fingers on her neck to locate the large vein. When I found it, I picked up the IV needle and slipped it under her skin. To my delight and surprise, I hit the vein the first time! I quickly hooked up the IV hose and soon had the calcium bubbling in just like it was supposed to do.

I heard Uncle Peter climbing over the gate behind me. "Good work, Evan!" he praised, when he saw how it was going. "Here, let me hold the bottle and you hold the needle. This is almost a two-man job."

"I think she'll make it," he declared when we loosened the halter and 307 lounged shakily to her feet. "I like the way you keep after the cows, Evan. Before long, you won't need me anymore."

"Yeah, I should have tried it myself before I called you." I was pleased with my success. "They say 'practice makes perfect,' but I never had much success hitting the vein before. I figured I might as well call you right away."

"Sure, anytime." Uncle Peter idly toyed with the empty calcium bottle. "I needed to talk to you anyway, Evan."

I braced myself. I thought I knew what was coming.

"We as a ministry met last evening to discuss a few issues in the church," he began, turning the bottle over and over in his hands. "We decided that if you do not show any positive changes in your conduct or attitudes before our fall council meeting, we are going to need to reevaluate your status as a church member. I do not need to tell you what our concerns are. I have already done that several times."

I stared at the ground mutely. Had it really come to this?

"Evan…" Uncle Peter hesitated. "What I have to say next will sound very unkind. But I want you to think about it. If you want to persist in this kind of rebellion, you can be glad your father died."

My mouth dropped open. "What?!" I gasped.

Uncle Peter did not back down. "I hear you are tired of everybody picking on you. But, Evan, your father always meant it when he said,

'No.' If you want to live a rebellious life, then you can be glad he is not here." He looked at me as though expecting a response.

"You're…you're…" I stopped, shocked at the word that was on the tip of my tongue.

"I know I sound unkind," Uncle Peter answered calmly. "But I have tried kindness over and over, and I cannot seem to get through to you. Evan, you have told me often through the years that you can't see how Jerry Diller can talk so disrespectfully about his father. Actions speak louder than words, Evan. What are YOU saying about YOUR father? Doesn't he mean anything to you?"

I felt like someone had slammed his fist into my stomach. Sinking down on the nearest straw bale, I put my head in my hands.

"I am sorry, Evan." Uncle Peter laid a gentle hand on my shoulder. "It hurts me to talk to you like this, but please…" his voice broke. He was silent for a while. "Think about your mother, Evan," he said finally. "She is worried about you. She lost her husband, and now she fears she is losing her oldest son. And she tells me that Douglas is already picking up some of your street language and begging to let his sideburns grow as long as yours. You are bringing her a grief worse than the grief she carries as a widow."

I sat there mutely, not trusting myself to speak. Is this what it felt like to have a father? Uncle Peter sighed and removed his hand from my shoulder. "I will keep praying for you, Evan," he promised huskily. "You are like a son to me, and I want to see you become the kind of man your father wanted you to be." He turned then and left me alone.

I don't know how long I sat there. Sandy came around eventually and poked her curious nose into my face. She was the dog Daddy had given to me twice. Seeing her brought back a sudden rush of nostalgic memories of my father. I broke down and cried.

Jenny helped me milk again that evening. She seemed to be in good spirits, singing one song after the next. I did not mind; I was not ready to talk much yet anyway. I had been doing some serious thinking ever since Uncle Peter left, and I had apologized to Mother. I actually found myself whistling a few tunes along with Jenny. Her mood was contagious.

"Thanks, Jenny," I managed, when the last shift of cows was exiting the parlor. "For this evening, as well as last evening." Her eyes lit up. She had lived with me long enough to know what a masculine apology can sound like. "I told Mother that it suits me to go to Clear View this evening. You coming along? You can keep your stickers, though."

She laughed. "Of course, I am coming along! And if you don't want a sticker, I will see to it that we have homemade ice cream for supper. I am sure you'll accept that! I think I still have time to make some."

As I dressed for church, I could not help comparing the pleasant atmosphere of our family at the supper table this evening with the strained atmosphere of the evening before. All because of me. What had I been doing to my family? What was Jerry doing to me?

As I pulled my belt out of the drawer, a feeling of disgust welled up inside of me. But what would people think if I quit wearing it now? I slipped it on. Just as I was about to buckle it, a picture of Daddy flashed into my mind. He was smiling at me. And he was wearing suspenders. "Doesn't he mean anything to you?" Uncle Peter's question slapped me in the face.

"This is it!" I muttered fiercely, pulling the belt back off. I had never felt comfortable wearing it anyway, knowing how Mother felt about it. Just for effect, I sawed it in half with my pocket knife and socked it into the waste can. "There!" What would people think? I knew what Mother and Jenny would think!

I felt sort of self-conscious when I went downstairs. Mother, however, seemed to understand. She gave me a quiet smile and waited to say anything until Jenny and Douglas had already gone to the car and we were alone in the house. "Thank you, Evan," she said simply. "It is good to know that I can trust the man of the house again. You have no idea how much this means to me."

The evangelist at Clear View used a phrase from Proverbs for his title. "The way of transgressors."

Yes, it is hard. The way of transgressors is hard. I speak from experience. And observation. As I write this many years later, I think of Jerry. He is serving prison time. He divorced his first wife. When he was incarcerated, his second wife left him, taking both of his children. There is a rumor that she will likely win the lawsuit she filed against him, pretty much wiping out everything he has. He is alone, abandoned, a wretched, miserable man. Isaac Diller, his father, has aged fast, but he is still the same generous soul that I always knew him to be.

Sure, since I am older, I can see that Isaac did have his faults, and perhaps in a way, I can understand Jerry's struggle to respect him. But Isaac Diller tried to do what was right. My own heart aches for him. I just don't see how Jerry could do what he did to his father. If I had had a father...

I did have a father. As I think back to the period of my life I have just told you about, I am still ashamed of the way I treated him. I thank God over and over that Uncle Peter and Jenny had the courage to confront me, and as it were, shock me to my senses. And that Mother, in her own quiet way, never gave up on me.

There is no grief which time does not lessen and soften. Cicero

Faith or Fear?

DAVID HEGE

"Faith of our fathers, holy faith—We will be true to thee till death." Nineteen-year-old Lavonda's thoughts were running deep as she replaced the songbook in the rack. She was not thinking about the faith of the medieval Anabaptists. No, this song always reminded her of the unflinching faith her own father had displayed in the last few months of his life.

"I want to be true," she told herself firmly. "I want to trust, and leave everything in God's hands. But oh, it is hard." Her pensive thoughts moved forward a few weeks to the day Denton and Janet were planning to become husband and wife. She and Denton had become very close in the years since Justin's marriage and Father's death. Her entire being rebelled at the thought of giving him up. "Arise, let us go hence," she thought dismally. "That is what Father would say. To be honest, I wish I could stop the clock."

"How can you do it?" she asked Denton a few days later.

"Do what?" he asked, puzzled.

"Get married," Lavonda said bluntly. "I mean, well, don't you ever think about the fact that she might die? Or that you might die and leave her alone? It makes me shudder just to think of it. To me, it seems safer not to marry. Not to become so attached."

"We-ell," Denton said slowly. "Like Father always said, if we are living for God in the present, we do not need to fear the future. God will work all things out for our good. If His will includes an untimely parting for us, I am sure it will be hard. But I choose to leave that in His hands. His grace will be sufficient if and when that time comes. Just ask Mother."

Lavonda shrugged. "I know you are right. And Father would smile at you and say, 'Let us go hence.' But not me. Guess I don't have enough faith, or something. Of course, I will not stop you from getting married if you are sure you want to, but for myself it will not happen. I have made a firm resolution that I will never marry. Never. No one. It is too risky. No matter who it is, any young man who asks me will get a firm 'No.' I really don't care if you tell everyone, Denton. It will make it easier for me and them if the boys know not to ask me."

"I advise you not to say that too loud." Denton looked almost amused at her passionate outburst. "You might regret it later, when God unveils His plan for your life."

He already has, Lavonda thought sniffing to herself. *Denton is just like Father. Just taking one day at a time and saying that God will plan the future.* She sighed. *I wonder if Denton is really as confident as he sounds? How can he help but think about what all could happen in the future if he marries? Sure, he is on cloud nine now, but surely he knows it could change in an instant. Then what? Gound zero. Or worse. It is just not worth it.*

Three weeks later, Denton brought the mail in. He gave Lavonda an encouraging smile as he handed her an envelope addressed to her in painfully meticulous masculine handwriting. Her face flushed when she saw it. "Take care of it, will you?" she pleaded. "I don't want it."

"Indeed not!" Denton said emphatically. "Well, maybe I should! That way the poor fellow would have a fair chance. I will be around later for more information."

"Who is it?" he asked her at the supper table. "Someone respectable?"

Lavonda sighed. "Doreen's brother. Linford."

"He is a very nice young man," Mother said softly. "Maybe God is ready to lead you further into His plan for your life. You need to take your time and think about this before you say 'no,' Lavonda."

"I'll say," Denton agreed. "I will be glad to answer this letter for you,

Lavonda. To me, there is no question."

"I have already answered it," Lavonda said tonelessly. "I had a sort of form letter already in my mind in case any boy ever asked me. I was hoping I would never need to send it, but it goes in the mail tomorrow."

"Is that kind?" Mother asked. "Just to return an answer that fast without taking time to consider what God's will might be for you? What will that make Linford feel like, if he senses you did not even think much about it?"

"Is it kind to make him wait when my answer is 'no'?" Lavonda retorted. "I have already thought this thing through many times. I do not want to marry. He might as well know." Suddenly, she pushed her plate back and got up from the table. "Don't make it hard for me," she pled tearfully. "You already know how I feel about it." Turning, she fled from the room.

Mother looked at Denton helplessly. "Times like this, I really miss your father," she sighed. "Maybe she does need a little more time to grow up yet."

Denton scratched his head. "I am going over to talk to Justin," he said. "We can't let her respond to Linford so carelessly. She is not even thinking! Imagine! A form letter, already prepared in her head! She needs to get rid of her mind block and think this thing through."

Justin listened silently as Denton poured out his frustration. "I knew this was coming," he said calmly. "Linford has been keeping in touch with us. He wanted to ask Lavonda six months ago, but I advised him to wait for a while. I did give him permission to ask, but warned him that Lavonda is very set against getting married."

"So, what are we going to do?" Denton asked. "Let her say 'no'? You know Lavonda. She is impossible to reason with once she makes up her mind."

"And so," Justin said quietly, "we do not reason with her. That is what she expects us to do. Her arsenal is ready, so to speak. Doreen and I have been talking this over. Lavonda has not really had a lot of contact with a two-parent home for over seven years. She dwells too much on Father's passing and Mother's widowhood...."

Denton was nodding in agreement. "...And she says marriage isn't worth it. You can expect a parting, and she doesn't want to face that possibility. Is she even ready for courtship with that kind of attitude?"

"Yet she is so grown up in a lot of ways. She would make an excellent wife for someone if she could just get rid of this mind block. What can we do to help her? Sitting down and talking straight won't get us anywhere. We both know that."

Justin nodded thoughtfully. "Let me run this past Doreen," he said finally. "If we boys take things into our own hands, we are bound to bungle something up."

Fifteen minutes later, he came back out of the house. "Doreen was not real impressed with Lavonda's attitude." Justin half smiled. "She thinks we should tell Mother not to allow Lavonda to reply to Linford just yet. She says Lavonda thinks a lot of Linford—deep down in, she wants to say 'yes'—but Doreen says the brains of a man won't be able to comprehend the evidence she has to prove this, so she won't try to explain." Justin's eyes twinkled. "Just tell Mother to stall Lavonda's response to Linford. Doreen and I will take care of things from there on. We have an interesting little plan up our sleeves. Just keep your eyes and ears open, and you should be able to figure it out."

The next morning, a quiet Lavonda arrived in the kitchen just in time for breakfast. Dark circles under her eyes spoke of troubled sleep. The meal was a silent one, each member of the family busy with their own thoughts. *Why did it have to be Linford?* Lavonda was lamenting to herself for the thousandth time. *It would be so much easier if it had been someone else...anyone else.*

"Lavonda," Mother said as she got up from the table, "I want you to know that I have never regretted the fact that I married your father. Yes, the parting was hard, and I still miss him a lot. But I would not trade those years together, or my children, for anything. I want you to spend more time thinking and praying before giving Linford an answer. Why don't you talk to Doreen? Ask her if marriage is worth the risks that you seem to think are involved."

"Please, Mother," Lavonda said, keeping her emotions carefully under control. "The sooner I get this settled, the happier I'll be. Marriage is not for me. Period. I made that decision years ago. I see no point in keeping Linford waiting. After all," she added lightly, "you'll need someone to take care of you in your older years." She forced an artificial giggle.

Mother did not smile. "It must be your decision. I will accept whatever you decide about Linford, but I will not allow you to mail him an answer today. That is not being fair to him, nor to yourself. Give it a week or so at the least."

Lavonda groaned as she passed the mailbox on her way to her job at the bakery. If only she could throw her refusal into the box and slam shut the lid. Then she could think about something else. *A week or so*, Mother had said. *Okay*, Lavonda decided, *I'll just forget about it for now and enjoy my day at work*. But her mind would not cooperate with her will.

Three days later, activity in the kitchen awoke Denton before his alarm clock rang. "What is going on?" he asked. "You didn't tell me you wanted an early breakfast. Going somewhere?"

Lavonda turned quickly to face him. "Justin and Doreen had a baby girl!" she exclaimed. "I wanted to call you, but Mother said to wait. A girl, Denton! Isn't that something? After three boys! They called her Lavonda Joy! I always thought it would be special to have a niece named after me!" Lavonda stopped, out of breath.

Denton was suitably impressed. "Lavonda Joy," he mused aloud. "With a name like that, she has a lot to live up to, doesn't she? Think she'll measure up to you, Lavonda?"

Lavonda ignored his jibe. "Doreen wants me to come to the hospital and stay with her this afternoon while Justin takes care of a few things at home. When they get home from the hospital, I am supposed to help her three days a week for a while. She thinks the boys will have a big adjustment with a baby in the house. I can't wait! Don't you envy me, Denton?"

"Not really," Denton answered. "Of course, I want to see the baby, and maybe even hold her if she doesn't cry. But honestly, I like 'em a little bigger than that. Two-year-olds are more the right size for me. They don't break as easily."

"Oh, isn't she sweet!" Lavonda gushed several hours later as Doreen handed her the little pink bundle. "Denton says he likes two-year-olds better than babies, but I'll take a baby any day. Don't you agree?"

"I like both." Doreen smiled at her enthusiasm.

"Of course, so do I. Oh, you little dear!" she could hardly contain herself. "Look! She opened her eyes. Hi, Lavonda! You and I are going to be best friends, okay? Oh, don't cry! Am I scary? There, now." To Aunt Lavonda's delight, the baby quieted down.

"I'll just take this one home," she teased Doreen. "You already have three boys."

"I don't think so," Doreen said with a chuckle. "But I will be glad to share her with you."

"You have to!" Lavonda squeezed the little bundle again. "She's just perfect, Doreen. A miracle." Both women were silent for a while. Both were thinking about Lavonda, though not the same one.

Lavonda thoroughly enjoyed her days as baby maid. Doreen let her bathe little Lavonda, as well as babysit the boys. "I don't want to dump all my dirty work on you," she told Lavonda one morning, shooing her away from a stack of dirty dishes. You keep the boys and the baby happy. I'll wash the dishes."

"No, I will!" Justin pushed his sleeves higher. "I don't want Lavonda thinking I don't do my part." He smiled at Doreen and escorted her to the recliner. "Take care of yourself, Mommy," he said, rearranging the cushions. "Can't have you wearing yourself out before your time."

You are jealous! Lavonda was startled at the thought. Justin and Doreen had been making no secret of the fact that they loved each other. She almost thought they overdid it at times, yet it reminded her of the way Father had cared for Mother, letting her drive the truck in the produce patch, making sure she didn't "wear out before her time." She found herself thinking about Linford again.

Several hours later her thoughts were still busy. Nights were always the worst. Tonight, a lingering whiff of baby lotion teased her mercilessly. *Get over it!* she scolded herself, flipping her damp pillow over. But she couldn't. Would it be a blessing to have someone to share life with, to help each other over the rough spots, to enjoy the good times, even if death parted the union in the future? How could a person know? Wouldn't it be safer to live a quiet life like Aunt Verna? Her thoughts ran on and on.

"Are you sleeping well at night?" Mother asked Lavonda the next evening. "You look so weary."

Mother's gentle concern brought tears to Lavonda's eyes. "Not really," she admitted.

"You still have a decision to make, don't you?"

Lavonda nodded miserably.

"Has Doreen ever said anything to you about it?" Mother asked, looking at her intently.

"No. I wonder if she even knows it yet. Listening to her, I get the impression that married life is the utopia of human experience. I never knew she and Justin were so...so." She groped for the right word. "Well, romancy, if you know what I mean."

Mother smiled. "Justin and Doreen are happy because they are in the center of God's will for them," she pointed out quietly. "That is a lesson you need to learn, Lavonda. No matter what life brings to us, there will be no real peace or joy if we do not submit to God's will."

"Aunt Verna is submitted to God's will, isn't she? And her life seems much safer. No husband or children to love and then lose."

"Maybe she doesn't," Mother agreed. "But think of the many people she has risked building relationships with! Why, she has friends wherever she goes. Aunt Verna didn't stick her head in the sand just because her beloved twin sister and her parents died. Think how lonely she would be."

"But...but isn't marriage different? Isn't the relationship closer?"

"In some ways, yes. But, Lavonda, you must learn to trust your future to God. He does care about you." Mother looked at her intently. "I can understand your fear of parting," she continued. "And it is not easy to love and then lose. But you must face your future and make this decision in faith. Allowing fear, rather than faith, to make your decisions in life will leave you a very miserable person. God will not force you to accept His plan for your life, but accepting His plan is the only way to find peace."

Lavonda was silent.

"I sense that you care deeply for Linford," Mother's voice was gentle. "Will you give him an answer of fear or of faith?"

Lavonda drew a deep, trembling breath. "Father would say, 'Let us go hence.' I am sure he would. We learned to know Linford's family quite well while Justin and Doreen were dating, and I know Father had a deep respect for them. If only I had Father's faith to face the future..." Her voice trailed off. "I need a little more time, Mother. Thanks for asking me to give more thought to Linford's request before sending him an answer. I have been observing Justin and Doreen's marriage and...and, well, they did not make a mistake when they decided to marry. I want to give Linford God's answer...and...I almost think I know what that is."

Mother flashed Lavonda a warm smile. "I think you do. Let us go hence."

Sorrow looks back; worry looks around; faith looks up.

Pulling Up the Roots

He set my feet upon a rock, and established my goings. Psalm 40:2

293

Pulling Up the Roots

SUELLEN J STRITE

Some years ago, I was working at cleaning up my strawberry bed. It was full of dandelions and thistles and ragweed… and, oh! lots of lamb's-quarter. The soil was damp and many of the weeds pulled out easily. But the August sun made the job tedious, and I felt my energy depleted before I was finished. I would pull for a while, then straighten my back and survey the bed. The clean section seemed small compared to the mass of weeds ahead of me. I wiped my wet forehead with my clammy handkerchief and bent to pull a particularly large lamb's-quarter. The thing reached to my waist, but I grabbed the base of that weed and gave several hard yanks. Suddenly the weed popped out, and I staggered backwards. Ah, that made a difference in the strawberry landscape.

It made a difference in my shoulder, too. Something other than the roots of the weed had popped. I could not finish weeding that patch. Sleep eluded me that night as the pain shot up to my neck and down to my hand. After several remedies, my shoulder worked its way back to normal. But I've never forgotten that lamb's-quarter, and I am more cautious when trying to pull one up by the roots; it might cause unnecessary pain.

Usually when there is a death, the widow's family tries to think of ways to make her life easier. Sometimes they are eager to move the widow here or there. Maybe if she moved off a farm there would be fewer decisions. Or if she moved onto a farm, the children would have more to do. A smaller house might cut back on expenses. Being closer to her parents may allow more support.

Sometimes other changes are suggested or forced upon the widow. Her husband's favorite tractor or horse should be sold. The big maple out front needs cut down. The teenagers must find jobs.

Maybe such moves or changes would make things nicer, easier. Maybe the change is even legitimate, necessary.

But we need to remember, unless we are the widow, we cannot fathom the pain that even small changes cause her, especially at first. And the pain reaches deeper than her shoulder.

Caution and discernment are needed when suggesting changes to the new widow. Usually after some time has passed, it becomes clearer if and when and how and where that uprooting should be.

Christmas

MARLENE R BRUBACHER

Christmas is hard
>   When we think of our loved ones now missing;
>   Remembering singing…and laughter…
>   And long-ago dreams.

>   But
>   Immanuel came
>   To be with us in all of our heartaches,

>   And even this Christmas,
>   The Bethlehem hope-star gleams.

Question 23

Do you have any thoughts to share about coping with the changes that come with being a widow?

Widows answer:

• Don't make quick decisions on big things, such as moving. Seek advice, even when sometimes the answer isn't what you hoped for. Never be in a hurry to sort clothes and make changes. My family was, and I do not think it was worth it.

• It was difficult to move. I waited nearly four years. I think it would have been harder to go through it all earlier. The wound of parting was not as raw after four years as I sorted and packed, stirred around in all those memories, sold "his" farm machinery, etc.

• I recommend waiting at least two years to move.

• We moved shortly before my husband died. We didn't have time to make many memories together at this house. That was hard for me to accept.

• It was bittersweet to leave the house where we spent 16 months of married life, welcomed our precious daughter, and enjoyed learning to know each other. Each person's situation is different. Our move was necessary so I could start my own business, and be close to my parents, so my daughter could grow up with my sister who was a half year younger than my daughter.

• After four years, I was okay with moving because our farmhouse was too big.

• We lived in our dream home only 1¼ years before my husband died. I waited seven years to move. Since my dreams were shattered, I could no longer enjoy the woods, pond, and beautiful house, so it was not difficult to move. I would recommend waiting a few years to make any major move.

• It was actually beneficial for me to move after one year since I was ready to get rid of his clothes and move things around and use his drawers for other things. It erased the memories of seeing him turn into the driveway after a day at work, his empty place at the table, and his favorite chair in the living room…sitting empty.

• I'm glad I stayed in the farmhouse for a few years before moving to a small adjoining house. There weren't so many changes at one time.

• We had planned to move before my husband died. His desire was to be buried in the new location if he died before we moved. He died in November, and my daughters and I moved the following August.

• We had nine children under ten years, which caused an overload when my husband died. Our boys spent much time at my brother's farm in the summer, and after school in the evenings. Our girls helped out here and there. It was not the way I chose…to have my children scattered… but it was best to have it that way to cope.

• We had to change the children's sleeping arrangements. We also had to sell most of our horses. But that was okay. A month or so earlier, my husband had told me what to do with them if anything happened to him, and I knew I couldn't go on raising them all by myself.

• We kept on farming but had to get rid of our horses, as they were not women's horses. That was not easy, but there was no other choice. We had neighbors coming in with their equipment and taking time to do our crops and it seemed they were actually enjoying themselves by trying to outdo each other…while my heart was weeping that we couldn't just still do it our own quiet, slow way.

• We rented my husband's band mill to his brother, since we could not use it. It was hard to see it go out the lane, headed three hours away. But I was sure my husband would be happy, because he always looked out for others.

• My hardest struggle was when I was asked by a widower to be his partner and marry him. Oh, I thought I couldn't bear it. I prayed and prayed. I knew I either had to find a job to support me and my little family, or accept his invitation to marry him and move to another state. Once I gave it up to God, I felt at peace to do His will. His will was for me to go.

• Little changes were hard, like leading in devotions, getting rid of his clothes, parting with his dialysis machine and medical supplies, getting rid of our old horse and trying out a new one. So many memories are tied up in the little things. By not dwelling on it; just doing the next thing and moving on with life makes things possible.

• I had to get used to people helping on the farm the first year after my husband's death. Later the farm was rented out. It was so hard to see other men running his tractor. I finally realized that I must accept what I could not change.

• Inviting guests to dinner and sitting around the table when my "table head" was missing to welcome them all and ask someone to lead in prayer was hard. I started inviting one of my married children when I have company, then my son or son-in-law fills that place.

• It was hard for me that I couldn't keep up with helping in our business of custom poultry processing. I was so engulfed in grief I don't even quite remember all the things I did when the children suggested I go for help. I received help on how to grieve, and was told that even the strongest people have to grieve. After going for help, which was tender, loving, and understanding, I have a desire again to be a real mom to our dear children. I am so thankful they can keep on with the business.

Dear Ones,

After the busy weeks of working toward our sale, the day is finally over. Even yet, the morning of the sale, I felt there was no way I could ever feel ready to do this—in many ways it was saying good-bye to our hopes and dreams of the future, as well as to the memories of the past. Yet I had to recognize that it was what my husband could do with those things that meant more to me than the things themselves...and at the end of the day there was a sense of relief in knowing that this was now behind us.

We are very indebted to you, our family, for taking charge of all the plans and preparations to make the day go smoothly. Thank you for shouldering that responsibility, yet being sensitive to our feelings—the emotions that run deep at a time like this. Only in the past weeks have I realized how comforting it has been to have all of my husband's things still around these past seven months since his death. Thank you for waiting this long to take this step. While our minds know that this has to be done, the heart would rather not have to face up to the realities that this drives home.

On reflecting on those realities, the word *incomplete* is the best way I can put my feelings into words. His short life...our marriage...our family...his business...all cut so short, so unfinished—as incomplete as the conversation we were enjoying, the sentence he was speaking, when he was taken from me so suddenly. To see his things—our dreams—sold off today stirs up all those unanswered questions again in our hearts.

Yet as his wife during the seven short years we had together, I was so often blessed and stabilized by his calm, matter-of-fact opinions about life...his acceptance of whatever life brought...taking things in stride. And while I am so thankful that he was spared the knowledge of how his earthly lifework and dreams would end, I just know that he would swallow and smile and be okay with it...if this is what God allowed, he wouldn't waste his time fretting and fighting against it. That assurance gives me courage to face life's struggles the way he would—and the way he would want us to as well.

Thank you for your time and sacrifices and support these past weeks...and this week especially. It was a lot easier for me to let the family go ahead with this than to see someone else assuming that role. God bless you for sharing and caring.

Sincerely,

"Violet"

299

Adjusting to Change

CHZ

Jesus Christ the same yesterday, and today, and forever (Hebrews 13:8). *For I am the Lord, I change not* (Malachi 3:6).

Changes! Life brings so many changes; some we like and some we wish would never come to pass. How thankful we can be that God remains the same; we can trust His promise that He will always be with us. *Lo, I am with you always* (Matthew 28:20).

We were just a typical family—father, mother, six sons, and two daughters—desiring to serve the Lord amidst the usual joys and trials of life. A new baby after almost five years seemed change enough for us. We had settled into a new routine when suddenly, with little warning, life was forever changed! My husband, the daddy of our home, was diagnosed with cancer, stage four melanoma. We were thrown into a medical whirlwind, with daunting, unfamiliar surroundings. With the diagnosis of such a life-threatening illness, it caused great sorrow in our lives. We just couldn't plan much of anything, because we didn't know when my husband would be in the hospital or when he would be feeling better.

At that time, our daughter, the oldest child in our family, was dating a young man who was becoming very special to all of us. It appeared that marriage was in the future, but how would a wedding ever fit into such a schedule? How could I as a mother of eight children, with the youngest just a baby, manage a wedding with a terminally ill husband? For the next several months we just took a day at a time, trying to focus on the moments rather than the hazy-looking future. Then my husband took a sharp turn for the worse and all our energies focused on his care, as it became evident that he would not be with us much longer. I am grateful that our daughter's special friend had the opportunity to request my husband's blessing on their marriage, someday in the future. For me, as wife and mother, it was very bittersweet. That blessing was important, but how does one combine such joy with the heartrending sorrow of impending death? Once more, as we had done so many times before, we relied on God's grace that never failed to see us through. Our daughter's friend was an encouragement to us over the time of my husband's death, as he shared in our sorrow in his steady, quiet manner.

After my husband's passing, that tremendous sense of heaviness lifted somewhat, although then the pain and grief and missing were becoming real. Less than three months later, our daughter and her friend announced their engagement and we were caught up in wedding planning. I could hardly grasp how we could really be happy, when at the same time our hearts were so burdened with sorrow. So many times, I thought how much my husband would enjoy this! Helping prepare the house would've been his delight. Sometimes, amidst wedding and house preparations, with a crying toddler who felt uncertain about all that was happening, I wasn't sure how we were going to make it through. And no husband to share it all with! I wondered, how did we get to this place in life and why are we here? But God was faithful, and our caring families and friends were a marvelous support.

As the wedding day approached, I was apprehensive. Grief is noted for coming in waves, and I just didn't know how to prepare for this special day, not quite ten months after my dear husband's death. Would the tears come uncontrollably or would there be this dazed, surreal feeling where I just can't quite comprehend what is happening? Sometimes God, in love, allows us to feel our pain, those deep searing throbs within the breast, so that we can experience healing. Other times, God, in mercy, carries us through, or even above, the pain so we can cope. The night before the wedding, the magnitude of our situation overwhelmed me. Our first child is getting married tomorrow; we have a wedding in *our* family and my husband, the father of the bride, isn't here to be a part of it! We will never share the joy of a child's wedding. Oh, the pain! The tears came.

Many tears. As I prayed and sought the Lord, He gave peace and rest. The next morning, I felt courage to face the wedding day with a very real sense of being carried. Not numb, but carried in those Everlasting Arms. The children and I were able to smile and enjoy the day. There were a few tears, but my husband was remembered in a positive way and we focused on joy. With God's help, the day was truly a beautiful experience.

After the wedding, here it was again—change! The newlywed couple left for their trip and we were struck with the thought that she doesn't live here anymore. The little chats we enjoyed with them as a couple each Sunday evening were missing. My husband and I had found those visits so special; then when he was gone, I felt they brought stability—someone to discuss events and happenings with. A child leaving home left another empty spot at the table to decide what to do with—that feeling afresh that someone is missing. We missed her presence breezing in the door after work, her help with housework, and just another lady in the house.

One night I was especially burdened with the cares of life, concerns for the children, adjusting to the change of a child leaving home…and this tremendous, on going missing of the one who had shared his life with me for almost twenty-two years. At last, I fell asleep and dreamed I was carrying a heavy burden. A staircase ascended before me and I started to climb, but partway up I simply could not take another step. The load was just too heavy. It was then, when there was no strength left, that the Lord picked me up in His strong arms and carried me to the top of the stairs. His Presence was so real, strong, and comforting. It was a confirmation that when I feel like I can't go on, God will give me grace. He doesn't always show us His strength in that way, but we can always be assured that He is with us.

Though we miss our daughter/sister, we are also happy. This leaving of home, for something happy like marriage, is a normal change in life. We can still spend time together, still talk and make precious memories. This is change, but a pleasant change—one that gives more than it takes.

May the changes we experience in widowhood change us more and more into the image of God, for His glory. For…someday, we shall all be changed in a moment, in the twinkling of an eye, at the last trump! Then we shall be caught up together with them in the clouds, to meet the Lord in the air: and so shall we ever be with the Lord. To God be the glory for ever and ever. Amen.

Changes...and the Unchangeable One

LMH

I did not face the huge changes of moving or of dissolving a business after my husband's death, but the many small changes wore me down bit by bit.

My husband and I used to take our children out and all do chores together; after his death I was so weak physically and emotionally there was no way I could milk cows. But this was a huge change in my routine...

My husband was a great ball-hitter, shooting the ball out over the barn roof, and giving the children a good time. I tried to bring a little normalcy into my children's life and helped them play ball one evening. We all discovered I am such a poor substitute...

My husband was the homework whiz. Who gets to help my daughter try to figure out her difficult science lesson when Daddy is no longer here? I do. And science makes no sense to me...

My husband used to be in the room with the other men when we were invited away for a meal. After his death, we were still invited away, but he was not with the men. One such time, my son's shoe was open. I bent to tie it for him, but he protested. "I want to go over to the men and have them tie it for me." Darts shot through my heart. If only he *could* go over to the men and let *daddy* tie his shoe once more...

My husband used to be the primary cardholder. I had a stressful half hour on the phone, trying to get our credit card changed over for me to be the primary cardholder. If my husband were here, I would not even *need* to be the primary cardholder…

My husband owned a self-propelled chopper. He had put hours into it to make it run properly. He had enjoyed using it. The decision was made to sell it. The morning it went out the lane was a hard morning for me. Yes, it was only a thing, yet it held sentimental value. It was like another part of my husband leaving me…

These were just a few of the little changes I faced, and grief made them into monsters in my life. Sometimes I felt I would suffocate from the weight of those monsters. Sometimes I felt so angry about it all, that I would go out and take a brisk walk or hoe thistles to release some fury. Sometimes I just cried and cried for all the little joys that had been, and were no more.

We can feel frantic about all the changes we need to face when death snatches our husband. We feel like we need to grab and hang onto anything, however unreasonable, so we don't face one more change. Yet, our human hands are incapable of stopping the ebb of time and the inevitable changes that come with it. How can we cope? How can we survive? We see change in every direction we look.

Except one direction…*up*. We must look up, if we are going to get through this. *Up* to the *One who changes not*! There is hope. There is healing. The Unchangeable One will not let us down. He *promised* not to give us more than He would help us bear. And He will not back up on His promise, for He is the Unchangeable One. He is Alpha and Omega, the Beginning and the End. The I Am, who will keep us in the hollow of His Hand, until He calls us up yonder where earthly changes can reach us no more.

When you feel suffocated, frantic, angry, and sad about all the changes grief has brought into your life, look *up*. Remember the Unchangeable One. Cling to Him.

The Widow's Answer

EVA METZ

In the quiet of her kitchen, a mother patched a pair of worn trousers, and listened to the glad shouts of the children at play in the yard, two boys and one little girl. Her children! Her heart swelled with contentment. They were healthy, happy children and were growing old enough to help with many little tasks.

But, oh, how much guidance they would need in the next few years! A shadow crossed her face. Must she do it all alone? What if she should be taken from them? Taken away, as their dear father, who had died just four years ago?

Who would feed them? Who would clothe them? Who would mother them? The questions blew hard on her wavering faith. They would be so alone.

"O God," she whispered. "What can I do? Surely You would not take me from them—but what if? Oh, show me what I can do."

As stitch after stitch fell from her busy needle, God showed her a way for widows and their children. She must give them something which would be theirs always. They must have a Friend who would go with them all the way, whether they had a father or a mother or not, so that when trouble came, as it surely would, they could go to Him.

I may not be here, she thought, *while they make their way among strangers. If they do not have God to trust, who will they have?*

She treasured her discovery as something valuable beyond price, and began to teach her children some lessons each day about their heavenly Father and His Son, Jesus Christ. As she saw them learning something of the One who would be their Friend as long as they followed Him, her burden became lighter. She knew that this was the dearest blessing she could possibly give her children. 🌸

Ready to Go

SHEILA J PETRE

I stand here, shawled in waiting,
Peering down the way.
Assured this morning's sunrise
Is the last to grace my stay.
    My useful days are over.
    I know He'll come today.

He told me He was coming
When living got too long.
When bearing got too heavy
Or storms came on too strong.
    My life has grown too painful.
    He'll come to right this wrong.

I stand here, shawled in waiting,
Peering down the way.
And baffled, as the sunset
Ends an eventless day.
    I want to go…but…maybe…
    He would rather that I stay?

God's promises are like rainbows: the darker the storm, the brighter they glow.

For Every Cloud,
a Rainbow

I was young, now I am old, yet have I not seen the righteous forsaken, nor his seed begging bread. Psalm 37:25

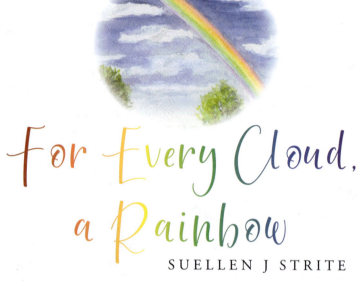

For Every Cloud, a Rainbow

SUELLEN J STRITE

Their names were Ida and Ruth, and as children we adopted them into our family. Or did they adopt us into theirs? They lived in the house at the end of my parents' farm lane. They walked up to our house to fill their potato bucket; we ran to their house to cut off garden tea. They gave us marshmallows and read us stories when we were young; we washed their car and mowed their lawn when they were old.

These short little ladies were the only children of John and Susie Eby. Neither of them ever married, so when they died, they left no posterity. They left no prosperity either, for they died penniless. But they did not live in vain. They left impressions and influences that helped shape many lives, including my own.

Ida and Ruth were born and raised during the Great Depression and they knew how to make do. Their feed-sack-fabric dresses were quite neatly patched and their black serviceable shoes were worn for many years. Their dry sink and old stone crocks spoke of an era when everyone lived more simply. Their house permeated with frugality, from the loaves of warm bread which Ida carefully took from her oven, to the durable rag rugs Ruth knitted on her loom.

With the money they saved, they were able to share with others. Every month, one of us children had the special privilege of going along to the grocery store with Ruth to purchase groceries for the "poor people."

When we got home, the groceries were divided out into brown paper bags and placed on a row of wooden chairs behind the kitchen table. One by one the poor neighbors in the community drove their old rattle-trap vehicles to the Eby home where Ida and Ruth handed them a bag full of flour, sugar, bread, and rice. They also had a little room to the side of their garage which they called "The Clothes House." They kept this stocked with clothes and shoes. Their poor neighbors all knew they were welcome to come and pick out what they needed for free.

They shared many buckets of home-baked cookies with busy Mennonite mothers, always counting how many cookies each bucket contained and writing the amount on the top. Between each layer of cookies, they laid a carefully cut piece of cereal box paper, never wasting an inch of the paper. They went here and there helping families peel peaches or make applesauce. And while their sharp knives were meticulously keeping the parings thin, they told stories of long ago.

One of the most inspiring accounts to me, was the one about the time their father John was a real peacemaker. John and his relative Preston (not his real name) were both farmers. Preston wanted to buy his farm and asked John to co-sign the legal papers. John congenially did so, only to discover later that it had not been a good idea, as Preston struggled to make ends meet. Eventually Preston's creditors came after their money. When he could not cough it up, they knocked on John's door. Naturally, John did not have that much cash lying around, so to keep peace with everyone involved, John sold his own farm to pay Preston's debt. This farm was the lovely Charolais farm with rolling green fields and an attractive white stone house; it was the old family place which John's father had owned before him.

John was good with figures and went to work as clerk at Wilson's, a little country grocery store. In time, he made enough money to purchase another farm between Clearspring and Pinesburg on Route 68. This farm was well peppered with rocks and cedar trees...a far cry from the scenic family homestead five miles away, along Route 40.

John never stooped to complaining about this unfair situation. In fact, John's family and Preston's family maintained a good relationship in spite of this ordeal. Ruth used to tell us, "There were never any hard feelings between us. Pop and Mother never treated Preston different from our other relatives. We went to Uncle Preston's and played with their children and we had nice times together." With a tilt of her chin and a shake of her head, she would go on to inform us that not everyone treated Preston with respect like Pop did. "Another man who had helped Uncle Preston would never go back to see him," she said. "He had us know that he wasn't going there just to sit on his own chairs."

"That wasn't Pop's way," Ida would add. Today, the old Charolais farmstead still stands…like a sentinel; it's a beautiful tribute to John's goodwill.

Ida and Ruth carried on that goodwill after John was gone. They could have felt inconvenienced and underprivileged. They spent their life giving, living with little, taking the worst end of the deal as their father had done. They shared God's love with the poor, yet many of their recipients never accepted Christ; they cast their bread upon the water countless times; yet they could have felt as if it was not returned unto them. In spite of their frugality, their money dwindled; their parents died, their uncles and aunts died, and some of their cousins died. They had no siblings, no children, no nieces, no nephews.

Yet they were content, always pointing out their blessings. "We have so much to be thankful for. We can't complain," Ida would say. "We have a bed, good food, a Christian home. What more could we want?" Ruth repeated countless times. They spent much time watching the birds and they remembered God's promise, "Consider the sparrows. Are you not much better than they? Will I not much more care for you?" They often remarked on the beautiful sunrises and sunsets, and they thought of the verse in 2 Samuel 23:4 which says, *And He shall be as the light of the morning when the sun riseth, even a morning without clouds.*" Many times, they called us to notice a magnificent evening rainbow. And we knew they were recounting God's promise in Genesis 9:13: *I do set my bow in the cloud, and it shall be for a token of a covenant between Me and the earth.* They had the blessing of many friends and a godly church, so that it could have been said of them as Paul said to Phebe: "I commend unto you [Ida and Ruth] our sister[s], which [are] servants of the church."

In spite of what they did not have in this life, they had the things that matter. In their heart of hearts, they knew they were laying their treasures in heaven where God will reward them (as well as all the faithful widows and their supporters) under the greatest rainbow and cloudless sky. 🌸

Question 24

Has God helped you in any extraordinary ways since you have been a widow?

Widows answer:

• God has been good; His promises are so true and steadfast for the fatherless and widows. Take it to heart and trust it! Our children were small and my husband was self-employed. God provided; time and again a donation was sent and we never once had to ask for financial help even when we were down to the last. Praise Him, trust Him, His Word stands sure.

• I struggled and rebelled at my new title of "widow" for quite some time. About a year after I was widowed, I read a children's story to my preschoolers. It encouraged families to visit widows. Soon after that, my children were playing dolly. They came to me in the kitchen where I was working and greeted me cheerfully with, "Hi, Widow!" They had come to visit me since I am a widow! Maybe it was hearing it from them so innocently. Maybe it was the fact that it did not bother them that their mom was a widow. At any rate, that was the turning point for me. God used my innocent children to help me accept my new title. Anymore, I use the word "widow" quite freely and I hope I never hurt any of my "newer" widow friends because of it.

• "One evening as I was lying in bed, I was feeling sad and lonely. I had a special experience that evening that I find hard to describe. It felt like God touched my emotional life with His healing. Who knows? Maybe miles away, one of my friends was asking God to reach me in a special way. I will long remember it as a gift from Him.

• Many times, God helped me financially. Sometimes money came in a card through the mail. Sometimes I would find money lying in different places after company left. Once my neighbor arrived in his Sunday best. My oldest son was away at a wedding and the rest of us were out trying to drag a cow that was down off the concrete, without actually knowing how. The kind neighbor took over, telling me he will help the cow. The next morning it was raining before we went out to milk, and here comes the neighbor to check on our cow. He even milked her out in that rain. Another evening we found a sick-looking raccoon in back of our house and a neighbor happened to be there at the right time. He shot it and took care of it for us. Yes, we had many gifts from God in many different ways. God cares. God provides. God loves.

• God has been so good to us since my husband has been called to Him. How can I say this? No, it is not easy. But God is good. It is just amazing how God looks out for us through His people. My husband was always concerned that he wouldn't leave me with a huge debt. He talked about it more than once, and I still do not know why. He was young and healthy. But when he made these remarks, I told him he didn't need to worry; it would all work out. I never gave it much thought that he would actually die young, but he did. Still, I did not worry; I trusted God to take care of us. And through the touch of God from others, the debt has all been paid. Over and over God provided through caring hearts. My husband would be so blessed to know it. Yes, God cares; He really does. I have had so many faith builders since I am on this journey of single parenting and widowhood that I could fill more than one sheet. Time is a factor for me not writing more: widows do not reach around, especially with eight children who all call, "*Mom*" at the same time!

• When my second son was fifteen, we were offered a poly furniture assembly (and making) to do in our garage. It has proved a tremendous blessing as the business increases. We can live and pay debt! I have a friend who sends me three hundred dollars every month for over two years now and it is still continuing. They are not even our church family. Extraordinary!

• I was really struggling about all the "whys" in my life when I had a dream one night and saw my husband sitting beside Jesus. Jesus was explaining to me the reason my husband had to die and, in my dream,

I understood it perfectly. When I woke up, I could not remember the reason, but that peaceful feeling was still with me. Also, when I was struggling with the question if I should accept my friend's offer of marriage, I was so afraid of doing the wrong thing. Then I had a dream of going through a tunnel with all my children on a little wagon. I felt burdened with my load and where I was going, when all of a sudden, my husband was standing beside me. I said, "Oh, I am so glad to see you! Now I do not have to marry someone else and move away." He said, "I came to tell you I am happy where I am and I want you to keep going with the plans you have." That made up my mind to marry my widower friend.

• My children were all under the age of seven and having a newborn and a business, my spare time was almost nonexistent. Friday rolled around and groceries were at an all-time low. I should have gone shopping…but *when*? Finally, Friday evening I had put the children to bed and sat down on my rocker to feed my baby. I was crying and talking to God. "Lord, is this really Thy will? I am *soooo* tired and I cannot do this anymore. Please send me something to show me You care for us." I fell into bed totally exhausted, and slept. Saturday morning someone called and said they wanted to drop something off. When they came walking in my door with a box of groceries I could have cried. There was everything in that box that I was out of: a gallon of milk, eggs, sugar, flour, rice, and more. God had answered the weary groan that my heart had no words for.

• During our marriage, I worked for an income a few short stints, but after he passed away, I soon realized I needed an income. I had payments to make and rent to pay besides the usual expenses of a household. I still had one daughter at home. One day in the grocery store, I was led to speak to a little humpbacked older lady leaning on a grocery cart and told her my situation. I said I have no expertise, but I could do housecleaning. She said her granddaughter is looking for someone to clean and with that contact I started cleaning for her and from that my jobs just mushroomed and I was able to support myself.

• I was scheduled to be hostess for our congregation one Sunday in June. I was low on fruit and wished for fresh strawberries to serve the guests. A lady who had no idea of my wishes brought me eight quarts of fresh-picked strawberries. Her gift filled my needs perfectly, at just the right time. I pray that friends like her would be blessed so much that they can hardly stand it!

• When my husband died, I had no idea God was going to give us another baby. I feel God spared me, because if I would have known, I don't think I would have been emotionally able to handle it. But by the time I knew for sure, I was ready to accept it.

• It was the Saturday evening after Christmas. Any given Saturday was a hard day, but this one, the day after Christmas, was twice as tough. The children were happy, though, and were playing a pop-in, pop-out game in a closet around the corner from where I was doing dishes. I was fighting tears all the while. Finally, it was too much—I sank to the floor. I had knelt down to put dishes away in an under-counter cabinet, so I was nearly there anyway. I sat there and gave vent to the flood of tears. Almost instantly, my baby (1½ yr.) came bounding around the corner, and crawled right up onto my lap. How did he know I needed comfort? I knew he had not seen or heard me crying with all the racket the children were making. Did an angel whisper to him? I will never know, but it blessed me then, and many times since.

• The extraordinary ways God has helped me since I am a widow might fill a book. So many times, He has sent a person at the exact time I needed help. One day I was feeling extra overwhelmed, bereft, and sorry for myself. I had depended on my husband to line up the taxi to take me or the children to appointments. Then he would go along. He handled business and money matters. This particular time I was having a toothache. I knew it had to come out. How many times I had leaned on my heavenly Husband, and this time was no exception. I turned to Him. But the devil whispered, "God promised to be your Husband, but He can't (or won't) really be one. He won't literally take care of you like your husband did. He won't get a driver, and go along to the appointment. See, the Lord falls short of His promises." But I handed everything to the Lord and asked Him to take care of me.

I questioned my neighbor who I knew needed to go to the dentist. Maybe God would work out that I could go with her. It did not work out. I felt miffed, and decided to just put up with the toothache like a martyr.

The very next morning my oldest married son stopped by and asked if I would ride along to town with him. He had to take his son to the dentist, as he had a toothache. His wife could not go along, and since the driver was a lady driver this time, he wanted me to go along for appearance's sake.

Dentist? I perked up. What dentist? It happened to be my own! I went along, the dentist was able to work me in and pull my tooth. As I rode home, I couldn't cease praising God and declaring I'll never distrust Him again. Every time such things happen my faith is strengthened. He really does take care of the widows.

• Our clock sang, "When the Roll is Called up Yonder," when my husband passed on. Later that evening I saw the most beautiful sunset ever.

Things often happen that I just know was the Hand of God. So often I am doing something and know God is with me. God is there like the air. God has been so gracious in healing my emotions with the help of many mentors who had caring hearts, helping hands, and praying tongues. When the one mentor was praying for me, she asked that our heavenly Father through His Son Jesus would send me a song, or verse, or show me a picture. Immediately the words were right there. I sang, "I love You, Lord Jesus, I Love You today, I Love You in spirit and mind…"

• Traveling by myself long-distance is one area that I sense a deep need of God, my Protector and Provider. One day I was traveling on the interstate to my daughter who lives three hours away. Suddenly my van was engulfed in smoke! I pulled to the side of the road, calling on my God for help. Shakily, I dialed my son-in-law and tried to explain my situation. He suggested I let the van sit for a while before trying to start it again. I did that, and when it started, I got off at the next exit and stopped at the first garage. Several hours later my van was hauled to my daughter's house and my question was, "What do I do now?" The mechanic, my sons, and son-in-law all recommended that I replace the van due to the high mileage. It was no accident that one of our church brethren who lived neighbors to my daughter had a van for sale. My sons recommended that I buy it. Because I had done some "out of the ordinary" banking that very morning, I had my checkbook along (God's provision) and was able to purchase the van and drive back home. My faith in my Provider and Protector was strengthened indeed!

• I have always had cold hands and feet, and in general am a cold person who has to warm up at night before falling asleep. I dreaded that first fall and winter after my husband was gone. How would I ever get warm enough to sleep? To my surprise, though I needed to use an electric blanket to get warm when I napped during the day, at bedtime my feet were always warm and comfortable. That blessing felt even more miraculous when I came to the second winter and I was cold like always before. God had provided that extra blessing especially for that first hard year.

In working through challenges with the children, I have been blessed many times over with answers when I was desperate for them. Whether it is a new thought that suddenly comes to my mind, a grandparent or schoolteacher's insight, or someone who has no idea of what we're working with who shares personal experience with one of their children, I have always been blessed.

> Who knows how one experience, so singularly horrible, can set in motion a chain of events that will bless future generations? Loss may appear to be random, but that does not mean it is. It may fit into a scheme that surpasses even what our imaginations dare to think. Gerald Sittser from *A Grace Disguised*

Dear Widow Friends,

I know a sweet sister who seems to have been a widow about all her life. She raised their five children on a goat farm in Florida. She grew lots of tomatoes to sell, and she kept boarders in the winter. She always has a smile for everyone.

I know another friend who is ten years my senior. She was only married six years. She raised their two children, worked as a nurse, and encouraged many in our brotherhood. She loves to sing and has such a pleasant smile for all.

My mother was widowed after thirty years of marriage. She sometimes felt cheated when she saw others traveling with their husbands and she was left alone, with her dreams of touring and traveling with Dad crushed at her feet. Instead of letting her loneliness overwhelm her, she took other widow ladies and single sisters on trips. She made hardtack candy to sell and took in ironing for an income. She helped with her grandchildren, snapped green beans, peeled peaches, and fed the birds. She was friendly to her neighbors, and had groups of ladies over and was their chief entertainer. She laughed and she gave other people lots of laughs. I never felt sorry for my mother; she laughed! She was happy.

But now...as I read her old diaries, I see that being a widow was real to my mother. Was she happy? Why did she laugh? What about my other two widow friends with their smiles? Are they happy?

Would I be happy if I were the widow? I don't see how. I think I would have a dull ache that would never quite leave. I think I would dream that my husband came back and then I would wake up and find it was only a dream. I think I would be lonely, and I do not like to be alone for too long. I feel sorry for all widows.

One widow told me, "Sometimes I cry buckets of tears; other times I am fine." Another widow said, "It feels like half of me is gone." Any widow who loved her husband while she had him (most did) will carry a sadness with her for the rest of her life. So, what are their smiles? Their laughter? Are these merely masks, covering up a bitter, angry heart?

Hardly. Not when their smiles are so sweet; their laughter bubbly and sincere. These widows have something bigger and better than happiness; they have joy. Way down deep under their sorrow, their loneliness, their dull aches, God has given them a little seed of joy.

God keeps His promises. He promised that *the joy of the Lord is your strength* (Nehemiah 8:10).

The smiling widows have chosen to look to God for comfort. They have chosen to love, to give. To forgive. To look for the good in other people. To stay busy. To pray. Chosen to believe in God, and look for His blessings in every trial.

In spite of their heartache, they have chosen to enjoy the simple pleasures: a baby's smile, children innocently playing, birds, clouds, sun, flowers, friends, hope, church family, relatives, hobbies, pets, snow sparkling on branches, a song, spring cleaning, heaven, Jesus, our Father, God Who is Love, His Spirit that breathes within, God's Word to us, a new friend, a road ahead, a bubbling stream, The Lord is my Shepherd.

The smiling widows have chosen to allow God's little seeds of joy to sprout and grow. They share it with others through their smiles and laughter. I am impressed. I am blessed. I am praying God will continue to sustain them. And you.

Sincerely,

"Zinnia"

Glow for Gloom

LYDIA HESS

Clouds loomed on the day of my friend's death; they were—and are—the tie between earth's gray and heaven's grandeur. And the double rainbow that evening—also one the next morning—painted promise…

When overhead is shrouded,
By thunderheads beclouded,
Some sudden shafts of sunlight shift the scenes;
Bold, brassy color marches
Across the sky in arches.
Sure hope, midst stormy climate, intervenes!

318

God Will Provide

JOANNE DETWEILER

"Twelve pounds, six ounces," the nurse announced as she took the baby from the scales and gave her back to Sarah. "She's growing nicely. Now she's ready for her first set of immunizations." After carefully explaining each of them to Sarah, the nurse cocked her head, dropped her voice, and shared in a confidential tone, "These shots are very expensive. But the government does have a program that provides these shots for almost nothing. You would only need to pay fifteen dollars per time. You can talk to the doctor about it, if you're interested."

Sarah smiled at the infant cuddled closely in her arms. The baby yawned sleepily and then returned the smile. But Sarah hardly noticed. Her mind was busy. *Very expensive…government program…fifteen dollars per time.*

Sarah glanced at her six-year-old daughter sitting nervously beside her. That would mean only thirty dollars for today's shots. It wouldn't be a hardship to pay that amount.

A sigh escaped Sarah's lips and her shoulders sagged a bit more. Financial concerns became increasing burdens since William was no longer here. His sickness and death had strained the back account. And now the responsibility of providing an income and making ends meet felt at times like the impossible Red Sea before her.

Accepting the government's help in paying for the children's immunizations would ease the financial burden some. Maybe under these circumstances it would be acceptable…

"Lord, what wilt Thou have me to do?" Sarah prayed silently.

The spiritual dialogue continued until the doctor knocked politely on the door, then entered the room. Sarah returned the doctor's greeting with a cheery smile and straightened shoulders. The question was settled and she was at rest.

"Did the nurse tell you that there is a program to greatly reduce the cost of these shots?" the doctor questioned kindly.

"Yes, she did," Sarah answered. "But I don't feel comfortable accepting government aid. I'm willing to pay the full amount myself."

"That's fine," the doctor agreed. "I know you people generally take that position. But under the circumstances, I wanted to be sure you know there is that option," she concluded sympathetically.

When the receptionist was finished filling out the forms, her fingers flew over the calculator one more time. Satisfied that the figure was correct, she slowly, apologetically announced, "The total for both girls today is $526."

Sarah blinked in surprise! That was a lot of money! But then her eyes widened in even greater surprise. For she had caught a glimpse of the deposit ticket she had prepared to drop at the bank on their way home. "Miller—$500," it read.

That check had come in the mail last week. William's uncle and aunt had called it a "love gift—to be used where needed."

Smiling, Sarah handed the payment to the receptionist. With a now-sleeping baby in one arm, Sarah took her older daughter's hand in her own, being careful not to jerk her sore arm, and headed for the van.

"God did provide!" her heart sang. "He had made the way through the Red Sea before I even got there. If I would have chosen to accept the government help, my bill would have been thirty dollars today. But this way, I only needed to provide twenty-six dollars, since God had already seen to it that I had the five hundred dollars to pay for the rest."

Receiving this kind of help from others is humbling and makes me feel accountable to them. But how much better it is to feel that responsibility towards a godly uncle and aunt than to the government! I know they will

continue to be an encouragement to us by their prayers and their faithful
example. What a blessing to be indebted to someone like them.

Two months later it was again time for the baby's shots. Sarah glanced at the checkbook balance before tucking it into the diaper bag. *I'm so grateful for the farm income to keep us going,* she pondered. *That provides for our basic necessities. And this money gift that William's cousin handed me at the wedding on Saturday should help to cover today's doctor visit.*

This time again the receptionist's voice sounded apologetic as she read the total amount due. "Three hundred twenty dollars," she said. Inwardly Sarah gasped. Three hundred dollars was the amount of that gift money. *This time I need to cover twenty dollars, just five dollars over the cost of what it would be with the government assistance.*

Sarah's faith was strengthened. God had provided so well these two times. Surely He was blessing her decision to trust Him to provide. She was eager to see how He would continue to open the path for her and the family.

The next time shots were needed, several small money gifts had come through the mail the week before the scheduled appointment. Once more, there was just enough to cover the costs.

The baby's first birthday had just passed when it was time again for another doctor's visit and more shots.

There's no money to deposit in my bank account today, Sarah mused as she drove to the doctor's office. *Did the Lord "forget" this appointment? I'm sure He didn't, but I do wonder how He is going to meet our needs this week. The funds are low and today's bill is going to use a sizable portion of what is available. But I know the Lord will provide,* Sarah concluded calmly. The thought of receiving government help did not even enter her mind this time. God had proven Himself faithful so many times, she was willing to just wait for His help.

Sarah set down the toddler beside her at the receptionist's window, and reached into her purse for the checkbook.

"Shall we schedule your three-month appointment right away?" the receptionist asked. And then her eyes twinkled as she added, "You can put your checkbook away! Your bill is being paid by someone else today. They said we may tell you that 'Someone who loves you wants to pay this bill.'"

Sarah's misty eyes hindered her from seeing clearly, but she thought she saw tears in the receptionist's eyes too. "Well! Tell them 'thank you' for me," she choked. The receptionist only nodded, not trusting herself to speak.

Then, regaining her composure, Sarah acknowledged, "God has been so good to us. He has been providing for us so well and it's so special when our friends allow God to use their money to help meet our needs."

"You have a lot going for you," the receptionist murmured. "You're much better provided for this way than you would be with any insurance or government program."

Sarah smiled in agreement. The Red Sea was open before her. The "walls of water" still loomed threateningly beside her. But she knew God had the power to hold those waters back and to lead her safely through on dry ground.

The days ticked away...thirty, sixty, ninety, and once again Sarah was on her way to the doctor's office. This time again she had a preschooler along who needed shots in preparation for school.

I wonder what the bill will be today, Sarah pondered. *Last year it was over five hundred dollars for two girls. The Lord didn't give me that much yet. But I know the Lord can provide more than that. I am eager to see what He does.*

Five hundred eighty-one dollars. The numbers relentlessly chased each other through Sarah's mind the next two days. *From where will that money come? Both an insurance company and the government would have been willing to cover some of the bill. But so far God has used family and friends to meet these needs. And they were the ones who also cared enough to help meet our physical, emotional, and spiritual needs. But these five hundred eighty-one dollars...*

Brother Galen's wife stepped up to Sarah after prayer meeting that evening. "Galen asked me to give this to you," she explained as she handed Sarah a white envelope.

Sarah's heart leaped. "Thank you," she replied simply, but with deep gratitude. *Might this contain the answer to our need?* she wondered.

At home in the living room that night, Sarah slowly, almost reverently, slit open that envelope. Breathlessly, she read the handwritten note tucked inside: "A gift from our congregation. We prefer if finances (especially a lack of money) do not add a lot of stress to your life. May God be your portion, Brother Galen."

"And here is the check," Sarah whispered as she held it up.

There it was in neat, black letters, "$585."

The Stretch of Road

JANICE ETTER

We drive from shafts of slanting light
Into a world of cloud
And all the sky's wide circle disappears.
The narrow stretch of streaming road
Is only just in sight;
A blowing shroud has blurred the glass with tears.

We straddle waves of stormy wind
To climb a rocky steep,
Remembering the cloudless joy of dawn.
With far to go, we do not know
What yet the skies may send,
And still we keep the road and journey on.

The Veggie Widow's Perspective

KRISTEN J HORST

M arji was selecting broccoli at the produce stand when she stopped, frozen, her newly wedded eyes wide. She stared at the women clustered by the strawberries.

"None of his business, I said." The lady's hands fluttered over the strawberry pints, never quite settling on a box. "He is always ruling what I do and I'm sick of it."

"You bet!" the lady beside her, who looked to be her sister, said. "My man told me…" On she went with her story, finishing up with "…and I told him to get lost."

Their voices jarred the walls and the vegetables and her heart. Marji redirected her gaze, but she wondered about Mervin, her husband for the last six weeks. She remembered the tiff they had last evening. Two hours later, it had seemed like such a small issue. They had eagerly apologized and made up. But in twenty years, when she was the age of these women, would their relationship be just as deteriorated?

A frosty, breezy fear exploded in her heart. She felt an urge to throw her vegetables down and flee. Just as she pulled the first head of broccoli from her basket, she heard a different voice, a soft wistful voice.

She looked at the source. Another lady stood at the checkout, glancing over her shoulder at the unhappy women. Marji followed the lady's gaze.

The other women still gestured vehemently, but she tuned them out. She wouldn't listen to their negative, unrepeatable language. But this other woman with the soft voice; she would listen to her.

So there Marji stood again, a head of broccoli in her hand, and watched the gray-haired lady pocket her change and glance again at the unhappy strawberry ladies.

Then the lady shook her head, just a little, and said to the cashier, "That's sad. My husband died four years ago." She paused, then added, "I still miss him."

The widow picked up her bags and with a final disappointed glance, walked away.

Marji straightened and smiled and plucked the broccoli back. She whispered a prayer for the widow, who had lost so much. That widow needed a special blessing because she had given so much.

She had given hope. 🌷

To a Friend Who Faced Death:

DONNA HESS

I know that spring will come, for my Redeemer lives.
His promise never fails—new life to all He gives.
The sun will rise again, the singing birds return.
Though winter seems so long, and hearts for summer yearn.
I know that good will come, from every seeming ill.
I trust Him. He's my Friend. He will be gracious still.

Working Together for Good

Adapted from a message by *ENOS RUDOLPH*

Romans 8:28

And we know…

…that **God is good.** The earth is full of evidences that remind us of the goodness of God. The Bible says much about the goodness of God. His goodness overshadows all that God does, all that He is, all that He allows. We know that God is good.

…that **God knows.** God sees more than just what can be seen on the surface. God saw every test and trial that Joseph faced in Egypt. God saw the challenges that Daniel faced in Babylon. Through it all, God was with them. No matter what it is, we know that God knows all about it.

…that **God is in control of everything.** In Job's experience, God knew what was happening and remained in full control, superintending every detail. The devil could not penetrate the hedge which God placed around Job. God heard every word that Job and his friends uttered, and God knew the truth. God always knows the truth. Because God knows, then *we know that all things work together for good.* No matter what happens, we know that God is still in complete control.

…that **all things work together for good…**

God has a sovereign purpose for each individual. God superintends the whole of our life. Within the scope of His purpose, however, God is not the author of every detail of our life. The devil is an intruder who forces his interruptions into our life in an effort to turn us away from God. He wants to make us bitter toward God.

The devil seeks to cloud the good by inserting doubts and fears. He provokes conflict and misunderstandings between brethren. The devil brought the trials into Job's life. He took his possessions and children. He caused Job's friends to misunderstand him. The devil is ever threatening the good that God intends for us.

God does intend good for each one of us. There is, however, a condition which we must meet in order to see and realize that good:

...to them that love God.

It can be a real challenge at times to love God, because we are closer to ourselves than we are to God. Self-love poses a real threat, and has many facets: self-pity, self-confidence, self-pleasing, self-complacent, and more. When self-love is present, it blinds us so that we cannot see or realize the good that God intends for us to have. Self-love makes so that the things God allows for our good seem to be against us. In Mark 12:30, we find the antidote for self-love: *Thou shalt love the Lord thy God with all thy heart, and with all thy soul, and with all thy mind, and with all thy strength.* For those who do this, *all things work together for good.*

Is our love for God affected when those around us make mistakes? God often uses our fellow men to bring His good to us. This adds complexity to our lives because men are faulty, short-sighted, and make mistakes. With the devil's assistance, these faults and mistakes can get between us and our love for God. Self-love looks at the faults and mistakes of others with a microscope, but keeps our sunglasses on when evaluating our own lives. Some of the greatest evidence of our love for God is when our love for our fellow men extends forbearance and forgiveness to them, and when we acknowledge our own humanity and the times others have needed to forbear with us. *All things work together for good to them that love God.*

We are constantly troubled by problems and perplexities. This is part of the travail of life on earth (Romans 8:22,23). Have there not been times when you wished to be done with this hardship once and for all? But...*we know that all things work together for good to them that love God.* Overshadowing all the problems and perplexities, tests and trials of life is the sovereignty of God. As He is working through the circumstances of our lives, He allows trials and tests for our refining. The devil often tries to tell us that life is not fair. He wants us to compare ourselves among ourselves and conclude that God is not being fair to us, personally.

From His vantage point, God sees more than the "big picture." We tend to be shortsighted. God, in His infinite wisdom, may withhold what seems good to us so that He can bring about that which He knows is the best for us.

God's promises are for our comfort and encouragement, and those who love God will claim them. God wants us to trust our lives to Him completely, and rest in His providential care. He wants us to draw near to Him, and ask Him to have His way in our life, (Romans 8:26,27).

In any given situation, those who truly love God can ask Him to make *all things work together for good* and then fully trust Him to do just that. *And we know that all things work together for good to them that love God* because He is their Father and He is all good and He is all-knowing and He is almighty and He is at work in their lives.

> *Suffering is not always sent to burn out the dross; it may be meant to burn in the promises.*

The Cat

ANONYMOUS

I must tell you about *the cat*. I am almost embarrassed to write about *the cat*, but I feel it is a significant symbol in my healing process.

On April 17, 2017, a lady stopped in with a yellow tomcat. She said he came out of the woods and makes trouble for her cats and would we give him a home?

Yes, we would. I put him in the barn. My husband grinned a "whatever grin" when I told him what the lady brought.

Four hours later I found my husband in the skid loader, and his life as I knew it was gone... Gone to eternity. From that moment, my life completely changed. Our married life had been rich and full of love. We had dreamed of Happy Golden Years together. Suddenly, those dreams were cut short.

Through that first long, hard summer, *the cat* stayed close to the barn. I think he used eight of his lives, as he dragged himself around with a broken leg. But he was tough, and healed up nice and fluffy. I wasn't really looking out for him; cats take care of themselves and my own life was so drastically changed.

Then winter came. The mornings were dark and cold and I needed to walk out to do chores alone. But I soon discovered I was not alone. Every morning this yellow cat would appear by my side and walk with me.

Sometimes he led the way, sometimes he followed, oftentimes he quietly walked right beside me.

Now I am not a cat person. I do not believe this yellow cat is anything extraordinary. Of course, I know he has no soul. But I do believe the same God who made all these creatures is the same God who notices the sparrows that fall…and is also able to place a lowly cat in a position that reminds me *daily* that God will take care of me. *The cat* was a physical object that I could see with my earthly eyes.

The cat had such dedication. Be it snowing or raining or bitterly cold, he appeared at my back door as soon as I stepped out. He was so prompt that I started to watch for him. Sometimes I chuckled at his loyalty. Sometimes tears fell as I thought of God and His ways to arrest my attention.

To others, it may seem childish and simple. That is okay. I have a special bond between me and God about this and I know He understands. *The cat* may not live another winter. He may get tired of walking back and forth for me. But for now, when he appears, I think of God and of His promise to provide where He saw fit to take away. 🌸

Cloud-Connection
LYDIA HESS

Shapeless vapor, gray and black,
Swirls in a band,
Scuttles in a pathless track;
Agitated heavens crack,
Booming in command.

Billows, full of murky breath,
Veil the lamp of God;
Yet beyond this fog of death
Fullest glory glisteneth.
Clouds join sky to sod!

Candlelight

S W

Flickers, and then sudden silence. The electricity was off.

"Mother!" Two-year-old Ethan clung to her skirt. "It's too dark!"

"It's all right, Ethan. Just a minute, and we'll light some candles." Marla Steiner drew the match sharply across the matchbox, and a flame flared up. The candlelight danced across the five anxious faces clustered around her.

"What happened?" six-year-old Krista wondered.

"A tree probably fell on the wires somewhere," Rosene supplied quickly with ten-year-old wisdom.

"Or maybe there was an accident!" Laura added.

Brian's eyes grew wide with fear. Ethan whimpered. "Mother, I'm scared!"

"Come, children." Marla swung Ethan up into her arms. "Let's read a story before bedtime."

"I wish Father were here," Krista said wistfully. "I don't like when it's so dark."

Marla laid the book down. She looked at the children, their faces drawn in the flickering shadows; Krista and Brian, crowding up against her elbows; and Ethan, his blond head warm under her chin.

Her children. Her fatherless children!

"Father isn't here," she began quietly. "He—"

"He's in heaven," Brian said quickly.

Marla smiled down at her eager four-year-old. "Yes, Father's in heaven. But do you know Who is with us right now?"

Rosene took a deep breath. Marla saw the conflicting emotions flit across her oldest daughter's face.

"God is!" Laura and Krista burst out together.

"And we never need to be afraid when God is with us. God is a Father to us." Marla gave Ethan a little squeeze. Around her, she saw the lines of fear melt away from the children's faces.

"Now, shall we read our story?"

Before the story was finished, the electricity came back on. Gleefully, the children made their rounds in the house to blow out all the candles. Then they all trooped upstairs to bed.

"Mother, I can hardly wait for tomorrow!" Laura's eyes shone above the blankets. "It will be so much fun to go to school again. And this year I will be in third grade!"

"School is a privilege, isn't it?" Marla smiled at Laura's excitement. "And this year Krista will be in first grade. I guess Brian will be my helper here at home."

She brushed the hair out of Krista's worried face. Impulsively she stooped and kissed her cheek. "Don't worry, Krista. You'll learn to enjoy school. And remember, God is watching over you."

The first day of school! Last night's candlelight questions came back to Marla as she sat at the desk for her morning devotions.

I wish Father were here, too, she admitted to herself. *I miss Brendon so much!*

A new school year was starting today. What would it hold? There had been so many unexpected hurricanes to beat her ship last year. So many storms!

Suddenly Marla felt very battle-weary. *How can I ever face this year?* she wondered silently. *What if it brings more wind and waves? I think my ship will sink!*

But I am not the Captain. The thought came clearly through her discouragement.

Of course! Marla took a deep breath. God had been faithful through each of last year's storms, and His peace had been a constant companion.

Surely, she could trust Him again.

But the children!

Her mother heart ached for her children. To send the girls off to school all by herself for the first time—no father's kind wishes and firm reminders…no father's encouragement to "Do your best!" …no father's help to see them through girlish relationship struggles…

And in the stillness of the morning, she wept.

"They need a father, Lord!" she cried. "And Brendon is not here to be that father. O Lord, hast Thou not promised to be a Father of the fatherless?"

Unconsciously she spread her hands. "Help me, Lord, to help them see Thee as a Father. A Father we can trust in. A Father who will protect and help us. May we all find the security of a Father in Thee!"

In the paleness of early dawn, she went quietly down the stairs to start the laundry.

Candlelight!

Marla drew her breath in sharply. Candlelight, reflecting off the bathroom mirror! Swiftly she crossed the silent kitchen.

Yes! A stubby candle sat calmly on the washstand, its steady flame reaching up…up within inches of the hand towel hanging from the wicker cabinet.

One quick puff, and the candle was extinguished. Little smoke curls twined silently around the towel, and sooty smoke marks stretched up across its blueness. The fibers were scorched almost to a crisp.

But it was still there! Weak with relief, Marla sagged against the wall. How very nearly the house had burned down last night! What a miracle!

And then it struck her—here was the answer to her prayer! Here was the proof—proof that God was watching over them.

She covered her face with her hands. "Thank you, Lord," she whispered brokenly. "Thank you that even children without an earthly father have a Father to find rest in! Help me to build their confidence in Thy omnipotence. Truly we are under the shadow of Thy wings.

"Reach out and touch all other fatherless children today as they go off to school. And grant their mothers rest, at home alone—with Thee.

"Go with us as we move through each today. And, O Father, thank you for the candlelight assurance!"

Tomorrow's Clouds

PHEBE J MARTIN

The clouds on the dark horizon
    Speak of a gloomy dawn,
And the shadows on my soul
    Tell of a hope nigh gone.
But today the sun is shining
    And the sky is bright and clear,
So I'll treasure its present pleasures
    And bury my foolish fears.
Today I will treasure the stillness
    Though it speaks of a coming storm;
Today I will bask in the brightness
    And warmth of a summer morn.
Today I will gather the calmness
    And the peace and the courage and grace,
That will give me strength for tomorrow;
    For whatever I need to face.

It takes real faith to trace the rainbow through the rain, but it takes the storm-cloud to make the rainbow. Mrs. Charles E Cowman

The Unclouded Day

Josiah K. Alwood

John F. Kinsey

1. Oh, they tell me of a home far be-yond the skies, Oh, they tell me of a
2. Oh, they tell me of a home where my friends have gone, Oh, they tell me of a
3. Oh, they tell me of the King in His beau - ty there, And they tell me that mine
4. Oh, they tell me that He smiles on His chil - dren there, And His smile drives their

home far a - way; Oh, they tell me of a home where no storm - clouds rise,
land far a - way; Where the tree of life in e - ter - nal bloom
eyes shall be - hold Where He sits on the throne that is whit - er than snow,
sor - rows all a - way; And they tell me that no tears ev - er come a - gain,

Oh, they tell me of an un - cloud - ed day; Oh, the land of cloud - less day,
Sheds its fra - grance thru the un - cloud - ed day; Oh, the land of cloud - less day,
In the cit - y that is made of gold; Oh, that land mine eyes shall see,
In that love - ly land of un - cloud - ed day; Oh, that land of love - ly smiles,

Oh, the land of an un - cloud - ed sky; Oh, they tell me of a home
Oh, the land of an un - cloud - ed sky; Oh, they tell me of my friends
Oh, the land of an un - cloud - ed sky; Oh, they tell me of the King
Oh, the smiles of His love - beam - ing eye; Oh, the King in His beau-

where no storm-clouds rise, Oh, they tell me of an un - cloud - ed day.
by the tree of life, In the land of the un - cloud - ed day.
on His snow-white throne, In the land of the un - cloud - ed day.
ty in - vites us there, To the land of the un - cloud - ed day.

335